Literacy with an
Attitude

Literacy with an

Attitude

Educating Working-Class Children in Their Own Self-Interest

Patrick J. Finn

STATE UNIVERSITY OF NEW YORK PRESS

The illustrations in this book were done by
Amy Finn Bernier

Production by Ruth Fisher
Marketing by Nancy Farrell

Published by
State University of New York Press, Albany

© 1999 State University of New York

Printed in the United States of America

For information address State University of New York Press,
194 Washington Avenue, Suite 305, Albany, NY 12210-2384

Library of Congress Cataloging-in-Publication Data

Finn, Patrick J.
    Literacy with an attitude : educating working-class children in
their own self-interest / Patrick J. Finn.
        p.   cm.
    Includes bibliographical references (p.   ) and index.

    ISBN-13: 978-0-7914-4285-2 (hardcover : alk. paper) —
978-0-7914-4286-9 (pbk : alk. paper)
    ISBN 0-7914-4285-3 (alk. paper). — 0-7914-4286-1 (pbk. :alk. paper)
    1. Working class—Education—United States.   2. Literacy—United
States.   3. Language arts—United States.   I. Title.
LC5051.F56   1999
370'.86'230973—dc21   99-26086
                                                                CIP

14 13 12 11 10

To Mary
I still bless the day I found you.

Contents

Preface

There have been times in history when the prospect of literacy in the hands of the have-nots has been a source of endless angst among the haves. Less than one hundred years after the invention of the printing press laws were passed in England forbidding anyone under the rank of yeoman to read the Bible. Later, when political pamphleteers appeared, taxes were imposed to make pamphlets too expensive for the poor.

But in America from colonial times universal literacy (except for slaves) has been the aim. Today we see illiteracy among the have-nots as the source of many social ills. One explanation is that we have come so far in our democracy that we have nothing to fear from the have-nots. We worry instead that the low levels of literacy among them make them a liability for the rest of us. The idea is that if we could raise their level of literacy they would join the haves. America would have no poor, just rich, richer, and richest.

An idea that is often associated with this point of view is that our schools offer literacy equally to all comers, but somehow the have-nots refuse to take us up on our offer. They're not smart enough or they're lazy or simply perverse.

That's not my explanation. My explanation of why literacy is not seen as dangerous among the working people and unemployed of the United States is that we have developed two kinds of education. First, there is empowering education, which leads to powerful literacy, the kind of literacy that leads to positions of power and authority. Second, there is domesticating education, which leads to functional literacy, literacy that makes a person productive and dependable, but not troublesome. Over time, political, social, and economic forces have brought us to a place where the working class (and to a surprising degree, the middle class) gets domesticating education and functional literacy, and the rich get empowering education and powerful literacy. We don't worry about a literate working class because the kind of literacy they get doesn't make them dangerous.

A conspiracy? No. The beliefs, attitudes, and behaviors of the poor have contributed as much to the present state of affairs as those of the elite. We all participate in this social system as if it were natural, the way things were meant to be. In the past twenty-five years many scholars have abandoned the fruitless search for heartless conspirators among the Carnegies and Rockerfellers and have been trying instead to figure out what happened—what social dynamics and mechanisms have led to the present state of affairs. The following are some of the mechanisms they have uncovered.

- Some minorities feel they have been wronged by mainstream Americans and that "acting white" is a betrayal of their people. They develop what sociologists call "oppositional identity." Oppositional identity appears among working-class whites to some extent as well. Talking and acting like a school teacher and valuing things school teachers value doesn't win you a lot of friends in working-class communities.

- Working-class children with varying degrees of oppositional identity resist school through means reminiscent of the factory shop floor—slowdowns, strikes, sabotage, and occasionally open confrontation. The result is the "pretend-school model." Teachers ask little of students in return for enough cooperation to maintain the appearance of conducting school.

- The discourse (ways of communication and the beliefs, attitudes, values, habits, and behaviors that underlie them—especially attitudes related to authority, conformity, and power) of working class communities is at odds with the discourse of the schools. This makes acquisition of school discourse and powerful literacy difficult for working-class children.

- Progressive methods, empowering education, and powerful literacy tend to go together. Traditional methods, domesticating education, and functional literacy tend to go together. Progressive methods are nearly impossible unless children want school knowledge and cooperate.

Contemporary social scientists believe that if we can understand these mechanisms, we can change them and bring ourselves to a different place, one where there is greater equity and justice. That would require that both the rich and poor get empowering education and powerful literacy.

When rich children get empowering education nothing changes. But when working-class children get empowering education you get literacy with an attitude. It's exactly the kind of literacy that the folks feared who outlawed Bible reading for common people three hundred years ago. There is an important difference, however. Three hundred years ago people could only imagine one social setup, the ruling class and the rabble. The fear was that literacy would make the rabble aware of the injustice they suffered, and they would attempt to overthrow the ruling class violently and take its place—same roles, same rules, only a switch in actors in the roles.

Today we understand that many social setups are possible. Roles and rules can be transformed so that there is greater justice and equity. We understand too, after two centuries of experimenting in democracy, that change is possible without violence. People can become conscious of injustice and inequity, and through disciplined, focused, and strategic action, they can bring about change. Such action both requires and promotes powerful literacy in those who struggle for justice and equity.

The status quo is the status quo because people who have the power to make changes are comfortable with the way things are. It takes energy to make changes, and the energy must come from the people who will benefit from the change. But the working class does not get powerful literacy, and powerful literacy is necessary for the struggle. How can the cycle be broken?

Teachers who see themselves as allies of their working-class students can help their students see that literacy and school knowledge could be a potent weapons in their struggle for a better deal by connecting school knowledge with the reality of working-class students' lives.

Just as "the labor organizer" appeared on the American scene as we changed from an agrarian to an industrial society and helped working people realize, harness, and use their power, "the community organizer" appeared on the scene after World War II as more affluent Americans fled the cities leaving the poorest among us behind. Community organizers can help working-class adults and older working-class students see that literacy and school knowledge could be a potent weapon in their struggle for a better deal, not a bunch of sissy stuff for which they have no use.

It's been done. Paulo Freire, an educator who worked with illiterate adults in the slums of Recife, a city in Brazil, pioneered this approach. He was successful enough to get himself jailed and later exiled by the military junta that overthrew Brazil's democratically elected government. He was welcomed back to Brazil only after years of exile, when a democratically elected government returned to power.

Grass-roots activism around schools is springing up all over the nation. People who have felt powerless are organizing and discovering their collective power. They are coming to realize that liberating education and powerful literacy is essential for their children. But demands for better schooling will not solve the problem alone. Teachers, parents, and older students need to understand the mechanisms that have subverted honest efforts to give working-class children a decent education. They must understand the relationships between society, culture, language, and schooling. They must understand the relationships between progressive methods, liberating education, and powerful literacy on the one hand and traditional methods, domesticating education, and functional literacy on the other.

In the first six chapters I discuss the subtle mechanisms that make liberating education and powerful literacy so difficult—oppositional identity and the inability of working-class schools to respond to the changing attitudes of working-class parents and students as high-paying blue-collar work disappears and parents begin to see education as the only chance for their children's survival. In chapters 7-10 I discuss the conflicts between working-class discourse and school discourse and the complications they cause. In chapters 11-15 I discuss the prospect of developing a pedagogy that makes progressive methods, empowering education, and powerful literacy possible with working-class students. This entails organizing working-class adults and older students around issues that are causing them pain and helping them realize that the struggle for justice and equity requires empowering education and powerful literacy.

Chapter 1

TITLE, AUTHOR, AND HARD-BITTEN SCHOOLTEACHERS

I considered several titles for this book. The first was *Educating Our Children and Handling Theirs*. This was based on the observation that schools have learned how to educate the children of the gentry and how to "handle" children of the working class—those who had been handled in school themselves.[1]

Jonathan Kozol's book entitled *Savage Inequalities*[2] traces the notoriously unequal results of schooling between rich and poor children to segregation (both on the basis of race and family income) and unequal funding. This book is also about savage inequalities, but the sources of inequality I examine are in fact so subtle that the average parent, teacher, student, and taxpayer are not conscious of them at all. I considered calling my book *Subtle Inequalities*, but I immediately realized that the inequalities I address are every bit as savage as Kozol's. It is the mechanisms that underlie them that are subtle, and so I tried a new title *Subtle Mechanisms, Savage Inequalities*.

However, as I discussed the book with others, the more I described the mechanisms, the more insistent they became in wanting to know what can be done about them. From the start, I had an answer: Paulo Freire. Freire was a professor at the University of Recife, a city in northeast Brazil. In the early 1960s he started an adult literacy program for the city's teeming, illiterate poor.

There had been numerous literacy campaigns earlier in Brazil, motivated by the desire to make the poor better workers, better citizens, and better Christians—classic reasons for literacy campaigns among the poor since the invention of the printing press. All of these previous campaigns had failed.

Freire believed that while the benefits of such literacy campaigns were obvious to the people behind them, they were not at all obvious to the illiterate poor. He took a different approach. Before he started to teach reading and writing, he asked his students to reflect on the concept of justice—a radical and dangerous thing to do in a country where a huge divide separated a small number of very rich and a vast number of very poor. He asked his students what they might do to secure justice and suggested that literacy would make them far better able to engage in the struggle they would certainly face if they tried to get a better deal. Then he was ready to talk ABCs, and so were they.

The literacy they acquired would not be literacy to become better citizens, workers, and Christians as the rich defined those roles for them; it would be literacy to engage in the struggle for justice. This was dangerous literacy, and for a while I considered the title *Making Literacy Dangerous Again*, alluding to the fact that after the printing press was invented, literacy among the masses was viewed with fear and trembling among the ruling classes of Europe.

But it also seemed to me that the literacy Freire wanted for the poor of Brazil was literacy *with an attitude*. That sounded to me like a great title for a book.

—⚬⚬⚬—

I was the eighth of nine children—six boys and three girls—in a blue-collar, Irish Catholic family in an Irish Catholic neighborhood on the south side of Chicago. The south side, which is predominantly African American now, was mostly white and mostly ethnic—Irish, Polish, and Italian. My father was Irish. There were also a number of Czechs who referred to themselves as Bohemians. My mother was Bohemian.

My father was a plumber and my five brothers became plumbers. I did not follow the family trade because of a birth injury that left my left arm slightly paralyzed. The family did not quite know what to do with me, and so I was encouraged to stay in high school until I graduated. I was pretty good at school, but after working two years in a minimum-wage, dead-end, white-collar job I think I astonished everyone by going to the local teachers college and becoming a teacher.

One of my first teaching jobs was at the Carol Jason Banks Upper Grade Center[3] in a black neighborhood on Chicago's south side. There were about four hundred eighth graders who were sorted by reading scores from the highest to the lowest and divided into fifteen classes, 8-1s being the highest, 8-15s being the lowest. But they didn't divide them exactly equally. While the 8-1s through the 8-13s started out with around twenty-seven students, the two lowest classes started out with only around fifteen. The theory was that the slowest students would get more attention in smaller classes. The reality was that as the year wore on there were spaces available in the "lower" classes to dump troublesome students from "higher" classes. And so by Christmas there were likely to be more than twenty students in the 8-14s and 8-15s, fifteen of whom were originally assigned because of low reading scores, and an additional five or six who were "sent down" because of discipline problems. You want to talk about a tough teaching assignment?

I taught double periods of language arts and social studies, and so I had only four classes. When I started, I had the 8–7s, 8–8s, 8–9s and 8–10s. Teachers with seniority had the higher classes. The younger teachers who had proven their ability to "handle" them had the lower classes. By the third year I had the four lowest classes, the 8–12s, 8–13s, 8–14s, and 8–15s. I was a huge success.

I was from the working class and I knew how working-class and poor kids related to authority. They expected people in authority to be authoritarian, and I gave them what they expected. It was an exhausting job, but my classroom was nearly always quiet. The children were nearly always working. The assistant principal told me once that he always walked visitors *slowly* past my classroom so that they could see what could be done with students in our school.

But, in fact I was schooling these children, not to take charge of their lives, but to take orders. I taught them to read and write a little better, and I taught them some facts about United States history, but control was uppermost in my mind. When I discussed discipline problems with other teachers, a frequent topic of discussion in the teachers' lounge, I would talk about my teaching methods as methods of control. I had work assignments on the board when the students entered the classroom, and so there wasn't a moment when they didn't have anything to do. I didn't say to an errant student, "What are you doing?" I said, "Stop that and get to work." No discussion. No openings for an argument.

I made the assignments easy so the least able students could do them. I had "extra credit" assignments for students who finished early, usually not too challenging, but time consuming. I corrected and graded and returned every paper by the next class so the students felt that completing assignments mattered, or put another way, students were punished with a zero if they did not do their assignments. But, of course, that meant assignments had to be easily correctable, fill in the blanks, matching, one- or two-word answers on numbered lines on spelling paper.

Mind you, we had our lighter moments. We wrote news stories that might have appeared on the front page of a Boston paper the day after the Boston Tea Party. We colored maps with crayons, showing which European powers laid claim to which parts of North America in 1789, the year our Constitution was ratified. We wrote Mother's Day poems. We wrote summaries of television shows telling why we liked them—this sort of thing, very rarely, however, because they took too long to grade. But the good times (if you could call them that) would come to a sudden halt if the students got too boisterous, a fact of which they were frequently reminded.

"Good students" were obedient students, students who followed orders. The assignments were so easy that all obedient students got good grades, but I gave plenty of bad grades to students who were not obedient, who did not do their assignments. Obedient students were not kept in from recess, but most days there were one or two disobedient students kept in from recess. Obedient students' parents were not called up to school, but on one or two mornings a week I met a parent of a disobedient student who had been summoned to school at 8:30 A.M. before classes began. Obedient students did not get suspended, but disobedient students were suspended at my request at the rate of about one a semester

I was very flattered when the assistant principal remarked that he brought visitors past my room "so they could see what could be done with our students," but I look back at it now with chagrin. It would have been more accurate if he had said, "so they could see what could be done *to* our students."

I must say that I did a whole lot more for these children than a number of "flower children" (this was the '60s) who came in with the message of universal love and not much appetite for the hard work that teaching, or even handling, children entails, and who were tossed out nearly literally on their behinds by the students in a matter of weeks.

On the other hand there was a woman who taught across the hall from me. Her name was Mrs. Kennedy. I can't remember her first name. I think we actually addressed one another as "Mrs. Kennedy" and "Mr. Finn." She was a strikingly beautiful black woman, a recent graduate of Fisk University. Her classroom was always orderly, but I never heard her raise her voice. If the students saw me as an easily provoked drill sergeant, they saw her as a den mother, a den mother who didn't put up with much nonsense, but a den mother.

I think Mrs. Kennedy might have been doing a better job of teaching than I, but not a whole lot better. All of us—teachers and students—were locked into a system of rules and roles that none of us understood and that did not allow for much in the way of education. And I do not mean in just the "low classes." For the most part, students in the 8-1s were also getting handled—schooled to take orders, to replace their parents at the bottom of the economic heap. My guess is that things are about the same today at Carol Jason Banks Upper Grade Center and thousands of schools like it throughout the country.

When I was twenty-seven, I married another teacher. At the time we were not entirely aware of it, but she was from a different world, a fiercely middle-class world—her father an accountant, mother a school teacher, one sibling, raised in a middle-class suburb, Methodist, Republican, educated at the University of Iowa (not an urban teachers college as I was), and she taught in the suburbs. Thus began a thirty-five year experiment in cross-cultural communication, which has been stormy at times and approached the shoals on a few occasions, but it has taught both of us that most of what goes on in cross-cultural communication when it doesn't go well (which is often) is subtle, covert, unconscious, and often insidious.

I was pretty tuckered out after eight years of handling poor children. During that time, I had earned a master's degree in English. My talent for things academic and probably the know-how of my middle-class wife led me to other pastures. I quit teaching elementary school and went to work at Scott-Foresman editing literature textbooks for a few years. A little later, I taught English at City College of Chicago (where a majority of the students were working-class) and began to work on a doctorate in education at the University of Chicago. It was here I began to read such people as Basil Bernstein and William Labov, people who dealt explicitly with the impact of class on communication style, language, and school success. For the last twenty-five years I have been on the faculty of the Graduate School of Education at the State University of New York at Buffalo, where I have a handful of students working for their doctor's degrees and a whole lot of students working for their master's degrees.

And so for nearly thirty years I have been reading, writing, thinking, debating, and teaching about literacy and language and schooling and how they are related to inequality in our society, and at the same time I have been thinking about and teaching teachers how to teach language arts in the elementary school.

—m—

Since I teach at a graduate school, my students are a little older than the average person would imagine. They tend to be getting on toward thirty, with a sizeable number getting on toward forty, because they are changing careers or they took time off to have children. Nearly all of them teach full time. My classes are scheduled at 4:00 or 7:00 P.M., and the students, brave souls, come to me after a full day of teaching.

A small number of them are overtly political and they sometimes disagree with my conclusions—some because they are farther to the right and others because they are farther to the left than I. But most of my students are not overtly political. They put me in mind of myself thirty years ago when I was teaching eighth grade and going to graduate school evenings.

My favorite professor was John Carter. He was a widely recognized scholar on Edgar Allen Poe, and he wrote a best-selling novel, *Full Fathom Five,* in 1965.[4] His father had been a physician, and he was raised in Oak Park, an affluent suburb west of Chicago. He sometimes talked to his classes about who he thought we were, and he would refer to us as "hard-bitten" Chicago school teachers.

We understood what he meant. First of all, he intended no disrespect. In fact, he admired us. Because we were mostly young we taught in the poorest neighborhoods. (Teachers moved to richer neighborhoods with seniority.) We wanted our students to succeed and move ahead, just as many of us had. We believed they could do it if only they would try. We knocked ourselves out every day and experienced little success, and so we blamed our students for not trying. That left us a little bitter.

John Carter found us problematic. He couldn't get through to us. He loved Shakespeare and Keats and Byron and Poe and he wanted us to love them as he did, and he succeeded to a degree. But there was always a practical, down-to-earth element in our makeup that defeated him. If getting a master's degree didn't mean a raise in pay, most of us would not have been there. We took the seminar in Keats rather than Shakespeare because it fit better into our child care responsibilities or our bowling nights. And although we did love literature (we could have gotten our master's degrees in psychology or any number of other fields and gotten the same pay raise) we had practical, down-to-earth reasons for studying it. Knowing literature enabled us to pass certification exams, and we looked forward to the day when we would teach in "better" schools where we might venture reading a Shakespeare sonnet in our classes.

We judged everything that John Carter, or any other professor, taught us by one criterion: How would it work in my classroom? That meant that anything that got a little too aesthetic was out. And we didn't think John Carter, or any other professor, had anything to tell us about what would work in our classrooms. We were out there in the trenches and we took no advice from anyone who wasn't out there with us. I think that's what John Carter meant when he said we were hard bitten.[5]

Many of my students are hard-bitten school teachers. They are practical and down to earth, and they judge everything I say by one criterion: How would this work in my classroom? They are dubious about whether I have anything to tell them about what would work in their classrooms. True, I taught school for eight years, but that was thirty years ago.

And because I teach education rather than English there is an aspect to our relationship that was not present in John Carter's relationship with me and my classmates. If John Carter rhapsodized over "Shall I compare thee to a summer's day," I could go along and smile at his naivete in thinking that "a summer's day" would be greeted by anything but howls on Chicago's south side. But when I suggest to my hard-bitten students that poor children are not being as well educated as they could be, they are not amused. They take it as a personal attack from someone who has been living in an ivory tower for the last thirty years, and they resent it—a lot.

—⟨⟨⟨—

So my getting through to these students is a good deal more complicated than John Carter's getting through to me. Benign amusement is replaced by thinly veiled hostility. Unlike my self-consciously political students who sometimes disagree with me on ideological grounds, these hard-bitten school teachers take differences of opinion with me personally.

My hard-bitten teachers have taught me a lesson that I, like many academics, needed to learn: Don't be so damned superior! Don't look down your nose at people out there teaching real children in real and sometimes dreadful circumstances. Don't question their intelligence, or their commitment, or their motives. I hope I have learned this lesson well enough so that I don't set up barriers between them and me such that they are not able to listen to my story and consider my position.

And so I think I've thought it through, and I hope I've learned to deal with the realities of teaching and not to be too smug while assessing problems and suggesting solutions, because no matter what the solutions are, it's hard-bitten school teachers who will need to implement them.

Chapter 2

A DISTINCTLY UN-AMERICAN IDEA
An Education Appropriate to Their Station

J ean Anyon studied fifth grade classes in five public elementary schools in rich neighborhoods and not-so-rich neighborhoods in northern New Jersey.[1] In one school, designated *executive elite*, family breadwinners were top corporate executives in multinational corporations or Wall Street financial firms. Their incomes were in the top 1 percent in the United States. In a second school, designated *affluent professional*, family breadwinners were doctors, TV and advertising executives, and other highly paid professionals. Incomes were in the top 10 percent for the nation. In a third school, designated *middle class*, breadwinners were a mixture of highly skilled, well-paid blue- and white-collar workers and those with traditional middle-class occupations such as teachers, social workers, accountants, and middle managers. Incomes were better than average for the United States but below the top 10 percent. In a fourth and fifth school designated *working class*, about one-third of the breadwinners were skilled blue-collar workers; about half were unskilled or semiskilled blue-collar workers, and about 15 percent of the heads of households were unemployed.

First Anyon noted similarities among the schools. They were nearly all white. They were all located in northern New Jersey and subject to the same state requirements. They all used the same

9

arithmetic books. They had the same language arts course of study. Two of the schools used the same basal reading series. There were startling differences, however.

In the two working-class schools, most of the teachers were born in the same city as the school but lived in better sections. Most of them were young and had graduated from the local teachers college; many of them were single.

In the working-class schools, knowledge was presented as fragmented facts isolated from wider bodies of meaning and from the lives and experiences of the students. *Work* was following steps in a procedure. There was little decision making or choice. Teachers rarely explained why work was being assigned or how it was connected to other assignments. Work was often evaluated in terms of whether the steps were followed rather than whether it was right or wrong. For example, one teacher led the students through a series of steps to draw a one-inch grid on their paper without telling them what they were making or what it was for. When a girl realized what they were making and said she had a faster way to do it, the teacher answered, "No you don't. You don't even know what I'm making yet. Do it this way or it's wrong."

While the same arithmetic book was used in all five schools, the teacher in one working-class school commented that she skipped pages dealing with mathematical reasoning and inference because they were too hard. The teacher in the second working-class school said, "These pages are for creativity—they're extras." She often skipped them as well.

In one working-class school they used a social studies textbook that was described by its publisher as intended for "low ability students." The teachers guide referred repeatedly to "educationally deficient students"—for whom the book was intended. The book was intended to provide a year's work, but there were only sixteen lessons consisting of a few paragraphs followed by vocabulary drill and exercises to check recall. However, these were not special education classrooms. In the two working-class school classrooms combined, the children's average IQ was above 100 and eight children had IQs above 125.

In the working-class schools, social studies instruction typically consisted of copying teachers' notes, writing answers to textbook questions, and craft projects, such as cutting out and making a stand-up figure of a cowboy roping a steer to represent the South-west when studying U.S. geography. Compared to the more affluent schools in this study there was less discussion of controversial topics such as labor disputes, civil rights, and women's rights and less attention to the history of these issues.

In language arts, the teacher gave each student a duplicated sheet entitled "All About Me" and directed them to write their answers on the lines following questions such as "Where were you born?" and "What is your favorite animal?" This activity was re-ferred to as "writing an autobiography." Children were presented with rules for where to put commas, but there was never any discussion of how commas made writing easier to understand or of the notion that punctuation called for decisions based on the in-tended meaning.

In science, children were routinely told to copy the directions for doing an experiment from the book. The teacher then did the experiment in front of the class as the students watched and wrote a list entitled "What We Found" on the board. The students copied it into their notebooks. A test on "What We Found" would follow.

Teachers made every effort to control students' movement. They often kept children after the dismissal bell to finish their work or to punish them for misbehavior. There were no clocks in class-rooms. Materials were handed out by the teacher and closely guarded. Students were ordered to remain in their seats unless given specific permission to move. When permitted to leave the room they needed a pass with the time and date.

Teachers made derogatory remarks regarding the students. A principal was reported to have said to a new teacher "Just do your best. If they learn to add and subtract, that's a bonus. If not, don't worry about it." A second grade teacher said the children were "getting dumber every year." Only twice did Anyon hear a teacher say "please" to a student in an unsarcastic tone. She heard "Shut up" frequently.

One fifth grade teacher said the students needed the basics— simple skills. When asked "why?" she responded, "They're lazy. I hate to categorize them, but they're lazy." Another fifth grade teacher who was asked why she had students endlessly copy notes from the blackboard in social studies replied, "Because the children in this school don't know anything about the U.S., so you can't teach them much." Another teacher said, "You can't teach these kids anything. Their parents don't care about them, and they're not interested." Another teacher answered when asked what was important knowledge for her students, "Well, we keep them busy." You have to keep reminding yourself that these children did not have low IQ scores. They were working-class children with average intelligence, some with better than average intelligence.

When Anyon asked these fifth grade students, "What do you think of when I say the word *knowledge?*" not a single child used the word *think*. Only one mentioned the word *mind*. When asked if they can make knowledge only one said yes.

In each category of school, Anyon observed what she called a "dominant theme." In the working-class schools the dominant theme was *resistance*. Students vandalized school property and resisted the teachers' efforts to teach. Boys fell out of chairs; students brought bugs into the classroom and released them; children lost books or forgot them; students interrupted the teacher. They showed no enthusiasm for projects into which the teacher put extra effort. They refused to answer questions and were apparently pleased when the teacher became upset. There was less resistance to easy work, and so assignments were rarely demanding.

According to Anyon these children were developing a relationship to the economy, authority, and work that is appropriate preparation for wage labor—labor that is mechanical and routine. Their capacity for creativity and planning was ignored or denied. Their response was very much like that of adults in their community to work that is mechanical and routine and that denies their capacity for creativity and planning. They engaged in relentless "slowdowns," subtle sabotage, and other modes of indirect resistance similar to that carried out by disgruntled workers in factories, sales floors, and offices.

—❧—

In the middle-class school, about one-third of the teachers grew up in the neighborhood of the school. Most graduated from the local state teachers college, and many of them lived in the neighborhood of the school. Some were married to other teachers, accountants, police officers, nurses, and managers of local businesses.

Teachers in the middle-class school seemed to believe that their job was to teach the knowledge found in textbooks or dictated by curriculum experts. They valued this more than knowledge taught by experience. For example, when a child said that the plural of *mouse* is not *mouses* because "it wouldn't sound right," the teacher said that was the wrong reason. The right reason was that *mouse* is an irregular noun, *as it says in the book.*

A social studies textbook intended for use in sixth grade was used in the fifth grade classroom in the middle-class school. According to the publisher, the purpose of the book was to introduce fundamental concepts. There were "understandings" from anthropology, economics, history, geography, or political science listed in the teacher's guide for each chapter.

Social studies classes involved reading the text, listening to the teacher's explanations, answering the teacher's questions, and occasionally doing reports. There was rarely sustained inquiry into a topic. The teacher rarely used a feature of the text entitled "Using the Main Idea" (applying main ideas to current events and personal situations), because she said she had enough to do to get them to understand the generalizations.

Knowledge in the middle-class school was "more conceptual" than in the working-class school. It was less a matter of isolated facts and more a matter of gaining information and understanding from socially approved sources. Knowledge here was like that in the working-class school, however, in that it was not connected with the lives and experiences of the students.

In the middle-class school, *work* was getting the right answer. Answers were words, sentences, numbers, facts, and dates. You could not make them up. They were found in books or by listening to the teacher. You wrote them neatly on paper in the right order. If you got enough right answers, you got a good grade.

You got the right answer by following directions, but the directions allowed for some choice, some figuring, some decision making, and the teacher explained the purpose of assignments and why the directions would lead to the right answer. For example, students were permitted to do steps "in their heads" rather than write them down. They were allowed to do division problems the long or short way. When reviewing homework they had to say *how* they did the problem as well as give their answer. Social studies consisted of reading passages and answering comprehension questions: who, what, when, where, and sometimes why. However, questions that might have led to controversial topics were avoided because parents might complain.

Work rarely called for creativity. There was little serious attention to how students might develop or express their own ideas. In a social studies project, the students were directed to find information on assigned topics and put it "in your own words." Many of the children's products had imaginative covers and illustrations, which were largely ignored by the teacher who graded on information, neatness, and the student's success in paraphrasing the sources used. Lessons that explicitly called for creativity and self-expression were "enrichment" and "for fun." They did not count toward grades.

The teachers in the middle-class school varied from strict to somewhat easygoing, but for all of them, decisions were made on the basis of rules and regulations that were known to the students. Teachers always honored class dismissal bells. There was little excitement in the school work, and assignments did not seem to take into account the student's interests or feelings, but the children seemed to believe that there were rewards: good grades lead to college and a good job. Remember, these were fifth graders.

When children in the middle-class school were asked what knowledge is, seventeen of twenty used words like *learn, remember, facts, study, smartness, intelligent, know, school, study,* and *brains.* When asked if they could make knowledge, nine said no and eleven said yes. When asked how, they said they'd look it up or listen and do what they're told or they'd go to the library.

The dominant theme in the middle-class school was *possibility.* There was widespread anxiety about tests and grades but there was a pervasive belief that hard work would pay off. These students viewed knowledge as a valuable possession that can be traded for good grades, a good college education, and a good job. There was more excited patriotism around holidays here than in any other school. There were frequent auditorium assemblies with a patriotic flavor. The feeling was that America is full of promise and these children were going to cash in on it.

Anyon observed that in the middle-class school the children were developing a relationship to the economy, authority, and work that is appropriate for white-collar working-class and middle-class jobs: paper work, technical work, sales, and social services in the private and public sectors. Such work does not call for creativity.

Such workers are not rewarded for critical analysis. They are rewarded for knowing the answers, for knowing where to find answers, for knowing which form, regulation, technique, or procedure is correct. While this kind of work does not reward creativity or self-expression, it usually pays enough to enable workers to find opportunities for creativity and self-expression outside the workplace.

—m—

In the affluent professional school the teachers came from elsewhere in the state. They all came from middle- or upper-class backgrounds. Most were women married to high-status professionals or executives.

Creativity and personal development were important goals for students at the affluent professional school. Teachers wanted students to think for themselves and to make sense of their own experience. Discovery and experience were important. In arithmetic, for example, students measured perimeters in the classroom and created questions for other students to answer. They collected data in surveys and did experiments with cubes and scales. They made a film on the metric system. In science, students experimented *in their own way* to discover the properties of aluminum, copper, and glass (which heats fastest, for example), and it didn't matter whether they got the right answer. What mattered was that they discussed their ideas. When students asked, "How should I do this?" teachers answered, "You decide," or, "What makes sense to you?"

There were, however, wrong answers. In arithmetic, six plus two was still eight and only eight. In science, the answer had to be consistent with observations. Students were required to have their observations and answers "verified" by other students before handing in assignments.

The social studies textbook emphasized "higher concepts" such as "the roles of savings, capital, trade, education, skilled labor, skilled managers, and cultural factors (religious beliefs, attitudes toward change) in the process of economic development," and the understanding that "the controlling ideas of Western culture come largely from two preceding cultures: The Judaic and Greco-Roman."

Students read and outlined the text and used it as a guide for "inquiry activities" such as baking clay cuneiform replicas, writing stories and plays and creating murals showing the division of labor in ancient societies. Several students had seen the Tutankhamen exhibit in New York—one had seen it in Paris.

They devoted a lot of time to current events because, according to the teacher, "they're so opinionated anyway, and they love it." Children often wrote editorials and brought in clippings on such topics as labor strife, inflation, and nuclear power. The teacher, however, said she had to be very careful of expressing her own opinion. "One year I had the superintendent's son, the mayor's son, and the daughter of the president of the board of education in my room—all at one time. I *really* had to watch what I said."

Knowledge in the affluent professional school was viewed as being open to discovery. It was used to make sense and thus it had personal value. School knowledge was presented as having relevance to life's problems. Unlike the situation in the working-class and middle-class schools, social strife was acknowledged and discussed.

In the affluent professional school, work was creative activity carried out independently. It involved individual thought and expression, expansion and illustration of ideas, and choice of appropriate methods and materials. Products were often stories, essays, or representations of ideas in murals, craft projects, and graphs. Students' projects were to show originality and individuality, but they had to fit with reality—that is, a creative mural could be marked down if it misrepresented the facts or concepts it was supposed to represent.

One assignment was for students to find the average number of chocolate chips in three chocolate chip cookies. The teacher announced gravely, "I'll give you three cookies, and you'll have to eat your way through, I'm afraid." When work was underway, she circulated giving help, praise, and reminders about getting too noisy. The children worked sitting or standing at their desks or at a bench in the back of the room or sitting on the floor.

In their study of ancient civilizations, they made a film on Egypt. One student wrote the script, the class acted it out, and one of the parents edited it. They read and wrote stories depicting ancient times. They did projects chosen from a list, all of which involved graphic representations such as murals. They wrote and exchanged letters with the other fifth grade in "hieroglyphics." The list goes on.

They discussed current events daily and were encouraged to expand on what they said and to be specific. The teacher's questions were designed to help them make connections between events in the news and what they were learning in school.

In language arts, they did not use textbooks because the principal thought textbooks hampered creativity. Each child interviewed a first grader and wrote a rebus story[2] just for that child. They wrote editorials about matters before the school board and radio plays that were sometimes acted over the school intercom. Lessons on punctuation stressed the relationship between meaning and punctuation.

Products of work were highly prized. The affluent professional school was the only school where Anyon was not allowed to take children's work away from the school. If possible, she could duplicate it and take the copy, but if it could not be copied, she could not have it.

Control involved constant negotiation. Teachers rarely gave direct orders unless the children were too noisy. Instead, teachers commented on the probable consequences of student behavior and asked students to decide accordingly. One of the few rules regulating children's movement was that not more than three children could be out of the room at one time. They could go to the school library at any time to get a book. They merely signed their name on the chalkboard and left the room when they needed to. There were no passes.

They sometimes negotiated what work was to be done. For example, children sometimes asked for more time before moving on to the next subject, and the teacher sometimes acquiesced. There is a remarkable footnote to this discussion. The teacher commented that she was "more structured" that year than usual because of the large number of children in the class who were considered discipline problems.

In the affluent professional school, work was not repetitious and mechanical, as it was in the working-class school; it was not knowing the correct answers, as it was in the middle-class school; it was being able to manipulate what Anyon termed *symbolic capital*.

The children in the affluent professional school had the least trouble answering the question "What is knowledge." Many of them used the word *think* and several alluded to personal activity having to do with ideas. ("Figuring stuff out." "You think up ideas and then find things wrong with those ideas.") When asked, "Can you make knowledge?" sixteen said yes; only four said no.

In the affluent professional school the dominant theme was *individualism* with a minor theme of *humanitarianism*. Emphasis in the classroom was on thinking for oneself, creativity, and discovery in science and arithmetic. But there was also a pervasive climate of mutual help and concern for one another and for humanity. The principal ended morning announcements with "Do something nice for someone today." Social class and class conflict were discussed in social studies, with a liberal spin. There was an entire textbook devoted to prejudice and discrimination. Eight of twenty students interviewed expressed antagonism toward "the rich," who they said were greedy, spoiled, and snobby. This is interesting in light of the fact that these students' family incomes were in the top 10 percent for the nation.

Children in this school were developing a relationship to the economy, authority, and work that is appropriate for artists, intellectuals, legal and scientific experts, and other professionals whose work is creative, intrinsically satisfying for most people, and rewarded with social power and high salaries. Although in the workplace they do not have complete control over which ideas they develop and express, affluent professionals are relatively autonomous. Their relationship to people who decide which ideas will be developed (the executive elite whom I'll get to in the next paragraph) involves substantial negotiation.

—⚉—

In the executive elite school, as in the affluent professional school, the teachers were women married to high-status professionals and business executives, but in the executive elite school the teachers regarded their students as having higher social status than themselves.

Knowledge in the executive elite school was academic, intellectual, and rigorous. More was taught and more difficult concepts were taught. Reasoning and problem solving were important. The rationality and logic of mathematics were held up as the model for correct and ethical thinking.

Social studies knowledge was more sophisticated, complex, and analytic than in the other schools. Questions such as good and bad effects of imperialism and the reasons for conflict between social classes were discussed. However, there was little questioning of the status quo. The present distribution of wealth and power was presented as natural and timeless—going back to the ancient Greeks.

Children were required to plan lessons and teach them to the class. Among other things, they were evaluated on how well they kept control of the class. The teacher said to one child who lost control of his classmates, "When you're up there, you have authority, and you have to use it. I'll back you up."

While strict attention was demanded during lessons, there was little attempt to regulate the children's movement at other times. They were allowed into the classrooms when they arrived at school; they did not have to wait for the bell, as in every other school in Anyon's study.

Students were permitted to take materials from closets and even from the teacher's desk when they needed them. They were in charge of the school office at lunch time. They did not need permission or a pass to leave the room. Because of the amount of work demanded, however, they rarely left the room.

The children were sometimes flippant, boisterous, and occasionally rude. However, they were usually brought into line by reminding them of their responsibility to achieve. "It's up to you." Teachers were polite to students. There was no sarcasm, no nasty remarks, and few direct orders.

When asked, "Can you make knowledge?" half the children in the executive elite school said yes; half said no. Compared with the affluent professional school children, these children took a more passive view toward the creation of knowledge. For many of them knowledge comes from tradition. It's "out there" and you are expected to learn it.

The dominant theme in the executive elite school was *excellence*—preparation for being the best, for top-quality performance. There was no narcissistic coddling here, but insistence upon self-discipline instead. The pace was brisker than in any other school and children were often told that they alone were responsible for keeping up.

In the executive elite school the children were developing a relationship to the economy, authority, and work that is different from all the other schools. They learned grammatical, mathematical, and other vocabularies by which systems are described. They were taught to use these vocabularies to analyze and control situations. The point of school work was to achieve, to excel, to prepare for life at the top.

—⟀—

The working-class children were learning to follow directions and do mechanical, low-paying work, but at the same time they were learning to resist authority in ways sanctioned by their community. The middle-class children were learning to follow orders and do the mental work that keeps society producing and running smoothly. They were learning that if they cooperated they would have the rewards that well-paid, middle-class work makes possible outside the workplace. The affluent professional children were learning to create products and art, "symbolic capital," and at the same time they were learning to find rewards in work itself and to negotiate from a powerful position with those (the executive elite) who make the final decisions on how real capital is allocated. The executive elite children? They were learning to be masters of the universe.

Anyon's study supports the findings of earlier observers[3] that in American schools children of managers and owners are rewarded for initiative and assertiveness, while children of the working-class are rewarded for docility and obedience and punished for initiative and assertiveness. Remember the teacher who said, "Do it this way or it's wrong."

This couldn't be more obvious when you compare Anyon's "gentry" schools—her executive elite and affluent professional schools—with her working-class schools. The surprising thing is where Anyon's middle-class school fits into this picture. Like the children in working-class schools, children in the middle-class school were schooled to take orders. They were taught that knowledge in textbooks was more valuable than their own experience. They were taught through traditional, directive methods to look up knowledge, not to create it. They were not taught to manipulate or direct systems, nor was there any effort to connect school knowledge with their daily lives.

On the other hand, Anyon's middle-class school was like her gentry schools in that students saw the knowledge that teachers had to offer as valuable—albeit for the future, for entrance into good colleges, and for procuring highly paid work. And since they valued the teachers' knowledge, they cooperated with the teachers to get it. The theme here was not *resistance*, as it was in the working-class school; it was *possibility*.

Twenty years after Anyon's study Robert Reich,[4] Clinton's first secretary of labor, analyzed America's workforce in the 90s. While Anyon classified Americans in terms of their incomes and the kind of work they do, Reich's analysis added a new criterion on which to classify workers: with whom do they compete for jobs—only other Americans, or with workers in other countries?

Reich identified the top 20 percent as "symbolic analysts." These are the problem solvers and creators of ideas and symbols. They are engineers, bankers, lawyers, writers, designers, and the fastest-growing category—consultants. Theirs is an international job market. The work done by an engineer in Chicago today might go to an engineer in Tokyo or Bonn tomorrow. The same is true of bankers, lawyers, writers, designers, and consultants. Americans educated in our best schools (those Anyon described as executive elite and affluent professional) perform very well in this international competition, and they command enormous salaries.

Reich classifies what I shall refer to as the working class (the bottom 55 percent of American workers) in two ways. He refers to "in-person service workers" and "routine production service workers." In-person service workers are in retail sales, hospital and health care, food services and security. Since these services are delivered to the consumer "in-person," these jobs cannot be easily exported. In-person service work is often characterized as nurturing work or women's work. It has always been and continues to be poorly paid. In-person service jobs make up a little more than half of the working-class jobs in America today.

Slightly less than half of the working class in America today are in "routine production service work." These are the foot soldiers of American industry—assembly line workers in the older "heavy" industries and in the newer electronics industries. These jobs are eminently exportable. While work in newer industries is cleaner and easier, shops are not unionized and the pay is remarkably lower. The number of well-paid jobs in older industries is declining while the number of poorly paid jobs in newer industries is increasing.

What's left is the approximately 20 percent whom I shall refer to as the middle class. Reich refers them to as government workers. These are the teachers, local and federal government employees, and, surprisingly, physicians paid through Medicaid and Medicare.

In the past twenty years numbers have grown at the top and bottom. The number in the middle has declined. Those at the top have gotten a whole lot richer. Those in the middle are in about the same place economically, and those at the bottom have gotten a whole lot poorer. Reich observed that among the fastest-growing occupations in America is that of security guard. Small wonder.

The question is, do the children of the elite and the middle class and the working class still attend schools like those Anyon described. The answer is, you bet! If there were later studies that did not support her findings or that showed a trend in a different direction, I would never have cited her in the first place. But the recent literature supports her conclusions.

In the early 90s, the faculty at California State University at Dominguez Hills (near Los Angeles) described schools attended by children who are disenfranchised because of social class, poverty, or cultural background in much the same way Anyon described the working-class schools in her study a decade earlier.[5] A colleague of mine regularly sends her students out to schools and asks them to compare what they observe to what Anyon observed. They invariably report that matters remain the same. In *Savage Inequalities*[6] Jonathan Kozol reports on schools in upscale communities like Winnetka, Illinois, Cherry Hill, New Jersey, and Rye, New York, and schools in impoverished communities like East St. Louis, Illinois, Camden, New Jersey, and parts of Washington, D.C., Chicago, and New York City. Nothing's changed, unless, perhaps, it's gotten worse.

In February 1998 I asked one of my classes to write papers comparing Anyon's findings to their own personal experiences. The following are excerpts from two of their papers.

I am from Amherst, New Hampshire. Amherst is one of the most affluent places to live in New Hampshire. About five years ago a high school was built entirely for Amherst families. Amherst originally was sharing a high school with a neighboring middle class town that was not as wealthy. Many parents and families in Amherst wanted a better education for their children, so as a result, a brand new high school was built. The high school was a major development in the town of Amherst, and people from other towns were moving to Amherst, just so their children could go to the high school. I would consider Amherst High School to fit into the affluent professional category. The methods of teaching almost duplicated the strategies taught at the affluent professional school in Anyon's study.

I did not attend the high school, because I went to a private school, but many of my close friends did and my younger sister does now. I was told the students were given extreme privileges and were taught knowledge in creative ways, rather than straight from a textbook. For example, students had their own smoking section, they called their teachers by their first name, there were no honor level classes, and a lot of material taught (from science to English) was done through projects involving the kids to the greatest extent. The students were also able to get away with a lot, because they questioned everything that was assigned to them. Parents were relentless in their persistence to have their kids receive the best education possible.

However, the town Amherst broke away from was left with mostly middle class students, because all the Amherst kids left. As a result, the high school resorted to more traditional styles of educating, which meant teaching straight from a textbook and not giving any choices or freedom to the students. Meanwhile, the Amherst students were receiving progressive styles of teaching and were being educated on how to become superior professionals.[7]

[At first] Anyon's conclusions seemed wildly radical and oversimplified to me. I was not willing to admit that limits so tangible and so obvious existed in classrooms in the United States. After all, America is supposedly the "land of opportunity" where you can achieve whatever career goals to which you aspire. This class culture distinction sounded as severe as the caste system in India. However, the more I remembered various teaching situations I have been in, the more clear class culture perpetuation became.

As a student teacher, I had the opportunity to teach in what Anyon would classify an affluent professional school and a working-class school. Although both schools professed progressive principles, the differences in the two schools were very apparent at the time. However, I never considered how the methods used to teach differed until reading Anyon's study. I find the correlations between my real life experiences and the study frightening. Reading about this type of class tracking in schools is one thing. Realizing that you have experienced it is truly another.

My experience in the affluent professional school was idyllic. The classes I worked with had many activities promoting independence and creativity such as Reading and Writing Workshops. Students had control of how to use their time, and all teacher directed lessons were mini-lessons taking no more than ten minutes of class time. These lessons were often based on questions that students had encountered during their individual reading or writing activities. Students could sit anywhere they pleased in the room, as long as they were working on their projects. All books read and all writing genres exhibited by the students were self-chosen. These conditions mirror Anyon's description of the affluent professional school.

Progressive principles were highly prized, and at each staff meeting, the principal began with the statement, "We are here to consider how we can best serve the whole child in each of our students." Staff went out of their way to interact with students individually in and out of class. All the teachers and administration lived in the school district or in adjacent upper class suburbs and most had attended private colleges for their teacher training. It was inspiring. This was how all of my education professors had told me our classes should run. The students flourished. Parents praised the program on Parent's night. They valued their children's creative efforts.

My next assignment contrasted sharply with the first. Before I began in the classroom my sponsor teacher told me that students at the school were not interested in learning, and were often out of control. She showed me lessons, complete with overheads she had designed instructing students on the proper steps to take if they felt they needed to leave the classroom. Everything was outlined in detail. The desks were always in rows. According to my sponsor teacher, the students "couldn't handle" working in groups.

The most effective way to have students take notes, my grade team told me one day, was to give them Xeroxed copies of the teacher's outline notes with some key words missing. This could have been the school Anyon observed in her study. The control and the bitterness directed at students were shocking.

The teachers in the working-class school lived within the community. In the time I was there, I met four teachers from two grade teams of six each who had graduated from this same school. Almost everyone had attended a state school for their teaching certification. While the affluent professional school's teachers were excited and motivated, the most common refrain I heard among the working-class school's teachers was that they planned early retirement.

The dichotomy still amazes me.[8]

And so I ask, "Those who are smartest and work hardest go furthest?" Who's kidding whom? When students begin school in such different systems, the odds are set for them. President Kennedy once said that he hoped that a person's chance to become president was not determined on the day he was baptized (referring to the fact that some said a Catholic could never become president). I'd like to hope that a child's expectations are not determined on the day she or he enters kindergarten, but it would be foolish to entertain such a hope unless there are some drastic changes made.

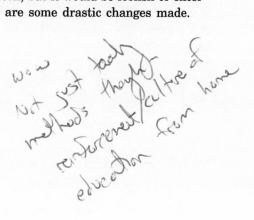

Chapter 3

HARSH SCHOOLS, BIG BOYS, AND THE PROGRESSIVE SOLUTION

D aniel Resnick[1] tells an interesting story about the history of American schools and how we got to where we are today. His story begins with the history of the catechism. If you didn't go to a parochial school or attend Sunday school, you might not know what a catechism is. It's a book that teaches religious doctrine in a question-answer format. I still remember the first catechism lessons I memorized, I think in first grade.

> Who made you?
> *God made me.*
> Why did God make you?
> *God made me to know Him, to love Him, and to serve Him*
> *in this life and to be happy with Him forever in the next.*[2]

Through memorizing page after page of such questions and answers I was taught those doctrines of the Catholic church that were deemed appropriate for children my age.

Catechisms appeared in the earliest days of Christianity and continued to be produced throughout the middle ages. Even after the Reformation the catechism continued to be a favored way of teaching religious doctrine. Luther's *Little Catechism* was translated into all the major European languages within a generation.

Similar books and methods were used in the first schools in Europe and in colonial America. *The New England Primer* with its hundred plus questions and answers was the most widely used reader in American schools before 1820. It sold more than two million copies in its many editions. Other school books followed suit, such as *A Political Catechism, Intended for Use in Schools in the United States of America,* which was published in 1796.

Early schools did not permit, let alone encourage, children to generate ideas or to argue about the truth or value of what others had written. Teaching from a catechism discourages questioning, interpreting, or reflecting on the significance of what was presented. "Writing" instruction consisted of copying portions of texts written by others—literally, in "copy books." The schools had no interest in recognizing or developing the independent authority of the student's mind, and they placed a great deal of importance on confirming the authority of received texts.

The frame of mind that gave us the catechism is the same frame of mind that gave us the American schools in the Traditional Era—from colonial times until after the Civil War.[3] The dominant aim of traditional education was to develop character and intellect in the young by teaching them long-established knowledge. The curriculum was narrow—reading, penmanship, spelling, arithmetic, plus a little history, English, grammar, and geography. Subjects were divided into small "teachable" parts and taught in rigid order—from easy to hard or according to some logical idea of what must come before what. Each subject was taught in its own time slot. Little attention was paid to common elements or similarities from one subject to the next. Emphasis was on learning facts and rules.

There was no attempt to relate the curriculum to the children's lives. The curriculum was fixed and followed down to the last detail year after year. The same material was given to all pupils, without regard for individual differences. The school day consisted of lectures, drill, memorization, recitation, and examinations. Interaction between pupils was limited to competition. Cooperation in doing lessons was likely to be seen as cheating. The teacher and the textbook were the only source of information. Students not occupied directly with the teacher were expected to keep quiet. Desks faced the teacher and were kept in straight rows. They were often bolted to the floor. Play was permitted only during recess.

If this all sounds pretty familiar, I'm not surprised. Traditional education has never disappeared, but the worst nightmare versions of it found today pale in comparison to the schools of the Traditional Era. These were the days of the school*master*. Before 1830, few women taught school. Women did not become the majority in the teaching profession until 1870.

The concept of educating a person to be a teacher was unheard of during the Traditional Era. People who could read and write set themselves up as schoolmasters. They were sometimes paid by individual parents, but almost from the beginning of the colonial period, some communities provided free schooling to those who wanted it and could take advantage of it. The teacher's continued employment did not depend on whether he had any particular talent for teaching; it depended on whether he could control the students.

Severity was considered a virtue. Teachers used a three-foot ruler and a flexible sapling about five feet in length "with force and frequency" upon both boys and girls, young and old, when they did not know their lessons or broke rules. During an inspection tour of the Boston schools in 1844, board members found that whippings in a "representative" school of four hundred pupils averaged sixty-five a day. They found "severe injuries" sometimes resulted from these beatings and that the offenses were often "very trifling." A famous historian commented that "There was little 'soft pedagogy' in the management of either town or rural schools before the Civil War."[4]

"Spare the rod and spoil the child" was a Bible text that received the most literal acceptance both in theory and practice. Even the naturally mild-tempered man was an "old-fashioned" disciplinarian when it came to teaching, and the naturally rough and coarse-grained man was as frightful as any ogre in a fairy tale.

In summer, unless the teacher was an uncommonly poor one, or some of the scholars uncommonly wild and mischievous, the days moved along very harmoniously and pleasantly. In winter, when the big boys came in, some of them grown men, who cared vastly more about having a good time than getting learning, an important requisite of the master was "government." He ruled his little empire, not with a rod of iron, but with a stout three-foot ruler, known as a "ferule," which was quite as effective. The really severe teacher had no hesitation in throwing this ruler at any child he saw misbehaving, and it is to be noted that he threw first and spoke afterward. Very likely he would order the culprit to bring him the ferule he had cast at him (it was a common occurrence to see in schoolroom walls "dents made by ferules hurled at misbehaving pupils' heads with an aim that sometimes proved untrue"), and, when the boy came out on the floor, would further punish him. Punishment by spatting the palm of his hand with a ruler was known as "feruling." The smarting of blows was severe while the punishment lasted, but this was as nothing to a "thrashing." The boy to be thrashed was himself sent for the apple tree twigs with which he was to be whipped. Poor fellow! Whimpering, and blinded by the welling tears, he slowly whittles off one after the other of the rough twigs. This task done, he drags his unwilling feet back to the schoolroom.

"Take off your coat, sir!" says the master.

The school is hushed into terrified silence. The fire crackles in the wide fireplace, the wind whistles at the eaves, the boy's tears flow faster, and he stammers a plea for mercy. Then the whip hisses through the air, and blows fall thick and fast. The boy dances about the floor, and his shrill screams fill the schoolroom. His mates are frightened and trembling, and the girls are crying. . . .[5]

"Big boys" were often the teacher's nemesis. Two fairly commonplace forms of disruption often cost the teacher his job and caused the school to be closed until another teacher could be found. The first was referred to as "putting out" or "turning out" the teacher. In 1837 more than three hundred schools in Massachusetts were "broken up" by rebellious pupils—and Massachusetts was always a leader in education. The situation was probably worse elsewhere in the country.

Turning out the teacher was described by Horace Greeley, of "Go west, young man" fame.

At the close of the morning session of the first of January, and perhaps on some other day that the big boys chose to consider or make a holiday, the moment the master left the house in quest of his dinner, the little ones were started homeward, the doors and windows suddenly and securely barricaded, and the older pupils, thus fortified against intrusion, proceeded to spend the afternoon in play and hilarity. I have known a master to make a desperate struggle for admission, but the odds were too great. If he appealed to the neighboring fathers, they were apt to advise him to desist, and let matters take their course. I recollect one instance, however, where a youth [the teacher] was shut out who, procuring a piece of board, mounted from a fence to the roof of the schoolhouse and covered the top of the chimney nicely with his board. Ten minutes thereafter, the house was filled with smoke, and its inmates, opening the doors and windows, were glad to make terms with the outsider."[6]

It seems that in the Traditional Period of American education, the schoolmaster needed to earn his wings every day.

Another widely reported problem was assaults upon the teacher. These sometimes resulted when the teacher's thrashing of a student got to such a pitch that the miscreant or others (the older boys again) began to protest. When shouts failed "forcible, if not indeed armed, intervention might be the result."[7] But assaults arose over other matters as well. One benighted soul was reported to have lost his job over a plan to demonstrate his physical prowess that went awry. He challenged several boys to wrestle during recess. "[H]e was downed successively by two or three and soon, as a result, lost control of the school, as they found they could handle him, and so concluded to have their own way."[8] The teacher was fired.

And brutalizing and humiliating students carried with them certain risks. And as we will see, these were not abandoned for purely altruistic reasons.

This was a time when public schools were not expected to include everyone. In 1850 fewer than half the nation's whites between the ages of five and nineteen were in school, and the number of nonwhites in school was negligible. This was before immigration from eastern and southern Europe and the white population was vastly more homogeneous than it is today.

The concept of individual differences was unheard of. If a student failed or dropped out, it was no reflection on the school. The student was thought to be stupid or lazy. In schooling, blaming the victim is not a new concept.

After the Civil War things began to change. Between 1850 and 1900 the population of the United States tripled. Nine percent of the population lived in cities in 1830, 25 percent by 1870, and 50 percent by 1920. With industrialization and urbanization, the extended family of the rural setting gave way to nuclear families living among strangers in an unfamiliar setting. Children who had commonly worked on farms, now worked in factories. But as sentiment against child labor in industry mounted, child labor laws were enacted, and children became unemployable. In Philadelphia in 1870, it was reported that "upward of 20,000 children not attending any school, public, private or parochial, are running the streets in idleness and vagabondism."[9]

Concern over delinquency, workers' fear of competition from cheap child labor, and some genuine regard for the welfare of children prompted a rising demand for compulsory education. Only Massachusetts had compulsory education laws before the Civil War. Vermont was the first state to follow suit, in 1867. By 1919 every state had compulsory education laws. It was now the responsibility of the schools to take in all children and keep them.

Enrollments soared and schools became overcrowded. Playgrounds, which had been all outdoors in the country, were confined, overcrowded areas in cities as the country urbanized. The student body was no longer homogeneous. Students varied in ability, religion, social status, place of birth, and language. Differences among white Americans, who had hailed largely from northwestern Europe before the Civil War, were dwarfed by differences among immigrants from southern and eastern Europe, Asia, Latin America, and the newly freed African Americans after the Civil War. By 1910 the proportion of students with foreign-born parents topped 50 percent in the nation's thirty-seven largest cities.

With compulsory education, control became the central problem of schools. Older children with no means of escape were even more prone to violent resistance toward the traditional teaching and discipline methods of the past. The assumption that a child who was not ready to recite lessons perfectly was simply lazy and deserving of a thrashing or expulsion no longer worked. Differences in what could be reasonably expected from different students became too apparent to ignore. Finding other means of control became essential.

Industrialization offered more promising kinds of employment for educated men than "keeping school." At the same time, with compulsory education, schools were becoming a big ticket item for taxpayers, and women could be paid less than men. By 1870 the majority of teachers were women and by 1920 more than 80 percent of teachers were women. The school staff was becoming more and more female. Simultaneously, or perhaps in response to the impossibility of continuing business as usual, public attitudes toward brutal treatment of children were changing and prohibitions against corporal punishment were written into most school districts' rules. Something had to happen, and it did. "Progressive" ideals were invoked, but ultimately subverted, to calm the troubled waters.

—〰—

The ideas upon which progressive education is built can be traced to the seventeenth century and the period referred to as the Enlightenment. Until this time the prevailing view was that human beings are inherently sinful. Enlightenment philosophers argued that man is not inherently good or evil; only his environment makes him one or the other, and so if you could make the environment consistently favorable, there would be no limits on the achievements and virtue of which individuals were capable.

Rousseau (1712–1778) applied this idea explicitly to childhood. He believed that children are endowed with potentials that should be nurtured and permitted to grow naturally in a healthy environment. Pestalozzi (1746–1827) and Froebel (1782–1852) took Rousseau's ideas and translated them into practice in elementary schools and in kindergarten. These ideas found their way to the United States as early as 1808, in a book by Joseph Neef, and found an influential champion in Horace Mann (1796–1859).

In an 1843 report to the Massachusetts Board of Education, Mann criticized the schools and called for reforms, including methods based on Rousseau's ideas and discipline based on love. Mann was immediately attacked by ministers who opposed his beliefs about human nature and by teachers who opposed his educational beliefs. The controversy succeeded in drawing widespread attention to Mann's ideas.

In the 1890s Joseph Rice toured schools in thirty-five cities and wrote a series of muckraking articles that attacked methods of teaching that were designed to "immobilize, automize, and dehumanize students." Lawrence Cremin, a distinguished educational historian, credits Rice's articles with starting the progressive movement in the United States.[10] About the same time, John Dewey (1869–1953), probably the best-known proponent of "progressive education," started the Laboratory School at the University of Chicago.

There are two central concepts of progressive education. First, schools should deal with the whole child—his or her personality, social skills and attitudes, and physical well-being—rather than focusing exclusively on his or her ability to master a narrow, traditional curriculum and parrot back answers. Therefore, education should be interesting, exciting, and enjoyable. Second, children are different. They have different experiences, abilities, and interests. Therefore, although the knowledge and skills included in a progressive curriculum might be quite traditional, they are not likely to be taught in a rigid order dictated by some concept of easy-to-hard or the logic of the subject. They are instead taught in an order dictated by the experiences, abilities, and interests of the individual children. Children are given some choice in determining what they will study and even in how they will go about learning.

Because progressive schools deal with the development of the whole child and recognize individual differences in students' experiences, abilities, and interests, traditional school activities such as reading, writing, and reciting are joined by expressive, creative, physical, and social activities. Art, music, crafts, shop, cooking, sewing, dramatics, and physical education all become part of the regular curriculum. Subjects are "integrated" whenever possible. For example, reading, writing, geography, history, and arithmetic lessons might be incorporated into an ongoing project determined by the students, such as studying the origins of ethnic groups represented in the classroom. Children's activities and learnings will vary. Courses of study (in history, for example) are viewed, not as something that must be covered by each child in a fixed and thorough manner, but as guides for facts, concepts, skills, understandings, and attitudes that might be developed as the teacher deems appropriate for the class and for individual students.

The teacher and textbook are no longer the sole sources of knowledge. Pupils go on field trips, utilize the library and audio-visual presentations, interview local citizens, and so on. Memorization and drill are replaced with efforts to lead students to discover general principles. Pupils are permitted to work independently and in small groups, move about the room, and engage in interesting projects, and a variety of methods and materials are used, including plays, murals, models, projects, games, audio-visual equipment, computers, and field trips.

When children do not do their lessons or don't do them correctly, teachers question whether students have the necessary background or previous knowledge, or they question their own methods or consider how they might capture the students' interest before deciding that the students are lazy or stupid. When, at last, punishment appears to be necessary, it is not physical; instead, it usually involves the loss of some sort of privilege and it is accompanied with sympathetic and constructive suggestions for behavioral changes and explanations of why they are necessary. The ideal is not discipline from above, but self-discipline. Willinsky defines "new literacy," a recent form of progressive education, as "those strategies in the teaching of reading and writing which attempt to shift the control of literacy from the teacher to the student."[11]

Teachers strive to be democratic and friendly. The classroom is informal. Desk and chairs are movable and they are frequently rearranged into circles, clusters, or lines depending on the activity. Distinctions between the school and other spheres of the students' life are minimized. Schools attempt to build on home and community activities with which children are already familiar. But, as we shall see, progressives had fairly upscale homes and communities in mind.

—⟋⟍—

Progressive education unintentionally offered the school an escape hatch from the crisis precipitated by compulsory education laws. Invoking principles of progressive education, schools were able to continue teaching the basics of reading, writing, and arithmetic in grades one through six, but there were now *flexible standards*. Less could be expected (and less demanded) of some students based on their "aptitude" or "intelligence." Everyone in the fourth grade class would move on to the fifth even though there might be a wide range of achievement among them. As early as seventh grade the curriculum would be diversified by adding such courses as shop, art, music, cooking, sewing, and auto mechanics.

The adoption of flexible standards and a diversified curriculum dovetailed with the growing testing movement and created a new profession—school counselling. Intelligence and achievement tests were used to assign students to "tracks" or "streams." An elementary school with sixty or seventy students in each grade might divide them into "low," "middle," and "high" classes, often based on their scores on standardized reading achievement tests. High schools developed academic, commercial, and vocational programs, which, despite protestation to the contrary, soon became identified as "high" and "low" tracks in the minds of everyone. Where schools during the Traditional Era selected students by a process of exclusion, schools in the Progressive Era selected students by differentiating them into different tracks or streams.

There are those who argue that the adoption of progressive ideas was the result of convincing philosophical arguments from scholars such as Dewey. There is no doubt some truth to this, but I generally favor the "escape hatch" theory, because after the dust settled we had arrived at the present system, which is pretty well described by Anyon's study of gentry, middle-class, and working-class schools reported in the last chapter.

Anyon's affluent professional school is about as good as it gets in terms of progressive philosophy and methods and her executive elite school had a progressive feel about it in terms of discipline, student autonomy, and teachers' attitudes toward the students. I would describe her middle-class and working-class schools as traditional schools with a "softened pedagogy," ones where lessons are a little less rigid, but not much, and the brutal assaults have all but disappeared.

—⟋⟋—

I would estimate that today about 20 percent of American schools, those attended by the offspring of the gentry, those whom Reich describes as symbolic-analytic workers, could be described as progressive. The remaining 80 percent, those attended by the offspring of the middle and working classes, are best described as traditional schools with a somewhat softened pedagogy. And I would expect the degree of "softening" to be related to the status of the parents—the higher the status, the softer the pedagogy.

But why aren't progressive methods, curriculum, and philosophy used in all schools? There is not a single reason. There are a lot of them. They're subtle and interconnected. I'll discuss them in the next several chapters.

Chapter 4

OPPOSITIONAL IDENTITY
Identifying "Us" as "Not Them"

You can't talk about the inequality built into the American school system for long before someone starts to tell you about his or her grandfather or great-grandfather or some ancestor who came here at the age of fourteen from Germany or Italy or Ireland with nothing and worked fifteen hour days and, although he died in very modest circumstances, sent his children to college. Of course, the point of the story is, "My ancestors made it through sacrifice and hard work, and anyone else who's willing to get off his dead ass can do the same."

Good point. Why have some groups seemed to prosper in America, while others have not? For example, in Stockton, California, in the 1930s the children of Chinese, Japanese, and Mexican American immigrants all experienced difficulty in school, probably because of their limited ability to speak English. By 1947, however, school failure had disappeared among the Chinese and Japanese but not among the Mexican American population. In fact, by 1947 there were two-and-one-half times more Asian Americans in junior college than one would have predicted based on the percentage of Asian Americans in the general population. In contrast, fewer than 5 percent of Mexican American students in eighth grade were expected to stay in school through junior college. The African American population in Stockton fared only a little better than the Mexican Americans.[1]

A 1983 study showed that Punjabi students did well in California schools despite the fact that, by and large, their parents held low-status, low-paying jobs, had little formal education, low English proficiency, and a culture regarded as backward by many Americans. Nevertheless, the average Punjabi boy did better than the average "American" boy in the same classrooms.

Studies consistently show that Asian Americans do better in school and score higher on standardized tests than African Americans, Mexican Americans, Native Americans, and Puerto Ricans. Latinos from Central and South America and Cuba perform better in school than Latinos from Mexico and Puerto Rico. In Britain, students from East Asia outperform students from the West Indies, despite the fact that English is the native tongue of most West Indians, while it is not the native tongue of most East Asians.

Maoris, who are indigenous to New Zealand, do less well in New Zealand schools than Polynesian immigrants to New Zealand whose language and culture are similar to that of the Maoris. In Japan there is a minority known as Buraku who tend to do poorly in school when compared with the dominant Ippan students. However, in American schools, Buraku and Ippan immigrants do equally well. Children of the Korean minority in Japan do poorly in school. Korean immigrants in the United States do as well as all other Asian immigrants. West Indian students do poorly in Britain, but they do well in the United States.[2]

John Ogbu[3] believes that all these puzzling facts disprove the common-sense theory that the more a minority is like the dominant culture, the better they will do in school. If that were true, why would immigrant Polynesians do better in New Zealand schools than Maoris who are native to New Zealand? Why would Koreans, whose culture and language is more like the Japanese than American, do better in American schools than in Japanese schools? Why do Mexicans and Puerto Ricans do less well in American schools than immigrants from elsewhere in Latin America? Ogbu believes that these puzzling facts can be explained by the history of the relationships between the minority and dominant groups involved. For Ogbu there are minorities, and then there are minorities.

Ogbu distinguishes between *immigrant minorities* and *involuntary minorities*. Immigrant minorities are people who have come to America for improved economic, political, and/or social opportunities. Ogbu identifies recent Chinese and Punjabi immigrants in California as immigrant minorities. Because of language and cultural differences, immigrant minorities initially feel they are discriminated against and their children experience difficulties in school, but they view these conditions as temporary situations that will improve probably over a single generation. Immigrant minorities in the United States compare their situation with that of their countrymen and -women "back home." If in fact they find the struggle in the United States to be more odious than the conditions they left, they have the option of returning home, as many European immigrants did in the late nineteenth and early twentieth century.[4]

Cultural differences exhibited by immigrant minorities existed before they came into contact with the American mainstream culture. For example, before Punjabis immigrated into the United States they spoke Punjabi, were Sikhs, Hindus, or Moslems, had arranged marriages, and males wore turbans. Punjabis continue to exhibit these characteristics more or less after they come into contact with mainstream Americans. Immigrant minorities perceive the mainstream to be different from themselves, not in opposition to themselves.

Immigrant minorities are willing to engage in "accommodation without assimilation." They encourage their children to "play the classroom game"—that is, to adopt the mainstream characteristics necessary for social and academic success in school without necessarily buying into the beliefs or meanings on which these characteristics are based. This is seen simply as expedient, not as a repudiation of their culture. They do it with confidence that they will be accepted or at least tolerated in the mainstream world and they will prosper. They don't mind that their culture is not represented in mainstream schools. They don't expect it to be. They send their children to public schools to learn mainstream ways and they trust that the schools will teach them what they need to know.

On the other hand, *involuntary minorities* are people who became Americans through slavery, conquest, or colonization and who were relegated to an inferior position and denied assimilation. They continue to experience failure in school for generation after generation. American Indians, African Americans, Mexican Americans, Native Hawaiians, and Puerto Ricans are examples of involuntary minorities in the United States. Maori in New Zealand and Buraku in Japan are examples in other countries.

Involuntary minorities experience discrimination as permanent. They have no "homeland" to return to. For Native Americans, this is their homeland. For African Americans, hundreds of years of slavery cut them off from Africa. They have nowhere to go back to in the sense that an Irish or Japanese immigrant can "go back." Puerto Ricans can only go back to an island dominated by United States mainstream culture. Although some recent Mexican immigrants can, and do, go back, many Mexicans are from southwestern states that were annexed to the United States through conquest. As a result, their relationship with the dominant group began as that of citizens in an occupied country to the occupying power.

Unlike immigrant minorities, involuntary minorities do not have peers "back home" with whom they can favorably compare themselves. When they make comparisons, it is with their ancestors before slavery, before the "discovery" of America by Europeans, before the United States' annexation of the Southwest and Puerto Rico, and they see themselves as worse off by comparison. They also compare themselves to mainstream whites and see themselves as worse off. They see newly arrived immigrant minorities move up generation after generation while they do not. They see themselves as oppressed.

Such situations result in what Ogbu refers to as "oppositional identity." Members of the oppressed group come to regard certain beliefs, skills, tastes, values, attitudes, and behaviors as *not* appropriate for them because they are associated with the dominant culture. Adopting these is seen as surrendering to the enemy. On the other hand, certain beliefs, skills, tastes, values, attitudes, and behaviors are embraced by the minority because they are *not* characteristic of the dominant group. The dominant group, in fact, may find them offensive. In short, if I perceive myself to be a member of an oppressed people, there are things I will reject because I associate them with my oppressors and to do them is to betray my people. In addition, there are things I will make a point of embracing because they are rejected by my oppressors. I embrace them as acts of freedom and defiance.

For example, a researcher named Perry Gilmore[5] went into a predominantly low-income black urban elementary school (very much like the Chicago school where I taught twenty-five years ago) to study a program called "Academics Plus." She was very surprised to learn that teachers, administrators, and parents alike focused on attitudes rather than achievement when discussing students' admission into the program. They identified two behaviors, that would definitely bar admission. One was called "stylized sulking" and the other "doin' steps."

Stylized sulking is a student response in face-to-face clashes with teachers. It is usually nonverbal and highly choreographed. It conveys rebellion, anger, and uncooperativeness. It is sometimes seen as a face-saving device. Stylized sulking differs for boys and girls. A girl will pose with her chin up, closing her eyelids for long periods and casting downward side glances, turning her head markedly sidewards and upwards, chin on her hand, her elbow supported by the desk. Striking or getting into the pose is usually performed with an abrupt movement that will sometimes be marked with a sound, either the elbow striking the desk or a verbal marker like "humpf."

Boys' stylized sulking is usually characterized by head downward, arms crossed at the chest, and legs spread wide. Often they will mark the silence by knocking over a chair or pushing loudly on their desk, assuring that others hear and see the performance. Teachers, both black and white, identified stylized sulking as a black thing.

Doin' steps occurs outside school rather than in the classroom. It involves chorally chanting rhymes punctuated with footsteps and hand claps. It is often full of taboos and sexual innuendo. Gilmore collected the following versions of steps based on what many will remember from childhood as a jump rope chant called "Mississippi." The children sometimes refer to steps as "Kookelater (crooked letter) Dances."

> MI crooked letter, crooked letter, I,
> crooked letter, crooked letter, I,
> hump back, hump back, I
> M for the money
> I if ya give it to me
> S sock it (to me)
> S sock it (to me)

> I if I buy it from ya
> S sock it
> S sock it
> I if I take it from ya
> P pump it
> P pump it
> I[6]

Another version was performed by fewer individuals and was viewed as an accomplished recitation by peers. The jeans theme made it a favorite.

> He, Deede, yo
> Spell Mississippi
> Spell Mississippi right now
> You take my hands up high
> You take my feet down low
> I cross my legs with that gigolo
> If you don't like that
> Throw it in the trash
> And then I'm bustin out
> With that Jordache
> Look in the sky
> With that Calvin Klein
> I'm gonna lay in the dirt
> With that Sergiert [Sergio Valente]
> I'm gonna bust a balloon
> With that Sassoon
> Gonna be ready
> With that Teddy
> I'm gonna be on the rail
> With that Vanderbail
> With the is-M is-I
> Crooked letter crooked letter I[7]

In doin' steps, each girl takes a turn. Each has her own style. Girls who were very good became captains who organized and instructed others.

However, the teachers, parents and administrators described stepping as "nasty" and as representing defiance and a bad attitude. Like stylized sulking, stepping was seen as a form of *black* expression and it was banned on the playground. A girl who had been a captain the previous year had given up stepping because she wanted to get into the Academic Plus Program.

But, you may ask, if they know that sulking and stepping is going to get them excluded from the Academics Plus program, why do they keep doing it?

First of all, they were aware that whites identified these behaviors as *black* behaviors and found them offensive, and so engaging in them was an act of defiance.

Furthermore, if these students adopted school-sanctioned ways of saving face in a standoff with a teacher or played hopscotch and jump rope like the girls who are acceptable to the teachers, they would not be who they are; they would be someone else—whites. And if they did make these concessions, would that guarantee that they would get into the Academics Plus program? And if they got into the program, would that guarantee that they would be accepted by mainstream society? Generations of blacks who have "acted white" have not been fully accepted into mainstream society, and have found themselves alienated from their own communities as well.

Robert Coles,[8] a child psychiatrist who has spent his life studying children, tells an interesting story in his book *The Spiritual Life of Children*. He had been interviewing Hopi children in a reservation school asking them such questions as whether they prayed, whether God spoke to them, and what they thought about God. He had carried on such interviews with children all over the world with pretty nearly uniform success, but after six months at the Hopi school he was about ready to admit failure and leave. The children answered his questions as briefly as possible and clearly were not interested in cooperating with him.

Finally, a Hopi mother who volunteered at the school said to him,

The longer you stay here, the worse it will get. . . . [T]hey won't ever want to talk with you about the private events in their lives in this building. They learn how to read and write here; they learn their arithmetic here, but that's that. You are asking them about thoughts they put aside when they enter this building. The longer you stay here and put them in a position that forces them to appear silent and sullen and stupid, the less they'll be inclined even to answer you. Maybe they think, "This guy isn't catching on!"[9]

After this conversation, Coles interviewed the children in their homes, and although there was no sudden miracle, within a month the children seemed altogether different. They smiled, initiated conversations, pointed out places that mattered to them, introduced Coles to their friends, and on their home turf, when he wasn't asking anything in particular, they shared some of their deepest spiritual thoughts. For these children, for these involuntary minorities, school was not and would never be their home turf.

When we're talking about oppositional identity in my class, I often do the following exercise. I ask my students what they would think of an American Methodist who converted to Shintoism (the national religion of Japan)? I don't get much of a rise out of them. A little weird, perhaps, but what's to think? Now let's imagine it's 1950 and Japan had won World War II and the United States is occupied by the Japanese. What would you think of an American Methodist who converted to Shintoism? Traitor! Or try these. A Palestinian converts to Christianity. Ho hum. To Judaism. Shocking! An American Irish Catholic turns Protestant. So what? A Catholic in Northern Ireland turns Protestant. Turncoat!

Why? Because in the first cases we are talking about people adopting a characteristic of a culture to which they feel more or less equal, a culture that has never oppressed their culture economically, politically, socially, or psychologically. In the second cases, we are talking about adopting a characteristic of an enemy. It makes all the difference.

Of course, religious affiliations associated with different groups are easy to think of, but the concept applies to many beliefs, skills, values, attitudes, and behaviors—such as ways of expressing resistance to people in charge (sulking) and forms of recreation (doin' steps).

For involuntary minorities, the dominant group is not only different, it is the enemy. Because cultural differences between them and the mainstream are oppositional rather than simply different, accommodation is difficult if not impossible. Cultural differences become cultural boundaries. Once a cultural identification is established *in opposition* to another, a border is established that people cross at their peril. "Border crossers" are likely to be censured by their own as traitors and they are not likely to be fully accepted by the dominant group.

Characteristics that facilitate school success are, of course, associated with the culture and language of the dominant group. To adopt these is to adopt the culture of the enemy. Furthermore, some beliefs and behaviors that involuntary minorities acquire in their cultures not only fail to prepare them for school, they can in fact be incompatible with the aims of the schools.

For example, Ron and Suzanne Scollon[10] did a study of the Athabaskans, Native Americans who live in Northern Canada and Alaska. Athabaskans have a high degree of respect for individuality. This makes them highly reluctant to interfere in what others know and believe. Therefore, they are not inclined to bring up a topic in conversation unless they are well aware of the point of view of everyone present regarding that topic. If a topic is introduced and you're an Athabaskan and you don't know where everyone present stands on the topic, you remain silent. Furthermore, in Athabaskan society, a person in an inferior position does not display his knowledge in the presence of persons in a superior position. Adults and teachers are expected to display knowledge and abilities; children are expected to watch and learn. As a result, whites see Athabaskan as unsure, aimless, incompetent, and withdrawn, and Athabaskans see whites as braggarts who talk too much.

Now imagine you're a six-year-old Athabaskan in a first grade classroom at "sharing time." Mindy, a white classmate, gets up and tells how she made candles at camp. In both Mindy's and the teacher's culture it is expected that children will display their knowledge for the teacher. They both have an idea of where Mindy's language development is headed—toward mainstream ways of expression that they both view as natural. However, you, an Athabaskan child, have little to say during sharing time. You feel your reluctance to speak is appropriate. You have an idea of where your language development is headed—toward Athabaskan ways of expression that you view as natural. But the teacher views your silence as a deviation from what's natural, and the teacher has all the power here. It is she who decides what's natural. Lucky for Mindy; too bad for you.

Now it's ninth grade. The teacher asks the students to write a persuasive essay: Should clubs dealing with religion be allowed to meet during school hours on school property? Mindy has been chugging along making progress toward the language style of her home, community, and school. She knows that she is expected to "generalize" her audience. It is not her teacher (who, in fact, is the only person who will ever read the essay) but a "general reader." Her arguments should not be addressed to a fairly devout Catholic, which she knows her teacher to be because she attends the same church, but to this general reader about whose beliefs she is to make no assumptions.

But you, an Athabaskan, have been chugging along making progress toward the discourse of your home and community—but not of the school. You are not to address topics unless you know your audience's point of view. How can you write to a general reader—whose point of view is by definition unknown to you? You are not to display knowledge to a person of superior status. Since the general reader may be of equal or superior status, how can you proceed? An Athabaskan cannot write a "good essay" without adopting values and social practices that are in conflict with her or his own.

Mainstream educators, especially those who keep talking about education as *the* answer to all our minority problems, seem to believe that if education were successful, the involuntary minorities would become fully assimilated. Their separate cultures would essentially disappear as, for example, the defining characteristics of Irish Americans at the turn of the century have all but vanished. Aside from the odd St. Patrick's Day Parade and Irish step dancing competition, middle-class descendants of the teeming Irish slums of turn of the century America are hardly distinguishable from other middle-class Americans either in their culture or *in their level of acceptance by other mainstreamers.*

But there's the rub. Involuntary minorities do not believe that they will be accepted even if they surrender their identity. And they have plenty of reason to believe they will not be accepted.

When we discuss Ogbu in my class, I ask my students to think about the students at the Carol Jason Banks Upper Grade Center, where I taught in 1965. The eighth grade students were divided by reading score into fifteen classes. Those in the top group—about twenty-five students—had reading scores at or a little above the eighth grade level. I ask them to think about them and to think about twenty-five eighth graders in the same year with exactly the same reading scores in Winnetka, an upscale suburb north of Chicago. Eighth graders are about fourteen years old. Today these students would be in their middle to late forties. Where would you expect to find them working and living?

My guess is that the nearly all the students from Winnetka went to college and are today professionals living in suburbs like Winnetka. It's possible, but it would be very surprising to hear, that some of them are in prison or on welfare or met a violent death. My guess is that eighth graders *with comparable reading scores* at Banks Upper Grade Center in 1965 are in a different place. One or two of them might have made it big. In fact Minnie Ripperton, who was gaining fame as a jazz singer until her tragic death from breast cancer in 1979, was in my class the first year I taught school. Probably some of these students are school teachers and police officers today. Some may have careers in the military. I would be saddened, but not surprised, to learn that one or two were on welfare or in prison or had met a violent death. On average, the benefits that our society has to offer would not be shared equally by these two groups of students whose reading achievement was identical when they were in eighth grade thirty years ago.

The connection between hard work, good grades, and life success that is so apparent to a student in Winnetka, is not at all apparent to a child in an involuntary minority. Adopting characteristics of mainstream culture costs them, and they have plenty of reason to believe that they will not be accepted into mainstream, white America.

"But," some of my students tell me, "that's all changed."

"Baloney," is my reply. In the O. J. Simpson case we learned that a Los Angeles policeman bragged about pulling over cars with racially mixed couples and finding reasons to give them citations. The media reported that many middle-class Americans were shocked. I wasn't shocked. I don't know of anyone, white or black, middle-class or otherwise, who was shocked. In 1996, Texaco promptly settled a law suit brought by minority employees for racial discrimination in promotions after tape recordings surfaced wherein top executives in the company jocularly referred to employees as "jelly beans" and commented that "all the black jelly beans seem to be glued to the bottom of the bag."[11] By and large, involuntary minorities do not believe they will be fully accepted by the mainstream even if they adopt mainstream culture, and there's plenty of evidence that this belief is fully justified.

In short, immigrant minorities (Hungarians and Asians, for example) see the characteristics of mainstream culture that are necessary for social and academic success in school as things they can adopt in particular circumstances without compromising who they are, and they have reason to believe that this course of action and effort in school will pay off in terms of success and acceptance in the mainstream world. Involuntary minorities (African Americans and Native Americans, for example) see adopting these characteristics as compromising who they are and as a formula for becoming alienated from their own communities, and they have reason to believe it will not pay off in terms either of success or acceptance in the mainstream world.

So sure, many mainstream Americans' grandfathers or great-grandmothers, or whoever, had a rough time and prospered, but they voluntarily entered a system under circumstances that did not set up a border between themselves and the mainstream. Simply expecting involuntary minorities to do the same is not only unfair; it doesn't help us get any closer to a solution.

I had a hard time trying to decide where to put this chapter in the book. I felt it should come early because it deals with the "My grandparents made it; why can't they?" argument which is the end of all discussion for many Americans. But I didn't want to introduce this chapter too early, because it seems to support the idea that poverty and illiteracy are solely the problem of nonwhite minorities. That simply isn't true.

In the late 80s, 12 percent of the white population, 46 percent of the African American population, and 40 percent of the Hispanic population were living in poverty. That sure looks like it's a nonwhite problem, doesn't it? But because whites outnumbered blacks by about five to one and Hispanics by about seven to one, there were 5.4 million whites, 4.6 million African Americans, and 2.8 million Hispanics living in poverty in the late 80s. Measures also indicated that around one-half of children classified as "educationally disadvantaged" were white. All other races made the remaining 50 percent.[12] The population I'm concerned about includes children of all races. In terms of raw numbers, I'm talking about as many whites as nonwhites.

Chapter 5

THE LADS

W hile Ogbu relates the concept of oppositional identity to involuntary minorities, a similar mechanism has been described by other authors dealing with working-class white populations who could not be described as either immigrants or minorities.

Paul Willis, an Englishman, wrote a great book[1] that opened with the words

> The difficult thing to explain about how middle class kids get middle class jobs is why others let them. The difficult thing about how working-class kids get working-class jobs is why they let themselves.[2]

Willis rejects the notion that working-class youngsters get working-class jobs because they are less intelligent or generally incapable of doing school work. He observed that high-achieving working-class students in England were very likely to wind up in low-income, low-prestige jobs while *low-achieving* middle-class students are very likely to wind up in higher-income, higher-prestige jobs.[3] How come, he wondered.

He studied twelve 14- and 15-year-old English working-class boys in a working-class school in a working-class town. They referred to themselves and were referred to by others as "the lads."

The most basic and obvious characteristic of the lads was their opposition to authority. Willis recorded the following conversation between himself and Joey, one of the lads, on the topic of teachers.

Joey: (. . .) the way we're subject to their every whim like. They want something doing and we have to sort of do it, 'cos, er, er, we're just, we're under them like. We were with a woman teacher in here, and 'cos we all wear rings and one or two of them bangles, like he's got one on, and out of the blue, like, for no special reason, she says, "take all that off."

WILLIS: Really?

Joey: Yeah, we says, "One won't come off," she says, "Take yours off as well." I said, "You'll have to chop my finger off first."

WILLIS: Why did she want you to take your rings off?

Joey: Just a sort of show like. Teachers do this, like, all of a sudden they'll make you do your ties up and things like this. You're subject to their every whim like. If they want something done, if you don't think it's right, and you object against it, you're down to Simmondsy [the principal].

WILLIS: You think of most staff as kind of enemies (. . .)?

Joey: Most of them. It adds a bit of spice to yer life, if you're trying to get him for something he's done to you.[4]

And here are Joey and Spansky, another lad, on the same topic:

WILLIS: Evans [a teacher] said you were all being very rude (. . .) you didn't have the politeness to listen to the speaker. He said God help you when you have kids 'cos they're going to be worse. What did you think of that?

Joey: They wouldn't. They'll be outspoken. They wouldn't be submissive fucking twits. They'll be outspoken, upstanding sort of people.

Spansky: If any of my kids are like this, here, I'll be pleased.[5]

The lads' lives seemed to be directed by a single principle: To defeat the official purpose of the school. When Willis asked them if they had any rules, they answered that their only rule was to break the "other" rules. In class there was a continuous scraping of chairs and sulking at the simplest request. The vaguest sexual double meaning was greeted with loud guffaws and obscene gestures just barely out of the teacher's view. Lads devised ways to get out of class, to attend class and do no work, to attend the wrong class, to roam the corridors, and to sleep—both in and out of class. They were aware that this was done with the connivance of the teachers "'cos they want to get rid of you, like." They sometimes went to class only because they were bored with wandering about.

They frequently violated the school dress code. The purpose of school dress codes is often to deemphasize sexuality, and challenging it had a special significance for the lads because they felt superior to other students in regard to sexual experience. Even the teachers acknowledged their sexual adventures. One younger teacher commented, "He [one of the lads] has had more than me, I can tell you!"

The lads not only smoked and drank, they flaunted it. Nothing pleased them more than to have a teacher see them smoking on school grounds and not report it. They took this as a sign of weakness on the part of the teacher and a victory for themselves. One lad walked up to a young teacher in a pub and said hello to him. The teacher was flabbergasted. He had been trying to pretend he did not recognize the boy, but he was put in a position of having to acknowledge him. The boy understood the situation very well. When the teacher failed to report him, he felt victorious and bragged about the incident.

The ability to "have a laugh" was another defining characteristic of the lads. They laughed to defeat boredom and fear and as a way out of almost anything. One lad reported

> (. . .) I don't know why I want to laugh, I dunno why it's so fuckin' important. It just is (. . .) I think it's just a good gift, that's all, because you can get out of any situation. If you can laugh, if you can make yourself laugh, I mean really convincingly, it can get you out of millions of things.[6]

A laugh can deflect the gaze of authority. It can turn submissiveness into cocky defiance, even while complying with the letter of a direct order from a teacher or boss.

Much of the lads' behavior can be seen as preparation for the shop floor. Clothing, drinking, smoking, sex, and cocky defiance all symbolized coming of age for the lads, and coming of age in a way that was reflected in their working-class culture, and counter to school culture.

People employed in factories are in a highly controlled environment. For many, survival depends on being able to take control of the situation. Slowdowns, goldbricking, extended toilet passes, unofficial job swapping, and even sabotage are mirrored in the lads' attempts to take control of classes, substitute their own timetables, and control their own routines and life spaces. The father of one of the lads expressed this clearly:

> Actually the foreman, the gaffer, don't run the place, the men run the place. See, I mean you get one of the chaps says, "Alright, you'm on so and so today." You can't argue with him. The gaffer don't give you the job, they swop each other about, tek it in turns. Ah, but I mean the job's done. If the gaffer had gi'd you the job you would. . . . They tried to do it one morning gi'd a chap a job you know, but he'd been on it, you know, I think he'd been on all week, and they just downed tools (. . .) They're four hard jobs on the track and there's dozens that's . . . you know, a child of five could do it, quite honestly, but everybody has their turn. That's organized by the men.[7]

Another aspect of the lads' mentality that can be traced to shop floor culture is valorization of physical strength and practical know-how and disdain for "useless" abstract or theoretical knowledge. One of the lads' fathers recounted a story about a "chap who was all theory" who was forever sending away for books. One day, one of the books came in a wooden box,

> and it's still in that box 'cos he can't open it. Now that in't true, is it? But the point is true. That in't true, that didn't happen, but his point is right. He can't get at the book 'cos he don't know how to open the box! Now what's the good of that?[8]

Of course parents' disdain for theory was conveyed to their children and so the culture of the lads was not simply different from the school, it was antithetical to the school. The lads valued practical knowledge and disparaged "theory." They viewed the art, music, and literature—everything that might be considered upper-class culture—with disdain. They valued violence, sexism, and racism as manly traits. This basic antithesis between themselves and the school bred contempt on both sides and the lads' definition of themselves was formed in part by what they were *not*. If this doesn't remind you of Ogbu and oppositional identity and Anyon's working-class school, it should.

The lads describe themselves as being rather tame until the age of twelve—a little older than Anyon's fifth graders. Then they said they just fell in together in activities involving alcohol and minor vandalism. But the faculty believed "the lads" came to be as a result of a combination of character defects among leaders and weakness among the led as the following school reports reveal.

> [Joey] proved himself to be a young man of intelligence and ability who could have done well at most subjects, but decided that he did not want to work to develop this talent to the full and allowed not only his standard of work to deteriorate, except for English, but also attendance and behaviour (. . .) too often his qualities of leadership were misplaced and not used on behalf of the school.
>
> [Spansky] in the first three years was a most co-operative and active member of school. He took part in the school council, school play and school choir in this period and represented the school at cricket, football and cross-country events.
>
> Unfortunately, this good start did not last and his whole manner and attitude changed. He did not try to develop his ability in either academic or practical skills (. . .) his early pleasant and cheerful manner deteriorated and he became a most unco-operative member of the school (. . .) hindered by negative attitudes.
>
> [Eddie's] conduct and behaviour was very inconsistent and on occasions totally unacceptable to the school. A lack of self-discipline was apparent and a tendency to be swayed by group behaviour revealed itself.[9]

However, Willis believed that neither the lads nor their teachers fully understood how the lads came to be. While he concedes that character defects may have played a part (the poor are no less susceptible to character defects than the rich), he believed that both the lads and the school they attended were the products of societal mechanisms that are so subtle that the teachers, students, parents, and families were unaware of them.

According to Willis, when schools operate the way they're supposed to, teachers and students enter into a bargain. Teachers have something valuable—high-status knowledge, that is, abstract, theoretical knowledge, the kind valued by the gentry. Not business arithmetic, but algebra, geometry, and calculus. Not the ability to read and understand contemporary "adolescent literature," but the ability to read, appreciate, and critique *A Tale of Two Cities*. It's a teacher's job to give such high-status knowledge to students. It's their profession. It's what they get paid for.

That being the case, students have something that is valuable to the teachers—cooperation. That's the deal, high-status knowledge for cooperation. Willis refers to this as the "basic teaching paradigm." I'd prefer to refer to it as the "real-school model." It's the model that operated in Anyon's middle-class, affluent professional, and executive elite schools.

In some schools, such as Anyon's affluent professional and executive elite schools, high-status knowledge is valued for itself. It is knowledge of one's own culture. In middle-class schools high-status knowledge is valued for what it "buys." It buys grades, diplomas, degrees, qualifications, and licenses. These can be exchanged for good jobs and high pay. So even though high-status knowledge is not seen as having value in and of itself, it is seen as valuable.

When the real-school model is working, it is the possession of high-status knowledge that gives teachers authority. Students grant teachers authority in exchange for knowledge. Under these circumstances, discipline is not a matter of punishing wrongdoing as much as it is a matter of maintaining a contract to which all parties have agreed.

But what happens when the value of high-status knowledge is called into question? What if students resonate with the fable of the man who ordered a book but could not open the box in which it was delivered? And what if, in addition, they see the school's qualifications and diplomas as irrelevant to their lives—present or future? What if they see school knowledge as antithetical to their culture and a threat to their identity, as did Ogbu's involuntary minorities, Scollon's Athabaskans, Coles's Hopi children, the sulkers and steppers, and the lads?

The school's first reaction to such a student body is to get tough, but this can turn quickly into brute force and brute resistance. Since teachers are always outnumbered, this has not been found to be a good solution. Next, schools adopt the students' definition of useful knowledge—practical know-how.

However, as knowledge becomes more practical, school itself becomes less necessary. Once children can read and write at a functional level they can learn practical things better at home, in the neighborhood, or on the job. It is well known that school "shops" are typically a generation behind industry. Kozol[10] reports on schools teaching typing on broken-down electric typewriters years after business has moved to word processing on computers, and he describes schools teaching auto shop without the electronic equipment necessary to find problems in modern automobile engines.

So the compromise is not quite successful. The school stops insisting on offering the high-status knowledge that students find useless or repugnant, but it cannot quite fulfill the promise of offering knowledge the students will find useful. And so the deal changes. Schools have little to offer, and so they ask little in return. They stop asking for real effort on the part of students. In return, the students offer enough cooperation to maintain the appearance of conducting school. Willis refers to this as the "modified teaching paradigm." I'd prefer to refer to it as the "make-believe school model." Under these circumstances, a "good student" is defined as one who has a "good attitude." This is consistent with Anyon and numerous other studies dealing with schools and social class: working-class schools reward students for docility and obedience rather than initiative and assertiveness.[11]

Most students in working-class schools cooperate, more or less. But some students decide not to cooperate. These are the students who are identified as having "a bad attitude" or simply "an attitude." They set up an opposition between themselves and the school that resonates with larger themes of their culture. In the case of the lads, some of these themes were racism, sexism, and contempt for theoretical knowledge.

Willis refers to this process as "differentiation." The students experience this as a positive, liberating development. They are freed from caring what the dominant culture thinks of them and flaunt their identity in an in-your-face manner. The schools experience this as a breakdown. Remember the sulkers and steppers.

Teachers are understandably outraged by the breakdown and see themselves as victims of inexplicable rudeness. Rather than seeing the logic of the lads' rejection of make-believe school, they see the lads as incapable of participating in school. This, coupled with their anger, often results in belittling and sarcastic retaliation. Teachers tend to be facile with words and so their remarks can be very cutting. For example, here are two remarks Willis observed teachers address to their classes.

> The "Midwich Cuckoos" is about children with frightening mental powers—that won't concern us here.[12]

> Y has just asked me, "Do you have to do both sections?" The first section is instructions. It's a good job you didn't have to learn to breathe, Y, you wouldn't be here now.[13]

These remarks are interpreted as insults not only to the students themselves, but to their families and communities.

And so the students' subversion escalates, and the teacher's retaliation increases, and neither teachers nor students are conscious of the logic that instigated the entire process. Locally, the lads appear to win. On a society-wide scale they lose. Locally the teachers appear to fail. On a society-wide scale they are successful in doing what is expected of them. They handle the lads with a minimum of violent disruption.

One of the teachers in Willis's study seemed to understand this more consciously than most. He said,

> I've never been one who thinks we are really teaching these lads. . . . I reckon it's careful containment. We give them little bits, you know, let them think they're big tough men getting their own way, but in all the important things they're doing what you want . . . you know, don't confront them, let them think it's going their way.[14]

Willis observed that "the most horrific breakdowns" occur when young teachers innocently try to assert the real-school model of high-status knowledge in exchange for cooperation and hard work. "Nothing," Willis says, "brings out the viciousness of certain working-class cultural traits like the plain vulnerability of the mighty fallen. Nothing annoys [administrators] more than being brought in to sort out the wreckage."[15] The most successful teachers are those who make few demands in return for enough cooperation to maintain the appearance of conducting school—the make-believe school model.

Of course the switch to the make-believe school model is done largely by stealth. The steps taken and the real reasons for them are rarely understood—much less stated—by the teachers, parents, and students involved. The official position of the school remains largely the real-school model: high-status knowledge for cooperation. To admit otherwise would be to acknowledge institutionalized inequality—savage inequality.

Of course, if you go into any school you'll find a certain number of students whom teachers dread having in their classes, and I'm talking about rich suburban schools and elite private schools. There is certainly resistance in all schools, but there is an important difference. If the students' larger community values school knowledge either in and of itself or for its credential-producing value, student resistance finds little affirmation in the community among parents and other adults, or even among other students by and large. There can be little serious oppositional identity between the students' community and the school when the students' community controls the schools.

In fact, Willis studied ten resistant boys from "a high-status grammar school" at the same time he was observing the lads. While all the lads left school at sixteen, the legal leaving age, eight of the ten boys from the high-status school remained in school until the equivalent of "graduation." The resistance of these boys did not result in academic self-immolation as it did with the lads. Willis observed that "once a working-class boy begins to differentiate himself from school authority there is a powerful cultural charge behind him to complete the process."[16] On the other hand, when students from the middle and upper classes begin to differentiate, there are powerful community pressures for them to abandon the process.

However, Willis observes that some nonconformist middle-class students struggle to make their opposition "resonant" with the opposition of the lads, and insofar as they succeed, their futures suffer. On the other hand, he says, insofar as working-class boys *reject working-class culture* and become free of its processes and assumptions, their futures are likely to be enhanced from a middle-class point of view. This is a much better model for explaining social mobility than any notion of intelligence or effort.[17]

Like Ogbu's involuntary minorities, Willis's lads adopted an oppositional identity. As a point of honor, they identified certain mainstream characteristics as ones they would never adopt and certain characteristics of their own—ones the mainstream found offensive—that they would never abandon.

But I don't want to detract from the plight of the involuntary minorities by suggesting that working-class whites face identical obstacles. Due to their different histories and different social and economic circumstances, oppositional identity has different outcomes for involuntary minorities and Willis's lads. Oppositional identity tends to leave involuntary minorities in serious poverty, while the lads were heirs apparent to their fathers' secure union jobs. Buying into the "enemy" culture presents different perils to the two groups as well. Since there are no racial or even ethnic differences between the lads and the bosses, the lads might stand a better chance of being accepted by the dominant group should they decide to cross the border, and perhaps there would be less a sense of betrayal of their own group.

This may suggest that working-class schools stand ready to implement the real school model any time students drop their oppositional identity and decide to cooperate; however, as the next chapters will demonstrate, once the make-believe school model is in place, it takes substantial pressure from outside the school to displace it.

CHANGING CONDITIONS—ENTRENCHED SCHOOLS

Lois Weis studied a high school in an American community somewhat like the English city where the lads went to school twenty-five years ago. There were many similarities, but there were also important differences—the most important being that in this city, which Weis called "Freeway," the steel mills that had employed Freeway breadwinners for generations in high-paying jobs had closed a decade earlier. Weis called her study *Working Class Without Work*.[1]

Weis never witnessed anything like a breakdown of order at Freeway High School. Students occasionally skipped class, but 94 percent of the students were in school every day. In some ways, however, Freeway boys were like the lads. When asked what they did not like about school, resentment toward authority was a major theme. Here we have a typical interview Weis conducted with a Freeway boy.

Tom: I don't like the principals. Most of the teachers are assholes.

LW: Why?

Tom: They have a controlling power over the kids, or at least they try to. Me, I won't take shit from no one. That's the way I am.

(. . .) Whatever they do, they can't bother me, 'cause when I get my diploma I can say what I want to them.

(. . .) The kids should have some rights. Like, let me say for one example, I know there's smokers in this school. A lot of kids smoke. (. . .) To solve all smoking problems with kids going outside and skipping classes, give the kids at least once a day a place to go to—a room—and have one cigarette or something. Five minutes a day.

(. . .) They [school authorities] play head games with kids . . . They think they can push you any which way they want.

LW: If they're pushing you around, why stay for your diploma?

Tom: 'Cause it helps for, like, a job or whatever. It's like a reference for this, this, this. It's like a key that opens many doors.[2]

On the other hand, Freeway boys were different from lads in important ways. First, the lads were confident that jobs like the ones their fathers had would be there for them when they left school. I suspect that Weis would have found many a lad in the Freeway High School twenty years earlier when the mills were open and an able-bodied man with a minimum of education could earn high wages doing dirty, dangerous, and physically demanding work—a "man's" work.

But the mills in Freeway had closed. Fathers found themselves unemployed or in safer, cleaner, physically less demanding jobs at much lower pay. The whole macho aura surrounding work in the mill was gone. The only jobs available that paid a "family" wage (one that enabled a *man* to retain the role of sole breadwinner in his family—a highly valued ideal among Freeway boys) required education beyond high school, and so Freeway boys did not express disdain for school and mental work as the lads had. They *said* they valued education, if only as a credential-purchasing commodity.

LW: What do you plan to do when you graduate?

Steve: Go to college.

LW: For what?

Steve: I haven't decided (. . .) I just wanna go. Can't get a job without going to college. You got to be educated to get a job, a good job; you don't want to live off burgers when you're old.[3]

Bill: My dad is a machinist. He needs one more day in the plant to get his twenty years. He's fighting now to get one more day.

(. . .) [I want to get to college] 'cause I see what happened to him. He's working for like seven/eight dollars an hour. Like [what] he used to get in the plant, compared to that, it's nothing. To get a better chance, you got to go to college.[4]

While 40 percent of the boys expressed an interest in going to college, only 27 percent of the seniors took the SATs, and the average scores for these students would not have gained them entrance to the state university. For most students this would leave open only the community college, which, generally speaking, prepares students for lower-status, lower-paying, white-collar work. Those who did not express an interest in college expressed an interest in *skilled* working-class jobs such as a mechanic, machinist, or tool and die maker. None of them expressed an interest in general, unskilled wage labor of the sort that does not require further training or education after high school. And so even these boys acknowledged the value of a high school diploma.

Girls at Freeway High School also expressed respect for education as a credential-purchasing commodity. In previous studies, working-class girls commonly expressed an "ideology of romance"—the belief that they will marry and have children with a man who will love them and take care of them, and that paid work is only something to do while waiting for Prince Charming. Not so with Freeway maidens. They thought first of establishing themselves in a career or job. Marriage and family were considered second, after a job or career was established. They rarely talked about marriage without mentioning the *probability* of divorce and the prospect of becoming the sole support of themselves and their children.

LW: Do you hope to get married; do you hope to have children?

Liz: After college and everything's settled.

LW: What do you mean by "everything's settled"?

Liz: I know where I'm going to live. I know what I'm going to be doing; my job is secure, the whole thing. Nothing's open. Everything's going to be secure.

Carla: Oh, I'm going to do that later [get married; have children]. I'm going to school to get everything over with. I wouldn't want to get married or have kids before that.

LW: Why not?

Carla: It'd be too hard. I just want to get my schoolwork over with, get my life together, get a job (. . .) I want to be independent. I don't want to be dependent on him [my husband] for money. Then what would I do if I got divorced fifteen years, twenty years, you know how people are and marriages. Twenty years down the line you have kids, the husband has an affair or just you have problems, you get divorced, then where is that going to leave me? I want to get my life in order first, with my career and everything (. . .) Maybe it has something to do with the high divorce rates. Or the stories you hear about men losing their jobs and not having any job skills, and you see poverty and I just don't want that. I want to be financially secure on my own.[5]

But although Freeway students had come to recognize the value of school credentials, they did not associate school credentials with acquiring knowledge. This was apparent in their attitude toward homework, as revealed from the following excerpts from Weis's journal.

[In a social studies class] **One student to another:** "Did you do this [homework]?"

Another student: "No, I missed it."

[Several others are saying they didn't do their homework.]

Second male: "Fuck. I remember in school and then forget at home." [He grabs the paper of another student and copies it.][6]

[In a social studies class] Mr. ——— walks around checking to see whether the worksheet is completed. They all show him the sheet. As I [LW] walked into the class, Charles was copying from someone. He had the two sheets on his desk. Ed shows Mr. ——— and I said, "Who'd you copy from?" He said, "Sam," and pointed across the room.[7]

[In a study hall] Nine A.M. Several students in the back of the room were either discussing homework, exchanging homework, or returning it after copying it. Technically, there is supposed to be no talking in study hall but almost everyone does.[8]

The language of "passing" dominated Freeway boys' conversation. Most students earned Cs and Ds and appeared to be satisfied. This was more true of boys than girls, which is ironic, since it was the boys who talked most about the importance of education in preparing for a job that earned a family wage.

[In social studies] **Jerome:** [comes in all smiles.] "This is my last day in this class."

Paul: "Did you pass?"

Jerome: "I passed . . . I got a 68. [65 is passing] I passed!" [He is very excited.][9]

[In social studies. Ed gets his test back. He got a 78, a C.] Ed: [Smiling] "I like to see those passing marks."[10]

[In social studies] Teacher passes the test back. Paul turns the paper over fearfully: "I passed!" [with great happiness; he got a 66; 65 is passing].[11]

According to Weis the appearance of order in the classroom "masked complete nonengagement."[12]

Teachers also referred to the benefits of schooling, not in terms of the inherent value of knowledge, but in terms of what a school credential will buy. The following is taken from a social studies teacher's lecture to the class.

Why does level of education prevent you from getting a job? Okay. If there are a hundred jobs on a page in the want ads, ten percent of these, you need an elementary education; forty percent of these jobs you need a high school education; forty percent you need a college education; ten percent of these jobs you need a college plus [education].

The door system works as follows: If you have an elementary education, you can knock on ten doors. If you have a high school education, you can knock on fifty doors. If you have a college plus, you can knock on one hundred doors. Each time you have a piece of paper, you can knock on more doors. Each time you get more education, you can *try* [emphasis his] for more jobs. If you have college plus, you may not get a job, but your chances are going to be better.

The people who live in the poor parts of town have less education and it is more difficult for them to get jobs.[13]

Some teachers explicitly stated to the students that the school credential was valuable only because the mills had closed. For example, Weis recorded the following incident in a social studies class. Notice the insult the teacher delivers that reflects on the students' fathers as well as themselves. It is reminiscent of the teacher's remarks regarding the "Midwich Cuckoos" in Willis' study.

[There is] a long explanation of the electoral system; national nominating convention; campaigns; and elections. Mr. Sykes then hands out a work sheet on the topic, "Answer the five questions on the bottom. I'll see if you understand everything. Take about ten minutes. . . . If the steel plant were still open you guys wouldn't have to worry about this. You could crawl into some coil for an eight-hour shift and fall asleep and still get paid for it. That's probably one of the reasons why the plant closed."[14]

In virtually all classes, knowledge was distributed top-down, even to the point of telling students what line to write on and where to put commas. The following were typical of lessons observed by Weis.

Okay. Open up to page 11 [in the textbook] and get your notebooks out. Skip a line and write "Listening Test—suggestions on how to use your time." There are four steps involved with this.

Roman Numeral I in your notes. Write down, "During the first reading." Number 1. "Listen to the topic, usually stated in the first two sentences, and for the supporting details. Pay close attention to the conclusion which often stresses the main ideas." [This is directly from the book.]

Roman Numeral II. "During your reading of the questions," and [write down] just what it has on your page 11 there, "Your primary goal at this time is to become as aware as possible of all the questions so you will know the specific information to listen for." Roman Numeral III, next page, page 12, "During the second reading, the two things you are asked to do at this time are to listen to the passage and to write the answers. Of the two, the listening is the most important. You must keep listening." Underline the last sentence.[15]

> **Teacher:** Take out your notebooks. The Title. "The Reasons for the Growth of Cities." Put that down. It is at the bottom of page 60. "A. Industrial Revolution"
>
> (. . .) Skip a line. Take the next subtitle [from the text]. "B. Problems Facing Cities and Urban Populations." Take the next five subtopics under that. Skip a line between each.
>
> **Joe:** Just one line between each?
>
> **Teacher:** Yes.
>
> **Sam:** Just the five?
>
> [Time passes]
>
> **Teacher:** The public health department has two main functions: 1) enforcing health codes, and 2) to aid, assist and help those people who do get sick and cannot afford it.
>
> Put down the functions [in your notes] and then put down a "dash"; then put down "money" and a question mark.[16]

There was never any discussion of the question raised by Mr. Simon regarding the state's ability to support public health. It was simply a point in the prepackaged notes suggested by a "dash," the word "money," and a question mark. Students may have had no idea what was meant by this and perhaps no interest in knowing.

This type of classroom routine was well established at Freeway High. Students wrote notes in their notebooks exactly as directed by teachers. They were later tested on the notes and if they passed, they got credits. When they accumulated enough credits they were awarded a diploma that theoretically bought them admission to further job training in the military (a popular choice for both girls and boys), a trade school, or college (which they viewed as trade school).

At no point in this process was there any discussion, much less serious discussion, of the ideas or concepts contained in the original material—the material from which the teacher extracted the notes. When students asked questions they were for the purpose of clarification—not of ideas, but of the form of the notes themselves ("Just one line between each?"). The routine allowed students no ownership of knowledge, nor did it include any opportunities to engage in analysis, synthesis, or evaluation of abstract, theoretical, high-status knowledge as was evident in Anyon's affluent professional and executive elite fifth grade classrooms.

The only challenge to an idea that Weis observed in the entire year of observation was in the following exchange in an English class.

> **Teacher:** Okay, take out your notebooks. In your notes, just skip a line from where you were. Number 1. *High and Outside.* Author is Linda A. Dove, Setting: A town near San Francisco.
>
> He proceeds to give them notes from the entire book, including characters, plot, and so forth, even though they read the book. [The form of "reading" the book was orally in class.]
>
> (. . .) Skip another line and we get into Carl Etchen, Niki's father, who has treated her like an adult from the age of fourteen by including her in his wine tasting and afternoon cocktail hours. He was trying to protect her from the wild party drinking of other teenagers. But he unwittingly *caused* [my emphasis] her alcoholism.
>
> **Holly:** How did he cause her alcoholism? [with skepticism; indicating that she understood that alcoholism is a disease and that one person cannot cause it to occur in another].
>
> **Teacher:** I know what you're trying to say. What we're trying to do here is get some notes for the end of the year [state exams]. Maybe I should change the world "cause."

Holly: No, no.

Teacher: No, you're making a good point.[17]

Note that the teacher does not engage the student in a discussion but capitulates and states explicitly that his purpose is not to stimulate thought or discussion but to present material to be memorized for an examination.

The suitability of this routine at Freeway High went almost entirely unchallenged by either students or teachers. One teacher talked about the possibility of a different routine, but in the same breath he told Weis that when he tried it he was called down to the principal's office, not to be encouraged, but to be chastised.

Freeway parents *said* they wanted their children to go to college, but they didn't *do* anything to make it happen, and looked on with equanimity when their children did not make any moves to actually enroll in college. This attitude has been the norm among working-class parents for generations, as attested to in a book on Chicago steel workers.

> Steelworkers may complain about the dirt and hours, but they take pride in their work. Sometimes directly, sometimes merely by example, their attitude is passed on. Key Wychocki [an informant in the study] expresses the contradictory emotions of a steelworker family, as he wryly notes that, "I can always remember my grandfather didn't want my father to work in the mill. And my father didn't want me to work in the mill. And I know I don't want my son to work in the mill. But, it was just taken for granted if your father was in the mill, you were in the mill. It was never thought of that you'd go anywhere else. Your father didn't want you to, but when you were of age and ready to go to work, he was the guy that got you the job, for crying out loud."[18]

This is thoroughly consistent with my experience. I talked about going to college all the way through high school and my mother (my father died when I was twelve) more or less acquiesced, but when I graduated from high school without having applied to any colleges and took a low-paying white-collar job there was no comment from anyone. I took a collection of night school courses in marketing and accounting and I suspect that everyone expected that this too would pass, and they would fix me up with a civil service white-collar job (we were not without "clout") when I settled down. But as I said before, I was something of a problem in that because of a birth injury, I could not follow the family trade— plumbing. My brothers, who were every bit as smart as I was, were marched right down to the union hall for an apprentice card the day they left high school. When I actually quit full-time work and part-time school for full-time school and part-time work, I received little encouragement. I always get a laugh out of my students by saying that my mother did not want me to go to college because she was afraid I would become an atheist and a communist, and so I went to college and became an atheist and a communist so as not to disappoint her.

But I think the dynamics of my failing to attend college right out of high school reflected a universal theme among the working class. My mother was proud of who we were and what we stood for, and she feared that if I went to college I would cut myself off and become different, and perhaps even become one of *them*—the social worker who lectured her for giving her children more oatmeal than they needed during the Depression, for example. This is a sadder memory, because once again mother was right—as was Thomas Wolfe who told us we can't go home again. I have not turned this into an anecdote to amuse my students.

But the situation in Freeway was different from all these, because of a huge structural change. The mills had closed. The way Freeway parents talked about their children going to college lost its tone of platitude and cliche and took on a tone of desperation. Their children *had* to go to college. Weis observed that the rejection of school and valorization of "man's" work has been a centerpost of the working-class male's identity for generations, but with the industrial economy crumbling around them, things changed. Working-class males no longer explicitly reject schooling. They even give lip service to the credential-purchasing benefits of education.

There was no hint from Freeway parents about fearing that their children would be turning their backs on a proud community if they went to college. Since the closing of the mill, there was no community to defend. It was gone. It was now a question of individual survival, and schooling was seen as the only way to survive. Although parents desperately wanted their children to go to college, they didn't know what to do about it any more than Chicago steelworker parents or my parents did a generation ago.

Parents blamed teachers and teachers blamed parents. The chief complaint of the parents against the school had to do with the schools' failure to help their children get into college.

Here are some parents' comments on the subject.

- I don't think they give them enough alternatives and tell them what is a good field to go into. They don't do enough testing on them.[19]

- Even for the SATs and stuff they were supposed to have some preparation for it and they didn't.[20]

- They really don't tell them anything. Like what scholarships are available or anything.[21]

- They could have preparation for SATs. I don't think they go into that enough. And probably more guidance.[22]

Teachers, on the other hand, blamed parents for not being involved in their children's education.

- [about parents] Just general negativeness toward education and educators. [To teachers] "You aren't doing anything for my kid. You aren't doing anything for me." Then they expect you to accept the burden of educating their children without them supporting you.[23]

- I don't think [parents] really care 'bout the kids and even this isn't saying too much for Freeway. A lot of people, I shouldn't generalize, like when we would have, just an example, PTA meetings in junior high, there would be more teachers than there would be parents.[24]

And teachers continued to blame students. One teacher expressed the following sentiments:

[A]s of tomorrow I'm going to be off for two weeks [at Easter break]. Then when we come back the kids aren't going to do any more work because it just shuts off. Before, they did very little [work]; now they're going to do none, and then the days are going to keep getting warmer, and warmer and warmer, and we are going to go through the graduation ceremony where a couple of us are going to stand back there and whistle the theme for the Laurel and Hardy movies as they are marching up to the stage. Because that's bullshit, too. And the kids are going to go up there with their paper caps and gowns; somebody's going to open up his gown as he gets his diploma and flash the whole audience wearing a bikini or cotton cock or something like that, you know, and at the end they're going to throw their little hats up in the air, somebody is going to get hit in the eye with one and that's it. That's what they think of education. It's a big fucking joke.[25]

It's important to notice that the parents were not unhappy with what their children were taught or how it was taught to them. They were unhappy that the school did not provide "preparation" classes where they would cram facts needed for the SATs in the same "copy notes, memorize facts, and take the test" fashion used to teach them everything else. However, Freeway High School did not offer the kind of education that would enable students to get high scores on the SATs and to succeed in prestigious colleges and universities. The makers of the SATs do their best to insure that success on the tests is the result of eleven years of schooling found in affluent professional and executive elite schools where intellectual autonomy, reasoning, mental agility, creativity, and high-status knowledge were taught and expected.

Weis suggests that a significant part of the problem at Freeway was that the teachers were working-class themselves, and were giving their students the only kind of schooling they knew—the kind they had received themselves. Every female teacher in the social studies department had a father, brother, uncle, or husband who had worked at the mills and every male teacher in the social studies department had worked at the mills at some point in his life. Some had been full-time, year-round employees in the mills before they became teachers. Previous work at the mills was viewed favorably by the school board and it was routinely mentioned on teacher employment applications.[26] Seven out of ten of the faculty had graduated from Freeway or from one of the local Catholic high schools. (Freeway is a very heavily Catholic city.) Seven out of ten of them had gone to one of three local colleges for both their bachelor's and master's degrees. A similarity of background between teachers and students is the rule in America rather than the exception. You may recall that this was true in Anyon's study as well.

The continuation of the make-believe school model—little demand for work in return for enough cooperation to maintain the appearance of school—in the face of a positive shift in student attitude and behavior may have been partly due to the fact that the faculty simply did not know what was being asked of them. If they went to schools like Freeway, as many of them had, their own schooling did not prepare them to employ the real-school model. If they were taught progressive philosophy and methods in their college teacher training courses, and they probably were, they would have been socialized into the "hard realities" of teaching in schools such as Freeway in their first years of teaching—by the students as well as the more experienced faculty.

—∿—

R. Timothy Sieber[27] did a study that sheds light on these possibilities. Sieber came almost by accident upon a situation where young upper-middle-class families (probably affluent professional) were moving into an Irish, Italian, and Puerto Rican working-class neighborhood in New York City and renovating classic nineteenth-century houses that are referred to as "brownstones." I will refer to these people as "Brownstoners."[28]

Although most Brownstoners sent their children to private schools, somewhere under 100 Brownstone children were in the public school—approximately twenty in each grade 1 through 5. The parents were apparently silk stocking liberals who felt obliged to send their children to public schools. However, unlike the parents of the Puerto Rican majority in the school (most of the Irish and Italians sent their children to the local Catholic school), the Brownstone parents did not send their children off to school and trust that the school would provide an appropriate education.

When Sieber came upon the situation there were four classrooms for each grade, labelled 1, 2, 3, and 4, ostensibly in order of the ability of the students. The Brownstone children were all in the 1 class in each grade. Other children were in 1 classes, but only on a "space available" basis after the Brownstone children were included. In these classrooms the progressive philosophy of education and methods of teaching would remind you of Anyon's affluent professional school. Classes were organized for part of each day in what was called an "open" atmosphere. Children worked in groups and had a measure of autonomy. Some initiative and creativity were allowed. Liberal amounts of time were given to creative arts: poetry writing, painting, sculpting, crafts, and creative dramatics. Materials were available in greater quantity than in other classrooms in the school. They had some materials that were probably not found in any New York City Public schools at the time.

Children formally addressed the class regularly, making reports, reading poetry, explaining their work, and carrying on debates. In the upper grades children led class recitations, taught lessons to classmates, and were sometimes permitted to give their peers seat work assignments. They were expected to give positive critiques of one another's performances. Control of verbal behavior and personal demeanor was greatly relaxed. Children could move about more and in some classes seats were never assigned. Children were permitted to initiate and carry on conversations with the teacher and their peers. Such "talking" was not permitted in other classes in the school. It was permitted here because the Brownstone children were considered by the staff to be "naturally more verbal."

Sanctions in Brownstone classes were "normative appeals" (We don't do that here, or, Everyone else is working; why aren't you?) or reasoning, and explicit moral teaching. In other classes discipline was accomplished through threats, taking away treats, supplies, materials, or privileges, and tight control over movement and student interactions. The superior status of Brownstone children was continually publicly affirmed. They occupied nearly all school-wide offices and public roles. They were chosen for academic competitions. Their art work went to district shows and adorned the pages of school publications. They were the lead performers in school plays. They were school monitors, crossing guards, and main office attendants. They sat in the rear of school assemblies—a position, they were told, "of greatest trust." They regularly received awards, prizes, and other forms of recognition during morning announcements, at assemblies, and at graduation.

But, Sieber discovered, none of this happened "naturally." It happened as a result of an energetic and relentless campaign on the part of the Brownstone parents, with considerable resistance from the teachers and some resistance from the other parents. And the battle wasn't over.

The Brownstoners were not natives of New York City. They had migrated there to work as professionals in law, architecture, advertising, finance, and the arts. Soon after the first Brownstoners purchased homes in the neighborhood, they formed a neighborhood improvement association whose activities centered around beautification, architectural restoration, and protection of the quiet residential character of the neighborhood. They soon selected a new name for the neighborhood, which replaced one that had working-class associations, and they had the area declared a Historic Landmark Preservation District.

Although only 20 percent of the Brownstone children attended the public school, the Brownstoners generally agreed that improvement of the public school was a key element in making the neighborhood attractive to further upper-middle-class settlement. The improvement association formed an education committee. First they gained regular access to the school. They organized a tutorial program for slow readers which brought them into the school on a regular basis. They volunteered to work in the school library. They studied school documents and gathered information on school practices and personnel. They invited school staff to late afternoon teas in their homes, pooling china, silver, and linens to impress the staff with their status. They made a concentrated effort to master educational jargon, which they believed the school staff used to exclude and patronize them.

When they arrived at the school there was a PTA, whose members included a handful of Puerto Rican mothers who were employed as para-professionals in the school and which was dominated by the teachers. In a well-orchestrated meeting, the Brownstoners elected their slate of officers and soon afterward redefined the PTA as a Parent Association; teachers were barred from membership. Brownstoners held all the nine positions on the Parent Association executive board except one, which they referred to openly as the "Puerto Rican slot." They claimed to believe that the Puerto Rican mothers were glad they had taken over because they were better at running an organization. The Puerto Ricans, however, said they were made to feel unwelcome at meetings and that when they attended they found that decisions had already been taken by the Brownstoners in secret. Although the Brownstoners blocked several attempts by Puerto Ricans to regain influence, they frequently referred to the Puerto Rican's apathy.

Before the Brownstoners arrived, students were "tracked" into four classrooms at each grade level based on scores on reading achievement tests. The Brownstoners' children tended to be placed in the 1 classes from the first, but as they established themselves they introduced an innovation, with the backing of the principal. Teachers of 1 classes were required to adopt more "open" organization and methods, and all Brownstone children were assigned to these classes because the new format was more in keeping with the progressive child-rearing philosophy of their parents. The Irish and Italians students who attended the school tended to cluster in the 2 classes while the Puerto Rican majority in the school were concentrated in tracks 3 and 4.

Everyone knew that some of the Brownstone children did not belong in the 1 classes on the basis of test scores, so the Parent Association began to downplay the hierarchical nature of the tracking system and emphasized that a "culturally appropriate curriculum," not test scores, was the operating principle for the tracking system. Soon afterward, the Parent Association succeeded in having the school drop the designations 1, 2, 3, and 4 and refer to classes by their grade and room number. The top second grade room was no longer designated 2-1; it became 2-107 (referring to the classroom number). The result of this was that the Brownstoners were guaranteed a place in the top classes and the spaces left available would be filled by the most able of the other children. You can be certain that the equivalent of the sulkers and steppers would not be counted among the "most able" regardless of their test scores.

As in Freeway, the teachers in this working-class school sprang from working-class roots themselves. They had mixed feelings toward the Brownstoners. They saw the children as bright and gifted, but as overprivileged and disrespectful. They saw parents as pushy, overbearing, and interfering. Many teachers whose seniority would have entitled them to teach the top class in a grade passed up the assignment because of parental pressure and interference. Teachers were particularly bothered by complaints about matters that they believed were trivial, among them, the teachers' tone of voice when addressing students.[29]

The teachers at Freeway did not know how to respond to the change in attitude on the part of their students and their parents. The Freeway parents and students probably did not understand what they needed, and they certainly did not know how to make the teachers respond to their newly found needs. On the other hand, the teachers who were suddenly confronted with the Brownstoners' children didn't know how to respond either, but the Brownstoners understood what they wanted and knew how to bring pressure to bear. They got results. The teachers were not happy and the parents were not entirely satisfied, but the experience does give us insight into one way a school might be transformed from the make-believe model to the real-school model. Parents can insist on it, but that will take some doing when the parents are like those from Freeway rather than the Brownstoners.

But take courage! What's at work here are subtle mechanisms that, once understood, are not entirely overwhelming. Working-class people tend to use language in certain ways and share values, attitudes, behaviors, and beliefs that make make-believe schooling almost a certainty for their children and make it nearly impossible for them to understand or bring about change. They can learn to use language in different ways and adopt values, attitudes, behaviors, and beliefs (those associated with the gentry) that will make the real-school model possible for their children and empower them to bring about change.

But this can only work if working-class people want to adopt different values, attitudes, behaviors, and beliefs, and as we have seen, oppositional identity makes the whole process problematic. Paulo Freire, the author of *Pedagogy of the Oppressed,* whom I mentioned in chapter 1, has suggested an answer to this dilemma: that we educate working-class children like rich children—in their own self-interest.

In the next few chapters I'll discuss ways of using language, on one hand, and values, attitudes, behaviors, and beliefs on the other that promote the make-believe school model and leave working-class people comparatively powerless. In the last few chapters I'll discuss Freire's solution to the problem of educating working-class children in the face of oppositional identity. Read on.

Chapter 7

CLASS, CONTROL, LANGUAGE, AND LITERACY

I n 1980 I was on sabbatical in Scotland. I was a visiting scholar at Edinburgh University working on a book on how to teach reading in elementary school. While there, I came across an announcement about a discussion group on the Brazilian educator Paulo Freire at the Workers Education Association of Western Scotland. The Workers Education Association's history goes back to the early-twentieth-century Fabian Society, a pacifist, left-leaning organization (right up my Quaker alley), including such worthies as George Bernard Shaw. It was later associated with the British Labour Party, and continues today as a somewhat independent organization.

I went, anxiously hoping to find a bunch of bricklayers and factory hands reading philosophy. Instead, I found a bunch of teachers and social workers, and, as advertised, they were reading Freire. I joined them.

It was a very important move. First, it introduced me to Freire. Second, I volunteered to address the group on what interested me at the time, the work of Basil Bernstein, an English sociologist who wrote about the British working and middle classes,[1] their language habits, how those habits affected their success in school, and the savage inequalities that resulted. I have come to see Freire as having the answers for dealing with the many subtle mechanisms

81

I discuss in this book, but I won't get to him until a later chapter. My Bernstein talk was about explicit and implicit language and how they are related to values, attitudes, beliefs, and behaviors of two groups—the working class and the middle class. That's what this chapter is about.

When we are with our family and friends we naturally use implicit language. We rely on shared knowledge, feelings, and opinions when speaking to one another. For example, a man looks at a sweater on a chair in his living room and says to his wife, "Did you tell him what I said yesterday?" She answers, "Yes. But he didn't do it." He says, "Don't feel bad. It's not your fault." Although this is a perfectly clear communication for the husband and wife, it leaves many unanswered questions for the outside observer. The two are relying on context (the sweater apparently identifies the person they are talking about), shared information, and shared feelings. This kind of language is engaged in by nearly everyone when dealing with others with whom they are intimate or at least somewhat familiar.

An explicit rendition of the conversation might go as follows.

> **Husband:** Did you tell our son, Richard, who seems to have left his sweater on the chair again, that I said I would turn him out of the house if he did not call my cousin John and accept the job John offered him?

> **Wife:** Yes, I told him, but he didn't do it. I feel somewhat responsible because I've spoiled Richard and now he's totally incompetent and without ambition.

> **Husband:** Don't feel bad. I think he would have been incompetent and without ambition even if you hadn't spoiled him.

Bernstein believed that the British working class habitually use implicit language and the British middle class habitually use explicit language for reasons that can be traced to their cultures. And because the language of the school is typically explicit, the middle class has a great advantage in school and the working class has a great disadvantage.

The cultural characteristics Bernstein examined were attitudes toward conformity, styles of exercising authority, the amount of contact with "outsiders," and responses to pressures from outside the community—that is, how people deal with government, institutions, and agencies.

Where conformity is expected, where sex roles are rigid, where opinions are dictated by group consensus, there is no need to explain one's thoughts, beliefs, or behaviors. Communication is frequently possible by alluding to shared opinions and beliefs rather than by explicitly expressing them. In such groups communication tends to be implicit.

For example, when the TV networks declared the results of the presidential election in 1996 a cheer went up at the Democratic Party election-watch party in Buffalo. Now, a cheer is a good example of implicit communication. The reason it communicated was that everyone in the room knew what it referred to (it was bound to the context) and everyone present was expected to hold the same beliefs and opinions on that topic.

It is possible that some at the party were not wildly enthusiastic about Clinton's victory. They may really have been interested in the election of their brother-in-law to the county legislature and voted for Dole, but where conformity is the dominant theme, only consensus views tend to be expressed, and they go unchallenged. Under these circumstances meanings need only be implied or alluded to rather than stated explicitly. People who habitually engage in groups where conformity is the dominant theme develop the habit of using implicit language and expecting it from others. Conversely, they get little experience with using explicit language.

The news of Clinton's victory at the League of Women Voters, where people recognize that they represent many political positions, might have been greeted by the odd cheer, but not by a collective cheer. And those cheering might expect to be taken on by others whose reaction was somewhat less enthusiastic. Everyone would have to make his or her position clear in such a situation since no one could assume they knew the others' positions precisely. Where a variety of opinions are expected, explicitness is required. People who habitually engage in these kinds of groups get into the habit of using explicit language and expecting it from others.

The style of authority that is characteristic of a community also affects language habits. In an authoritarian setup, authority is invested in *position*—do what your father, the boss, or the teacher tells you because they are your father, the boss, or the teacher. In an authoritarian home or community there is little need for explicit language to control subordinates. On the other hand, in a more democratic setup, orders are based on reasons and decisions are made more *collaboratively*. While those in authority may not encourage their subordinates to demand reasons, they are willing to discuss reasons for rules and decisions when they are challenged. Therefore, in a collaborative home or community, there is continuous need for explicit language.

Here we have two vignettes involving fathers and their teenage sons, demonstrating authoritarian and democratic styles of authority.

Authoritarian Style

Pop: Be home by 11.

Son: Why can't I be out till 11:30?

Pop: Because I said so.

Collaborative Style

Pop: Be home by 11.

Son: Why can't I be out till 11:30?

Pop: Because the streets are dangerous after 11.

Son: But they're not any more dangerous at 11:30 than at 11:00. Can't I stay out till 11:30?

Pop: No. You need to get up for school in the morning. Make it 11.

Son: But a half hour isn't going to make any difference.

Pop: I said 11, and that's that!

Whether the style of authority is authoritarian or collaborative is a matter of degree. In the first scenario the father had reasons that the boy probably understood: The streets get more dangerous later at night, and the boy has to get up for school in the morning. But this is not said, it's *implied*. In such relationships, much that is understood goes unspoken, remains implicit.

In the second scenario the father does not immediately resort to authoritarian statements. He states a reason explicitly, which gives the boy an opening to state explicitly what's wrong with the father's reason. This leads the father to defend his reasons or state a further reason, which in turn leads the boy to respond. Finally, the father resorts to his authority, but not before several explicit statements are exchanged.

We have no reason to believe that the one father has more concern for his son or that one father has less of a sense of his authority. The difference is in the style of authority. One style encourages the habit of implicit communication while the other style encourages the habit of explicit communication.

A third characteristic of groups that affect habits of communication is isolation. Where individuals rarely have occasion to deal with strangers, they tend to rely on allusion to shared experience for communication; where individuals must communicate with strangers frequently, they learn they cannot rely on shared experience; they cannot be sure of what the other person knows or thinks.

A number of years ago a group of sociologists went into a town in Arkansas after a devastating tornado—people had been killed and millions of dollars in property was destroyed.[2] When they interviewed people, they found that some people said things such as, "Well, it hit the Jones place and killed all of them and then it swung around down the creek and wrecked the church, but no one was in it." People such as the local doctor or the district judge were apt to say, "Well, the tornado first touched down three miles south of town. It hit the house of a family called Jones and killed them all—the parents and four teen-aged children. It then swung east and destroyed the Congregational church."

One version of that story assumes that the listener knows where the Jones place is, who the Joneses were (how many is *all*?), where the creek lies, and what church was down the creek. The second version makes none of these assumptions. The second version is much more explicit than the first.

According to the study, the difference between the people who did these two kinds of reporting of this incident was their relative isolation. People who were rarely in contact with others from outside their town, neighborhood, or place of work simply had no practice with talking to people who did not know where the Jones farm was or who the Joneses were, and so they didn't have practice at using language that did not rely on shared information. They were in the habit of using implicit language, and they expected it from the people with whom they usually talked. Such communities have been referred to as "societies of intimates."[3] The habit of communicating through implicit reference to shared information reinforces feelings of intimacy.

On the other hand, people who were explicit and did not rely on shared knowledge were people whose occupations and position in the town led them into frequent contact with people whom they did not know, people who lived far away, who were from different ethnic, social, and economic backgrounds. They moved in what has been referred to as a "society of strangers."[4] This led to the frequent necessity of using explicit language. They came to use such language habitually and to expect it from others.

The fourth characteristic of homes and communities that affects habits of communication is the prevailing attitude toward power in relation to the broader society. How do people in a community deal with government, institutions, and agencies? Where powerlessness is the dominant theme (You can't fight city hall!) there is little occasion to make plans, express them to others, and convince others to follow them.[5]

My first real dose of political activism came with the effort to nominate Eugene McCarthy as an anti-Vietnam war candidate for president on the Democratic ticket in 1968. My wife and I were invited to attend a meeting in a neighbor's basement where we were to learn how to gather signatures for a petition to put McCarthy delegates to the Democratic convention onto the ballot. I was an elementary school teacher at the time and I had fairly undisturbed working-class attitudes toward conformity, authority, and feelings of power. I had been married for only a few years, and, of course, it was my middle-class wife's idea to get involved with the McCarthy campaign. My response to the war was more along the "You can't fight city hall" lines—which is, of course, implicit and context dependent.

I went to the meeting with a pretty clear picture of what I thought would happen. I expected that an "expert" would get up and tell us what to do and answer a few questions, and we'd all go home. To my dismay, the meeting lasted for hours. One of the organizers got the meeting started and said only a few words about the petitions he was holding, when someone made a comment about the injustice and immorality of the Vietnam war. I thought everyone in the room had the same opinion on this topic; otherwise, why would we be here, and so I was surprised that the topic was even raised. But suddenly everyone wanted to say *why* she or he thought the war was unjust and immoral. Some thought it was because our boys were dying for a cause that did not involve the vital interest of the United States. Others were upset because of the psychological damage that our boys were suffering because they were faced with killing innocent civilians. Others insisted that the damage was spiritual as well as psychological. Others were upset about the Vietnamese being killed. Others thought the war did not pass St. Augustine's test for a "just war." Others thought all war was immoral, St. Augustine be damned.

I didn't think it was important that we decide which of these views was most defensible, or even that they should be mentioned. I wanted the expert to tell me how to get the damned signatures and go home. I wasn't used to "wasting my time" like this and I resented it. In the neighborhood where I grew up, people did not have meetings to oppose anything that the government did. It was commonly believed that there was petty corruption in the city government, but living in an Irish Catholic neighborhood we believed we had "clout," (a word that originated in Chicago), and therefore we got a little more than we deserved, and so we had nothing to complain about. If we were annoyed that garbage collection was not as good as it was in Mayor Daley's neighborhood, or that our streets went unrepaired longer than other neighborhoods, we'd say, "You can't fight city hall," or "It's not what you know, it's who you know," or "It's all politics." Now these are colossally implicit statements. There is a world of presumably shared knowledge and attitudes behind each of them. They do not invite challenge, discussion, or nuance.

If we did get upset enough about something that "the powers that be" (another highly implicit phrase) were doing, we didn't form alliances among ourselves, much less with comparative strangers. We went to the Democratic precinct captain whom we thought of as being one of us, but having access to power. He knew the right people. We didn't have to go into details in expressing our complaint to the precinct captain since we rightly believed that he knew us well enough to understand our concerns. To this day I can picture and I remember the name (Harry Painter) of our precinct captain, but I don't think I ever saw or knew the name of the alderman who represented our ward.

In communities where people feel powerless, they have very little necessity for using explicit language. They get into the habit of using implicit language and they come to expect such language of others. The people I found myself among in 1968 had a different attitude toward power. They thought that what they knew and believed counted, that they could fight city hall, and that they had the political savvy to get what they wanted or at least put up one hell of a fight.

They were accustomed to joining together with comparative strangers (often absolute strangers) to bring pressure to bear on institutions—even the military-industrial complex and the United States government. They were used to dealing with strangers, and so they understood the need to state their positions explicitly, to find common ground, and to plan unified action. They were not used to being dealt with in an authoritarian manner, and so the man who called the meeting could not tell them to pipe down and listen to the expert.

Getting them to *act* together was the hard part. When ten of them met to discuss a problem, there were ten interpretations of the problem and ten plans for solving it. Developing consensus and a plan where each would play a part demanded explicit language and lot of it. In communities where people feel powerful, they get a lot of practice in using explicit language; they get into the habit of using it, and they come to expect it of others.

I have become accustomed to the discussions that I considered a waste of time in 1968 and now I frequently engage in them myself. I have entered a new culture, but it wasn't easy. I still get bored with such discussions and find those who seem to thrive on them a pain in the neck—an implicit, context-dependent bit of analysis to be sure.

Of course, you see where all this is going. If you're poor, you're likely to feel powerless and be accustomed to a society of intimates where conformity is expected and where parents, teachers, and bosses are authoritarian. As a result you are likely to be accustomed to using implicit language and unaccustomed to using explicit language. On the other hand, if you're rich you're likely to feel powerful and be accustomed to a society of strangers where nonconformity is expected and where parents, teachers, and bosses are collaborative in their exercise of authority. As a result you are likely to be accustomed to using explicit language.

Of course, rich people don't use explicit language constantly. Although they spend a lot of time in a society of strangers, they also have families and friends among whom they can be as implicit and context dependent as the most working-classed of the working class. The conversation about the son who is incompetent and without ambition might have occurred in the home of the CEO or a floor sweeper at General Motors.

Nor is the working class incapable of using explicit language. There is a story of a woman who was on the first day of a job as a collector at a rural exit on a toll road. A motorist asked how to get to the Friendship Baptist Church, and she told him to turn left at the pond. The person breaking her in overheard this and pointed out that the pond was dry in August, so the motorist would not know when he had come to it. The toll collector laughed and said she just hadn't thought about that; she was accustomed to talking to people who knew where the pond was—wet or dry. Thereafter she referred to a different landmark to identify the road that led to the church, and she became accustomed to the fact that, when giving directions, she could not rely on motorists' knowing what she knew about the community.

When it comes to schooling, the working class suffers because of the dynamics of class and language in two ways. First, their habitual use of implicit, context-dependent language, and their relative lack of comfort in using explicit language puts them at a tremendous disadvantage in terms of acquiring higher levels of literacy that rely on highly explicit language. Second, their style of authority and their attitude of powerlessness in dealing with institutions and agencies explain why they wind up in classrooms like Anyon's working-class classrooms, those in Freeway High, and in the classrooms where the Irish, Italians, and Puerto Ricans remained in the Brownstoner's school. Conversely, class-related attitudes and behaviors regarding authority and power explain why the Brownstoners were able to get a kind of education for their children that leads to admission in upscale colleges, but the Freeway parents were not.

The language of the school, especially the language of school books, is explicit. The explicit language that more affluent children learn at home prepares them for the ever so much more explicit language of the school, particularly the language of books. The implicit language that working-class children become accustomed to at home doesn't. Children's scores over time on standardized reading tests bears this out. At the end of first grade, when reading tests are essentially tests of word recognition, there is a statistically significant but low correlation between children's reading scores and the status of their parents' occupation.

The language of first graders' books is not like regular books; it's not like the language typically associated with school. It is context dependent—usually about pictures on the same page. It's personal—childhood centered. It does not contain information children are not already expected to have. It's about puppies that get lost and trips to the supermarket with mother. It's redundant. It is much more repetitive, in fact, than normal speech.

But by fourth and fifth grades the language of the texts becomes more and more like the language of regular books. It's impersonal. It has information children are not expected to have. It's about topics that are far removed from everyday life—like the history of the Civil War or the process of photosynthesis. It's accurate, precise, and explicit.

By fifth grade the correlations between reading scores and the status of parents' occupations are considerable.[6] Not that all working-class children do poorly or that all rich children do well, but it would be very safe to bet that the average reading score for one hundred randomly selected affluent kids would be considerably higher than the average reading score for one hundred randomly selected working-class students. It's here that more affluent children's familiarity with explicit, context-independent language pays off, and it's here that the working class's habitual use of implicit language becomes a real handicap.

As working-class children progress through school, their reading scores fall farther and farther below their actual grade level. We presume they don't have the basics, and we give them more phonics. They don't need more phonics. They need to be introduced into and made to feel welcome in a community where explicit language makes sense, where it's necessary—a community where nonconformity is tolerated and even encouraged, where authority is exercised collaboratively, and where students do not feel powerless, where they have choices regarding the topics they will study and the materials they will use and where they are given freedom to work with others (preferably from backgrounds different from their own) and to move around the room.

This describes affluent professional and executive elite classrooms and the kind of classrooms the Brownstoners were trying to get for their children. The style of authority and use of power in such classrooms is similar to that which tends to be found in professions and at the management level of corporations and institutions. The people involved have a pretty clear idea of who gives orders and who takes them, but power, authority, and control appear to be, and often are, diffuse—distributed and rearranged in subtle ways. This is the style of authority and control that you might expect to find in many affluent professional, executive elite, and Brownstoner's homes. Therefore, when progressive, collaborative methods are used with children from professional and managerial homes they have a reasonable chance of working.

But what of students who come from less advantaged communities? Their parents are not professionals or managers. They are hardhats or factory or clerical workers or tradespeople or unemployed. They live in a world where lines of authority are clear and ever-present. Their cooperation is garnered more often by threats of reprisals than by appeals to self-interest. In such an atmosphere cooperation is grudging. Resistance often lies just beneath the surface.

The lads, the Freeway High schoolers, and Bernstein's working class expect insistence on conformity and authoritarian control in school. They are likely to view a progressive, collaborative classroom as one where no one is in charge, and that spells trouble.

"Successful" teachers in working-class schools are often working-class themselves, like the teachers at Freeway high school, the teachers in the Brownstoner's school, and myself thirty years ago, who share the students' attitudes toward conformity and authority. Or, like some of the teachers in the lads' school, they are middle-class teachers who take their cues from the students and give them what they seem to expect and to which they respond well. Conformity is demanded; the teacher is authoritarian; the children are given little or no choice, no freedom to move, no power. Because the children are all from the same background, there is no possibility that they might learn to communicate with others who are unlike them, but it wouldn't matter if there were children from different backgrounds since they are seldom permitted to work with one another. The classroom replicates the students' homes and communities.

Of course, working-class, middle-class, and gentry children often find themselves in the same schools and classrooms. My wife made an interesting discovery a number of years ago when she videotaped reading classes in a first grade classroom in a small town in western New York where there was a wide spectrum of social classes in the same classroom. When the teacher began the reading lesson with the "top" reading group, numbering about nine, she called the children to the reading circle; she sat down in her chair a few feet from the nearest child and said, "Open your books to page forty-two." She waited and watched as they opened their books and said something like, "Now who can tell me about the picture." And the lesson was under way.

When it was time for the "bottom" reading group, the teacher was suddenly on her feet. As she called this group to the circle, she moved around the room. She tapped children on the shoulder, picked up reading books and handed them to children, and ushered them to the reading circle. There were only six children in this group. The teacher pulled up her chair to where she could *reach* them all and said something like, "Open your books to page nineteen." But while she was saying it, she reached over and turned pages, gently pushed a child into a sitting position, said to another child, "That's good," because the child had her book opened to the right page and was seated properly, and finally the teacher put her finger on a word in a child's book and said, "Begin reading there."

Now this woman was a marvelous teacher. It was a pleasure to watch her. She was conscientious, creative, hard working. Her affection and concern for the children were obvious and genuine. She was quite clearly exhausted at the end of the three reading groups every morning, and most of her energy was spent on the bottom group. But what she was doing was relying almost entirely on explicit language to communicate with the top group. In the bottom group she was communicating to a large extent through manhandling the children and her language became very implicit and context-bound.

It is not unusual for the same teacher to conduct a very progressive, collaborative lesson with the top group and very traditional, directive lesson with the bottom group. Even when the method used in the two groups is ostensibly the same, the teacher's attitude toward conformity, her or his style of authority, and the amount of choice and freedom of movement and collaboration between the students changes dramatically between the top and bottom groups.

We were doing research on children in this class and we knew a lot about them. The children of the doctors and bankers tended to be in one group, while the children of the postal and steel workers were in the other group—and I don't need to tell you which was which. Of course, the segregation was not complete. In situations like this you will find some working-class children in the top group, and some more affluent children in the bottom group. When teachers make "ability" reading groups, they consider standardized test scores, particularly at the beginning of the year. But as the year progresses other factors are considered.

As I said, the top group had nine children and the teacher exercised a collaborative style of management, one that I would associate with more affluent homes. Children who did not respond to this style, those who were disruptive or nonproductive in this group would soon be reassigned. If they were very disruptive, they would probably wind up in the bottom group where there were fewer children and where the teacher's style was much more authoritarian. And so the working-class children tend to gravitate toward the bottom group, regardless of their reading scores, and the more affluent children and border crossers tend to gravitate toward the top group regardless of their reading scores

This is not the result of racism or class warfare. In fact, these were all white children, and I don't think the teacher had any nefarious motives. She just responded to the language and behavior of the children without, I am sure, a thought of their parents' occupational status. She did what she thought any good teacher would do.

The resulting inequality—empowering education for some and domesticating education for others—is about as savage as any I can think of, but it's much harder to pin down. It is much more difficult to know where to direct your anger. The easy (but I believe incorrect and ultimately self-defeating) answer is to shout conspiracy. But subtle mechanisms deny working-class children access to higher levels of literacy work so well—even when there are competent teachers and reasonable resources—that there is no need for conspiracy. Savage inequalities persist because a lot of well-meaning people are doing the best they can, but they simply do not understand the mechanisms that stack the cards against so many children.

Of course, this is all a little too pat. Affluent people can be very authoritarian and insistent on conformity, and poor people can be very collaborative and tolerant. Rich people can be very intimidated by institutions and agencies and poor people can be ready to take them on at a moment's notice.

So, Okay, it's a little stereotypical, but my students frequently comment on how much it helps explain what they see every day in their classrooms. Some seem to regard it as an epiphany, the old "scales dropping off the eyelids" phenomenon. I thought of it that way twenty-five years ago when I first read Basil Bernstein, and although Bernstein has his detractors, I haven't seen anything that's changed my mind since.

Chapter 8

WHERE LITERACY "EMERGES"

Okay, you're convinced that the cards are stacked in favor of the gentry and against the working class, but there's more. For several decades linguists, psychologists, and educators have been observing infants from birth and noting their earliest communication with others (usually their parents, more usually their mothers), the beginnings of language, and finally their involvement in written language—all of this before school age, and for some children, long before school age. As we will see, this process, which is referred to as "emergent literacy," is ideal preparation for success in school. It's all quite wonderful but, alas, the whole picture is based on observing the child-rearing practices of the middle class and the gentry.

An idealized version of "emergent literacy" looks like this. Only hours after birth, children react differently to spoken language than to other sounds—even rhythmic sounds like music. Infants show more interest in people than in inanimate objects. In the first several weeks of life, children show a preference for looking at human faces and respond differently to familiar and unfamiliar faces. Infants direct their earliest and most elaborate spontaneous behavior toward people.[1]

The emergence of conversation can be traced to the first few weeks of life. From birth the parent is attentive to the gestures, vocalizations, and changes of gaze initiated by the child and responds to them. Molly may fling her hands up near her face, and her mother imitates her and says, "Whoops!" Molly spits up milk, and her mother wipes her mouth saying, "What a little piggy!" The parent looks at the infant and, following the child's gaze, points at, touches, or picks up the objects the child is looking at. This kind of interaction is believed to be the beginning of conversation. In repeated "conversations" revolving around the routines of feeding, changing, and bathing, words are frequently matched with ongoing activities.

The cries, gurgles, coos, and vocalization of newborn infants are undoubtedly instinctual. Although they may have no intentional meaning for the child, parents constantly watch for meaningful signs. When Harry cries, does he need a clean diaper? Does he want to be held? Does he need to be burped? When Sarah coos, is she happy to see Mommy? Does she feel comfortable in her fresh diaper? Does she like being cuddled?

Adults impose meaning on the sounds and behavior of the child and respond with appropriate behavior. Child-initiated behaviors are followed by parental responses in regular and repeated patterns. Soon the child begins to act as if he or she has caught on to the relationship between behaviors he or she initiates and the response of the adult.

Soon children cry *because* they want their diapers changed; they coo and smile *because* they feel warm and dry and safe in their father's arms; they look from their mother's eyes to the toy on the floor *because* they want her to look there too. As early as six weeks, parents begin to interpret the child's facial expressions and changes of gaze as both meaningful and intentional.

Language begins when a particular vocalization takes on a particular meaning (or meanings). When little Sarah begins to say *uh, uh* when she wants to be picked up and *ba* when she wants milk, another monumental event has occurred. She is using speech sounds to communicate meaning. That is language, in a sense, but there is one more hurdle to jump. Children are born into societies that have language. There are conventional words for expressing meanings such as "pick me up" and "give me milk." Children apparently notice that everyone around them has words for certain meanings that are different from their own. When Sarah abandons *uh, uh* in favor of *up* and *ba* in favor of *milk*, she's got language.

Researchers have collected hundreds of hours of audio tape of toddlers with their parents to gain insights into language acquisition. Here are a few examples.

First we have Mark, age twenty-three months, in the kitchen with his mother and younger sister Helen. Mark is looking in a mirror and sees reflections of himself and his mother.

Mark: Mummy. Mummy.

Mother: What?

Mark: There . . . there Mark.

Mother: Is that Mark?

Mark: Mummy.

Mother: Mm.

Mark: Mummy.

Mother: Yes that's Mummy.

Mark: Mummy. Mummy.

Mother: Mm.

Mark: There Mummy. Mummy. There . . . Mark there.

Mother: Look at Helen. She's going to sleep. (long pause)

(Mark can see birds in the garden.)

Mark: Birds Mummy.

Mother: Mm.

Mark: Jubs. (Mark's word for birds)

Mother: What are they doing?

Mark: Jubs bread.

Mother: Oh look. They're eating the berries, aren't they?

Mark: Yeh.

Mother: That's their food. They have berries for dinner.

Mark: Oh.[2]

Mom's utterances are simple in form and restricted to topics arising from the immediate context. She comments on topics Mark introduces. She follows his lead by asking questions, restating what he has said, and adding new information to support and extend the topics he has introduced. This practice is called "leading from behind" or "scaffolding." Notice that when Mom introduces a topic ("Look at Helen."), Mark makes no response and she drops it.

Researchers have questioned parents such as Mark's mother about their intention to teach their children in conversations like this. They reply that their aim is not to teach, but merely to communicate effectively. They speak in simple utterances so their children will understand. They question and rephrase to check on what the child means and to keep the conversation going. However, when they use words that may be new to the child (such as *berries*), they exaggerate them and repeat them.

Two months later Mark and his mother are in the kitchen again and they have noticed a neighbor working next door in his yard.

Mark: Where man gone? Where man gone?

Mother: I don't know. I expect he's gone inside because it's snowing.

Mark: Where man gone?

Mother: In the house.

Mark: Uh?

Mother: Into his house.

Mark: No. No. Gone to shop Mummy.

(The local shop is close to Mark's house.)

Mother: Gone where?

Mark: Gone shop.

Mother: To the shop?

Mark: Yeh.

Mother: What's he going to buy?

Mark: Er—biscuits. [cookies]

Mother: Biscuits, mm.

Mark: Uh?

Mother: Mm. What else?

Mark: Er—meat.

Mother: Mm.

Mark: Meat. Er-sweeties. Buy a big bag sweets.

Mother: Buy sweets?

Mark: Yeh. M—er—man—buy. The man buy sweets.[3]

Once again Mom scaffolds or leads from behind. She takes Mark's topic and, realizing he has invented a reason for the man's disappearance, helps him to develop an account of a shopping trip by asking what the man bought. The resulting "story" is a collaborative effort.

Five months later the following conversation took place.

Mark: All right you dry hands.

Mother: I've dried my hands now.

Mark: Put towel in there.

Mother: No, it's not dirty.

Mark: Tis.

Mother: No, it isn't.

Mark: Tis. Mummy play. Play Mummy.

Mother: Well, I will play if you put the top on the basket.

Mark: All right. There. There. Play Mummy. Mummy come on.[4]

In this short exchange Mark regulates his mother's behavior ("you dry hands") and gets her to do something for him ("Mummy play"). These are forms of persuasion. It's interesting that Mark responds appropriately to Mom's conditional sentence ("I will play *if* you put the top down on the basket"), which seems like a pretty tall order for a two-and-one-half-year-old, but he doesn't supply articles (Put **[the]** towel in there), a task that seems so easy. But Mom does not focus on his mistakes and failures. She focuses on the jobs he is attempting to accomplish with language and cooperates by responding in both language and in action to his meaning.

Next, we have Nigel, a two-year-old who had been at the children's petting zoo with his father earlier in the day. While he was petting a goat, it began to eat the lid to a cup Nigel was holding with his other hand. The keeper rushed over and said the goat must not eat the lid—it would not be good for him. That evening Nigel started a conversation with his parents.

Nigel: Try eat lid.

Father: What tried to eat the lid?

Nigel: Try eat lid.

Father: What tried to eat the lid?

Nigel: Goat . . . man said no . . . goat try eat lid . . . man said no.

Then, after a further interval, while being put to bed:

Nigel: Goat try eat lid . . . man said no.

Mother: Why did the man say no?

Nigel: Goat shouldn't eat lid . . . (shaking head) good for it.

Mother: The goat shouldn't eat the lid; it's not good for it.

Nigel: Goat try eat lid . . . man said no . . . goat shouldn't eat lid . . . (shaking head) good for it.[5]

Nigel is trying to tell a story, but he is not quite up to it. His parents ask questions and repeat his not-quite complete sentences, and in the end, he gets it together, more or less. His parents count it a great success. They don't feel they need to work on his last version of the story. It's a terrific accomplishment, and when he's ready, with their scaffolding, he'll improve on it. In both Mark's and Nigel's homes the parents try to help the child accomplish his goals and their efforts are collaborative rather than directive.

In homes like these, exposure to books seems to flow naturally from the talk parents engage in with their children. For example, next we have two-and-a-half-year-old Emily on her mother's lap. Mom is holding a book entitled *Rosie's Walk*.

Mother: *Rosie's Walk* by Pat Hutchins.

Emily: Pat Hutchins.

(Mother reads that a hen named Rosie went walking in the yard.)

Mother: What's happening?

Emily: What?

Mother: What's the fox doing?

(Picture shows the fox jumping toward a rake.)

Emily: He's trying to catch Rosie.

Mother: Do you think he's going to catch her?

Emily: No.

(Mother turns page.)

Mother: What happened?

(Picture shows the fox hit by the rake.)

Emily: He banged his nose.

(Mother reads that Rosie walked toward a pond.)

Emily: Uhmm.

Mother: What will happen next?

(Picture shows the fox falling in the pond.)

Emily: He's gonna splash!

(Mother reads that Rosie walked by a haystack.)

Emily: Uhmm.

Mother: What happened?

(Picture shows the fox covered by hay.)

Emily: He fell in a "stick" of hay.

Mother: And Rosie kept right on walking.[6]

This exchange continues in a like manner as the book describes Rosie's walk past a flour mill, under a fence, and past a beehive. As soon as the book is finished Emily asks for more and chooses another book.

Emily: This one.

Mother: Which one? This one? *Good Night Owl?* [In a formal reading tone] *Good Night Owl* by Pat Hutchins. This one's by Pat Hutchins, too. She wrote *Rosie's Walk*.

Emily: She wrote it by Pat Hutchins![7]

Soon children like Mark, Nigel, and Emily begin to "read" books to their parents. They look at the pictures and the print and take on a distinctive "reading" voice and they intone the story they have learned by having it read to them over and over again, sometimes word for word. They recognize print around them and begin to "read" it. When shown a Crest Toothpaste box by an experimenter, three-year-olds reported that it said "Brush your teeth," "Cavities," and "Its called Aim." Some of them even said "Crest Toothpaste."[8]

They begin to "write" as well. When asked to "sign" their art work, they produce marks in a line, and they produce approximately the same marks each time they are asked to sign. By the time they are in kindergarten they have some pretty sophisticated notions about writing. A five-year-old kindergartner named Ashley[9] "wrote" a "story" that looked something like Box 8.1.

When her kindergarten teacher, asked her to "read" the story, her intonation and delivery conveyed the idea that the letters at the top of the page are the title and the drawing is the story itself. Ashley "read" the story as follows:

The Runaway Elephant
The elephant squirted her and the girl couldn't find the elephant. But she finally found the elephant and they were friends again.

Ashley's concept of "story" includes introducing characters and narrating some action. She has even introduced a problem and a resolution. Her concept of writing a story is to make marks on paper that represent the story she has created. She has shown an

Box 8.1

understanding of conventions—the title comes first at the top of the page followed by the story itself. For a child who can't write, Ashley shows a remarkable understanding of story form and literary conventions.

This research shows that some children exhibit reading and writing behaviors in the informal setting of home and community long before they start formal school instruction. Such children take to school like a duck takes to water. They thrive with teachers who encourage them along their path of discovery, rather than insisting that they be "introduced" to the sounds of the letters *c*, *a*, and *t* before they are presented with the word *cat*. Even if they have a more traditional teacher they wind up in the top reading group where the teacher is more collaborative and where the children are given more freedom.

Rosy picture, eh? But unfortunately, we all know that not all children have the idealized experience portrayed in the emergent literacy literature. For example, Shirley Brice Heath[10] observed people in two communities[11] in South Carolina. One was a community of professional people in a small city; the second was a community of white textile mill workers who lived nearby. Adults in both communities placed high value on success in school and urged their children to "get ahead" by doing well in school. However, the children in the two communities had very different experiences in school.

Heath refers to the professional small-city folks as Maintowners. They include both African Americans and whites. Their social interactions center, not on their immediate neighborhoods, but on voluntary associations such as the Elk's Club, Masons, YMCA, Junior League, churches, and tennis and swimming clubs across the city and region.

Maintowners are in constant contact with strangers in their occupations. They turn to professionals for advice about everything from marital problems to landscaping. They make phone calls to people they do not know to get information, complain about service, and make demands on officials and politicians.

Maintown children form associations and friendships with the children of their parents' friends and associates. They spend practically no time hanging out in the 'hood. Their out-of-school activities—music and dance lessons, Boy Scouts, Indian Guides, baseball, swimming, tennis, horseback riding—are planned as rigorously as the school day. Because of their numerous out-of-school opportunities, Maintown children acquired an air of accomplishment and entitlement. It was quite clear that Maintown children are at ease in a society of strangers and that they sense that both themselves and their parents are not without power.

Maintown children grow up in an environment awash in reading and writing and reference to print. Adults around them read in many different circumstances. They read alone and in silence for pleasure and for instruction. At other times they read movie ads, game rules, or instructions for putting new purchases together in the company of others and they talk about what they are reading with those who are present. On other occasions they read aloud from newspapers, magazines, or letters from friends and family.

They rely on print rather than a face-to-face network for information and advice. They choose movies on the basis of reviews; they choose tires on the recommendations of consumers' guides.

Both men and women write both friendly letters and business letters. These include ongoing correspondences, summaries of the year's events to be included in Christmas cards, complaints about products or services, and lobbying letters written to politicians, officials, and newspapers. These letters are often followed or supplemented with phone calls or meetings. Adults do a great deal of work-related writing at home. Managers draft reports and memos and write letters. Teachers bring home students' assignments and work on them and make lesson plans. Dinner table conversation refers to consulting professionals about writing tasks—a lawyer to write a will and a real estate agent to write a lease.

There are frequent discussions of writing "for the record." Maintowners formalized and spelled out in writing rules for group activities such as block clubs, church clubs, and senior class trips to Washington. Minutes of club meetings, signed petitions, news accounts, and letters are referred to and held up as having more authority than memory of what was said.

There is a great deal of discussion of schedules in Maintown homes. Rides need to be arranged. Dinner has to be fitted into everyone's schedules. A bulletin board by the telephone and datebooks carried by the parents are used to record decisions. These written entries have greater authority than anyone's memory of what was said.

Maintown babies come home to their own room outfitted with a crib, playpen, bookshelves, dresser, toy box, and rocker. Parents place great importance on getting the child on a schedule of a morning and afternoon nap, three meals a day, sleeping through the night. They consult baby books to confirm their notions of when these routines should be accomplished as well as when the child should sit, walk, talk, and be toilet trained.

They consider babies conversational partners, not just from birth, but almost from conception. Expectant parents address comments to the baby in the womb. As soon as the baby is born, they talk to it. Older brothers and sisters are encouraged to talk to the baby. No one except the parents and immediate family is expected to fondle the infant. Talk is the preferred means of communication.

From the start, a new baby's physical and verbal environment is oriented toward literacy. Babies are given books. Their rooms are decorated with murals, mobiles, and stuffed animals that represent characters from books.

Questions account for almost half the utterances of mothers addressed to preschool children, and the most frequent of these are "display" questions—ones where the adult has the answer but wants the child to display its knowledge. Most of these questions are repeated again and again and on similar occasions, bed time, book reading time, or a romp with daddy before dinner. By age three, children begin to have experiences that their parents did not share, at play school or Sunday school for example. Children are asked questions about such activities, and they are expected to give truthful answers in straightforward narrative form.

Mothers begin to read to children as young as six months, and from that age, although they cannot yet talk, children give attention to books and acknowledge questions about books. The adult says, "What is that?" The child attends to the picture and makes a sound. The adult says, "That's Pooh Bear. What does Pooh Bear like?" The child attends to the picture and vocalizes and the adult says, "Pooh Bear likes honey."

With the onset of speech, book reading sessions take on the characteristics of the one reported between Emily and her mother reading *Rosie's Walk*. They are similar to other conversations between parent and child, except now the topic is not whatever the child wants it to be; it must refer to the book. At the end of these sessions, adults often ask children about their likes and dislikes and what they think about events depicted in the book, but they do not insist on answers.

Around age three, adults begin to discourage a child's interactive and highly participative role in book reading. Children learn to sit and listen and to hold their questions until the story is over or until the adult signals a break in the reading.

From the time they start to talk, parent-child conversations allude to books. Parents take every opportunity to relate ongoing events to books. When they see a fuzzy black dog on the street the mother asks, "Do you think that's Blackie [a dog in one of the child's books]? Do you think he is looking for a boy [Blackie was looking for a boy to own him in the book]?"

Maintown children learn that talk about books suspends a lot of rules. When they engage in book talk, they can interrupt adults who are conversing; they can say things that are not true, and they can divert attention from otherwise troublesome matters such as a plate of uneaten food.

Books and book-related talk count as entertainment. Waiting in the doctors' office or travelling on a bus, parents read to their children. If a book is not available, they talk about objects as if they were pictures in a book. What is it? What is it like? What features of it make it similar to or different from other objects the child knows about?

Around age three, Maintown children begin to attend Sunday school and nursery school. Here they learn to sit with others and listen until the story reader signals that it is time for questions or discussion. Then they can talk to the teacher or group as long as they stay on the topic and do not interrupt one another. They are permitted to talk to each other as long as they do so briefly, quietly, and on the topic at hand.

Factual questions about the content of the story are often followed by questions such as, "How do you know?," where children are expected to relate what they have learned to specific portions of the text or pictures. For example, the teacher might ask, "Whose bed did Goldilocks fall to sleep in? Can you find that picture?" Finally, children are encouraged to share knowledge that they are reminded of by the story—the mention of a desert reminds a child of his visit to Arizona; a story about a dog triggers pet stories—but they learn to hold such contributions until the end of the lesson.

Reading lessons in school are very similar to bedtime story routines in Maintown. First come factual questions—Who, What, When, Where? Only after these are answered do they proceed to "reason" explanations—Why, Why not, How? And finally they address questions of feeling—Did you like it? Why or why not? How did it make you feel? Thus, Maintown youngsters learn the Maintown way of taking meaning from books and Maintown ways of talking about the meaning taken from print. For Maintowners this seems natural. It's the only way they know, but since nursery school, kindergarten, elementary school, high school, college, graduate school, professions, management, and Western forms of wielding power are based on this model, it's the only way they need to know. In Maintown it is true that the hand that rocks the cradle rules the world.

Maintown seems like a case study for the cultural characteristics that lead to habitual use of explicit language. Authority in the home tends to be collaborative rather than authoritarian. Parents and children live in a society of strangers where little can be assumed about what your communication partners know or what they believe. Parents feel powerful. They make complaints and demand answers. The many privileges afforded children give them an air of entitlement.

I've been talking about the way culture affects language, but there is another way of thinking about culture and language—not as separate things but as parts of a larger package that linguists refer to as "discourse." The common meaning of *discourse* is "conversation," but as linguists use the term it includes not only talk but also all the things that are behind it and underneath it. James Gee suggests that we "think of a discourse as an 'identity kit' which comes complete with the appropriate costume and instructions on how to act and talk so as to take on a particular role that others will recognize"[12]

Every discourse involves values, attitudes, behaviors, beliefs, ways of learning, and ways of expressing what we know, which persons must accept and conform to in order to operate within the discourse. If they do not accept and conform, they are not operating within the discourse

We all get one discourse "free" at our mother's knee, so to speak. This is our primary discourse, the discourse of face-to-face oral communication with those close to us in the community where we start life. The primary discourse I acquired in my large, Irish, Catholic, working-class, big-city family was somewhat different from the discourse I would have acquired in a large, Italian, Catholic, working-class, big-city family, and very different from the discourse my wife acquired in her small, generic "American," Protestant, middle-class, suburban family.

As we sally forth we acquire secondary discourses, those of the playground and Sunday school for example. Discourses are sometimes defined or arrived at in contrast or opposition to other discourses. The male chauvinist discourse and the feminist discourse are each defined in many ways in contrast or opposition to the other. The same is true of the discourses of management and labor, doctor and patient, student and teacher, for example.

Categories we are born into such as gender, class, and ethnicity determine to a large measure the secondary discourses to which we will be exposed, and our ability to acquire the secondary discourses to which we are exposed is determined to some extent by the degree to which the secondary discourse, is similar to our primary discourse. But dissimilarity is not the main impediment to acquiring a secondary discourse as we saw with Ogbu's immigrant minorities such as the Punjabis whose children seem to have little difficulty acquiring the discourse of the school. The real impediment to acquiring a secondary discourse is the degree to which it is in conflict with our primary discourse as we saw with Ogbu's involuntary minorities and Willis's lads, whose primary discourses are in serious conflict with the discourse of the school.

The primary discourse of the Maintowners is similar to and congenial with school discourse. Therefore, it's easy for Maintown children to acquire school discourse (so easy in fact that it seems natural).

The discussion of emergent literacy presented at the beginning of this chapter is in fact a description of how children in middle-class and gentry homes acquire the discourse of their communities—not only language and the way it's used, but the attitudes, beliefs, behaviors, and values that underlie language and the way it is used.

This discourse is consistent with school discourse. It is particularly consistent with the discourse of progressive classrooms as described in the affluent professional and executive elite schools.[13] How can these children fail? Even if they are not particularly bright or energetic, most do all right in school and in the affluent professional and executive elite world for which their classrooms prepare them.

But, alas, the story is different for the children only a short distance away in Roadville.

Chapter 9

WHERE CHILDREN ARE TAUGHT TO SIT STILL AND LISTEN

Only a few miles from Maintown is a working-class commu nity of textile workers, which Heath refers to as *Roadville*.[1] The people of Roadville like their town the way it is. Its rural setting gives them opportunities for hunting and fishing and offers a slow pace of life. They value their solidarity, their sameness. They believe that they are closer to each other and to their churches than people in other parts of the country. They are a community of intimates. One woman commented, "We, uh, mamma used to talk about how we [members of the community] were cut from the same pattern. We all knew what to expect." Another added, "We learned at church and at home too that things were either *right* or *wrong*; you did things the *right* way and you were *right*. You did wrong or said wrong and everyone *knew* it was wrong. Most everybody accepted that. Those that didn't just didn't fit in at all."[2]

Most Roadville parents regularly attend fundamentalist churches where they are reminded frequently to be strict with their children and to raise them the "right" way. Gender roles are clearly defined. Men support the family. Women stay home with the children, especially when the children are young. Even when women work outside the home, men are defined as the bread winners. Men decide on large expenditures for recreation and maintenance of the house; women decide on appliances and furniture.

Once beyond the age of two, boys and girls are separated for play. Beyond early ABC books and books of basic objects, toys and games are sharply differentiated for boys and girls. With the exception of toys for the very young, such as a post onto which rings of graduated sizes can be placed, educational toys are segregated as well. When they are older, girls help their mothers cook, can, freeze, and take care of younger children; boys help their fathers gardening, doing house repairs, painting, and working on the car, boat, and camper.

Roadvillers respect authority. They say, "Spare the rod and spoil the child," and they mean it. Talking back to parents is severely punished by strapping. They believe old folks know more than young folks, and men know more than women, although women are generally better educated than their husbands and are more likely to attend adult education classes. In Bible study, Roadville adults like to have the pastor, the person with authority, lead the discussion.

Stories play an important part in Roadville. Stories are usually told in response to an invitation. "Has Betty burned any biscuits lately?" or "Brought home any possums lately?" are invitations to tell a story, one the speaker has heard but others in the group have not. The focus of a story is a transgression, a deviation from the behavior expected of a "good cook," "good hunter," or "good handyman."

The point of a story is often left unspoken. You don't say, "George is a bit of a know-it-all," although that's the point of the story. Everyone present knows that, and they are all good enough friends to have a laugh on George and yet remain his friends. They will not tell a story behind George's back that they would not tell in his presence.

In telling a story, individuals show they belong to the group. They know and accept the norms that were broken. One story triggers another and each reaffirms the familiarity of everyone in the group with the experiences being recounted. Stories are expressions of conformity and solidarity.

Roadvillers do not rely on print the way Maintowners do. They prefer to look to their own experience or the experience of one of their own for guidance. When Roadville families get a new game, they rarely look at the directions. Usually one of the children has played the game at a friend's house and he or she teaches the game to the family. In assembling toys, fathers often look at the directions, but then proceed by using "common sense." There is no discussion as the toy is assembled, except for an occasional implicit, context-dependent utterance such as "That doesn't look right." Women tend not to try recipes that have not been tried by friends, and when they do they usually make substitutions or change the directions, relying on the friend's experience rather than the printed word.

As in Maintown, babies in Roadville are typically brought home to their own room decorated in a nursery rhyme motif with a bed, changing table, dresser, book shelves, and toy box. During the first three months, a great deal of emphasis is placed on keeping a schedule for eating, napping, changing, bathing, and bedtime.

Mothers assign intentions to their babies' crying—because he's hungry, uncomfortable, or overtired—and talk to them from birth. Young mothers at home alone with their infants often strap them into their infant seat and move them from room to room talking to them as they work. All the parent's friends and relatives are expected to talk to the baby when they meet. Men who do not are forgiven for being ignorant about babies. Only little boys are not expected to talk to a baby belonging to a relative or family friend.

Parents scaffold their children's early attempts at language as we saw with Mark and Nigel, but there is an interesting switch. Unlike Mark's mother, who always scaffolded his meanings and dropped topics as soon as he lost interest, Roadville parents are more likely to stay with a topic long after the child has gone on to something else. Heath records an example of a mother and child who were making Christmas cookies. The child bit the head off a snowman cookie and said "noman all gone." This prompted a sixty-word monologue on the part of the mother despite the fact that the child showed no interest and chattered on about other topics concerning cookies, but not the snowman.

Adults invite children to tell stories to other adults and they carefully monitor them. Stories are to be told in strict chronology and any exaggeration is considered a lie. Important details, *as the adult remembers them*, are to be included.

For example, what follows is a transcription of a dinner conversation involving Sally, a four-year-old, her mother, and a teenage brother. Sally and her mother had been out that day and had a flat tire. Mr. Jones, the gas station man asked Sally to "help" him by counting the lug nuts as he took them off the bolts and put them into the hubcap. Shortly afterward Sally found a wounded cricket and built a fence of small sticks around the cricket and talked to it while Mr. Jones fixed the tire.

Mother: Can you tell your brother what you helped Mr. Jones do today?

Sally: We went to get gas, 'n there was this cricket, and he was in a field. I found some sticks to make one.

Mother: But wait, wait, why did we go to the gas station?

Sally: Mr. Jones helped us!

Mother: Yes, but why did Mr. Jones have to help us? Come on, you know what happened.

Sally: We couldn't go to the store. The car broke. 'n I found a cricket.

Mother: What broke on the car?

Sally: The tire broke.

Mother: And did you help Mr. Jones fix the tire?

Sally: Yes. The cricket was fun, but I had to leave 'im. I took down the fence.

Mother: Well, let me tell you what happened to us....[3]

Parents "taking over" in parent-child interactions is a marked departure from the middle-class model we saw with Mark and Nigel. Heath believes it stems from the fact that Roadville parents have a different attitude from middle-class parents regarding communication with their toddlers. Middle-class mothers scaffold to keep the conversation going. Roadville parents are much more conscious of their responsibility to teach the child to "pay attention, listen, and behave."

In Sunday school, children are also told "moral" stories, ones where a child is offered a clear-cut choice between right and wrong and does the right thing. These are followed by pertinent Bible passages. Occasionally children are asked to recount similar choices that they have made, but situational ethics—what if a person had to do a bad thing or something worse would happen—are strictly discouraged. When children start to suggest "what ifs" the teacher tells them to "pay attention to what the story says and don't go wandering off somewhere and making things up."

Play with toys by adults and preschoolers has strong elements of both language interaction and manual manipulation. While playing with rings that fit on a pole parents ask, "Where does this go?" "Does this go on next?" A father playing with a toy work bench might say, "This is a hammer, see, I'm gonna hammer Bobby's shoe. Hammer goes bang, bang." Bobby is then asked, "What's this, Bobby? Where does it go? How does it go [what sound does it make]?" and Bobby is expected to repeat the response exactly as it was taught to him.

Parents later tell the children stories connected with toys such as the work bench. The stories have morals or lessons such as "Don't put screwdrivers into electric sockets," or "Don't pound a hammer while daddy is sleeping." When an infraction occurs the parents asks, "What did I tell you?" and the child is expected to repeat the story and its moral.

By the time children reach age four, emphasis on educational toys and playing with children diminishes. Fathers begin to teach their sons to play ball and generally roughhouse with them. Language is either absent or implicit and context dependent when parents teach their children to do such things as hold a bat, wear a baseball mitt, make Jell-O, or sew an apron. Adults say, "Do it this way. This way! Not like that." "That looks right." "Next time, be more careful." Children say, "Want me to do it like this? Is this right?"

The way things are done at school in, for example, science or shop—listing materials, taking one step at a time, and so on—is not seen as having any relevance to doing tasks at home. Although occasionally an annoyed parent may say, "Can't you read? What are you going to school for?" the domains of home and school are kept separate by both the child and parents by the end of the primary grades.

Most one-year-olds are active participants in book reading. They find letters from their alphabet blocks in their ABC book. They name pictures and parts of pictures. They imitate sounds of characters in books. Although Roadville book-reading episodes are similar to those of Maintown, Roadvillers do not relate book reading to other events in the day. They do not, upon seeing a thing or event in the real world, remind children of similar things or events in a book and launch a conversation on the similarities and differences.

By age three, nearly all the children can pretend to read. They associate print on boxes and packages with the items they contain—Bugles, Animal Crackers, Crest Toothpaste, and so on.

For Roadville children there are three overlapping stages of experience with print before school. First they are introduced to discrete bits and pieces of books—the alphabet, simple shapes, basic colors, and commonly represented items in children's books such as apple, baby, clown, and doll. Parents ask questions and expect the answers they taught the children. If adults decide that a dog in a book is a *dog*, other answers—*a puppy, a mutt,* or *Blackie* are counted as wrong. During this stage there is full participation by the child who sometimes poses the questions and pretends to read to the adult.

During the second stage beginning around age three, books with story lines are introduced such as *The Three Bears* and stories with characters from Sesame Street. Parents and Sunday school teachers expect children to sit and listen to a story and not participate either verbally or physically. Bedtime stories become something of a struggle as the stories get longer and the mother's objective includes teaching the child to "learn to listen."

Around age four, the third stage begins. Children are given activity books such as follow the dots and push out and paste shapes and letters. They are taught to print their names and draw straight lines and stay in the lines in their coloring books. The children are constantly reminded that these are things they will need to learn before they go to school.

Also around age four, children begin to go to bed later and without any special routines. Many children are enrolled in church nursery schools. At this point parents comfort themselves that they have taught them "right" and set them down the road for school, which they must now travel alone.

Roadville parents seem to follow the emergent literacy script when their children are infants. Mothers attend to their babies' every sound and gesture and adults speak to infants from birth, but soon after they deviate from the script Mark and Nigel's parents seemed to be following. In conversation they follow the child's lead, but try to keep the child on the topic long after he or she loses interest.

Their book-reading episodes are not like Emily's experience reading *Rosie's Walk*. Parents start with alphabet books rather than stories and focus on teaching letter recognition. They are strongly focused on teaching the child to "pay attention, listen, and behave" from the start. Characters from books are not referred to while engaging in other activities with the children. Older children are taught to concentrate on *who, what, where,* and *when* questions in responding to stories. They are not taught to answer *how* and *why* questions, and they are explicitly discouraged from considering *what-if* questions.

Children's writing-like activities are confined to printing their names, drawing straight lines, and staying within the lines while coloring. A Roadville four-year-old is not likely to "write" a story like Ashley's "The Runaway Elephant."

When Roadville children go to school, they usually do well in grades one through three. They arrive at school knowing their alphabet, colors, and shapes. They sit still and listen and answer *who, what, when, where* questions. They do well in reading workbook exercises that focus on parts of words and specific information from the story. When the teacher asks at the end of a lesson, "What did you like about the story?" few Roadville children answer. When she asks, "What would you have done if you had been Billy [a character in the story]?" most Roadville children say, "I don't know."

As they proceed through the grades, they continue to handle basic lessons satisfactorily, but they flounder when the lesson calls for independent action or thinking. When asked to make up a story they repeat stories from their reading books. They rarely provide emotional or personal commentary in recounting real events or book stories. They do not compare two items or events and point out similarities and differences.

Most Roadville children find hypothetical questions impossible. For instance, a fourth grade class is studying the culture of Hopi Indians on their reservation. The teacher asks what customs of the Hopi Indians might cause trouble if they moved into the city.

Roadville children answer by listing all the customs of the Hopi Indians *on the reservation*. All the "what ifs" have been drilled out of them.

Thus, by the time they reach fourth grade, the knowledge and habits that served them well in the primary grades begin to fail them. The teacher's talk and much of the material students are required to read become more and more explicit and context independent. The teachers' questions and assignments call for independent thinking and creativity, and the bulk of Roadville students have no way of keeping up.

Consistent with other studies of working-class students,[4] average and even good Roadville students do only the minimum of what is asked of them in school. They never seem to see the point of most of what they are asked to do. They see school as a place where you have to look up definitions all the time and then have a test, but they see no reason for using a word whose definition they learned in conversation or even in a school written essay.

Schools generally fail to help Roadville children see the relevance of school work to their lives. Although Roadville parents talk about the value of school, they often act as if they don't believe it. One woman talks of the importance of a "fitting education" for her three children so they can "do better," but looks on with equanimity as her sixteen-year-old son quits school, goes to work in a garage, and plans to marry his fifteen-year-old girlfriend "soon." In another family one daughter is going steady and everyone expects she will quit school and get married when she turns sixteen, and a son talks of going to college on a baseball scholarship, but admits he hates school. Yet the parents of these children talk about the prospect of their children going to college without any hint that they see a contradiction between their aspirations and their behavior.

By the time Roadville children reach high school they write off school as having nothing to do with what they want in life, and they fear that school success will threaten their social relations with people whose company they value. This is a familiar refrain for working class children. It is a milder version of the oppositional identity Ogbu described in involuntary minorities.

Roadville seems like a case study for the working-class discourse community described by Bernstein. Roadvillers live in a community of intimates where conformity is expected. Parents are authoritarian. Language is implicit and context dependent. The point of stories is implied, not stated. When parents teach children, they *demonstrate* skills and say context-dependent things such as, "Do it like this."

The discourse Roadville children acquire in their homes and communities is dissimilar and in serious conflict with the discourse of the progressive classroom as described in the affluent professional and executive elite schools. This is not simply because of differences in language habits but because of differences in the beliefs, behaviors, values, and attitudes that underlie language habits. What we see here is a clash of discourses. On the other hand, their primary discourse is very similar to the discourse of Anyon's working-class school, Freeway High School, and in the classrooms where the Irish, Italian, and Puerto Rican children remained in the Brownstoners' school.

That explains why people keep saying that traditional directive methods "work" with working-class children. No one seriously thinks these methods *educate* anyone. They keep the lid on, while giving the children a kind of domesticating literacy, which prepares them to take their parents' places in society. It's our old friend economic reproduction, and when you understand it, it just won't do.

Chapter 10

THE LAST STRAW
There's Literacy, and Then There's Literacy

W hile nineteenth-century anthropologists divided the world's people into primitive and civilized societies, twentieth century anthropologists have divided them into oral and literate societies. Oral societies are described roughly the same way primitive societies had been—as small, homogeneous, regulated by face-to-face encounters rather than impersonal laws, and having a strong sense of solidarity. Literate societies are described roughly the same way as civilized societies had been—as large, diverse, logical, scientific, technological, having a sense of history, regulated by impersonal laws, and sacrificing solidarity somewhat in favor of individualism. It is a short step to conclude that literacy *causes* the characteristics attributed to literate societies.

Havelock[1] gave us a brilliant example of a people who emerged from a "primitive" to a civilized state shortly after the widespread introduction of literacy—the ancient Greeks, no less. Havelock argued that during Homer's time the Greeks fit the description of a primitive society. They passed down their values and knowledge through spoken epic poetry, which, in the absence of writing, was limited by human memory. To facilitate memory, the epics were recited in a heavy metrical rhythm. Characters, actions, and events were stereotypical. The teller and the audience identified closely with the story to the extent that they "came under the spell" of the poem. Under such conditions, new ideas or challenges to existing knowledge and beliefs were difficult, if not impossible.

But then, around the time of Plato, literacy in an alphabetic script became widespread. What was written could be seen as a text, an object to be examined. It's hard to "look back" at what you're listening to, especially if you are caught up in the rhythm of an epic poem, but you can look back at a written text. It's common-place for students who first begin to write fairly lengthy papers to be surprised to find that what they wrote on page twelve is inconsistent with what they wrote on page two. With experience, writers are no longer surprised; they expect this to happen. Writing permits us to reflect on our knowledge and beliefs, notice inconsistencies, and work them out.

Writing also permits us to lay texts side by side and compare them. This enables us to find inconsistencies in knowledge and beliefs that might go undetected in an oral culture. And with writing there is also less tolerance for inaccuracy because writing permits us to check facts and sources and rewrite before "sending" the message in ways that speech does not permit.

Because writing can be moved away from the writer, the writer is apt to be unfamiliar with his or her audience. A writer cannot gauge the distant reader's knowledge, beliefs, and opinions with the accuracy that is often possible in speech. Therefore, with writing, facts are more likely to be stated explicitly; descriptions and explanations are apt to be more precise, and arguments are more apt to be reasoned in greater detail. Is it any wonder, Havelock asks, that philosophy, science, and history burgeoned in Greece following the introduction of widespread literacy?

Others, engaging in similar reasoning, concluded that societies become large, diverse, logical, scientific, technological, become regulated by impersonal laws, acquire a sense of history, and sacrifice solidarity in favor of individualism once literacy becomes widespread in a society. It's a short step from believing that, just as literacy causes the transformation of a primitive society into a "civilized" one, literacy causes a similar transformation of individuals within a society.

There are well-known correlations between various kinds of trouble and low levels of literacy. Juvenile delinquents, criminals, people on welfare, high school dropouts, the chronically unemployed, teenage parents, and people having minimum wage jobs tend to have low levels of literacy. This painfully obvious observation leads many to believe that illiteracy causes social ills and literacy cures them.

The War on Poverty during the Johnson administration was essentially a literacy program. The idea was that if children of the unemployed, the underemployed, and those employed at minimum wage jobs learned to read,[2] they would, like Plato's Greeks, discover inconsistencies in their thinking and begin to engage in higher levels of thought. They would begin to produce texts that are explicit, nonredundant, accurate, and logical. As a result, they would learn to deal with and become part of powerful institutions such as schools, big government, corporations, and professions that are built on and require this kind of literacy. They would, in short, get jobs or get better jobs and poverty would disappear.

But what happened when we taught the children of the poor to read and write but found that they did not become explicit, concise, accurate, and logical in their talk and writing and they did not understand texts that had these qualities? We thought, "We haven't made them literate enough." And we kept drilling phonics and spelling and grammar lessons into seventh and eighth graders and high school boys and girls thinking, if we just get them literate *enough*, the rest will happen.

The trouble was, and is, that basic literacy does not lead automatically to higher forms of thinking, either in societies or in individuals. Widespread literacy has occurred in numerous societies where a golden age comparable to that of Greece did not follow. One of the most remarkable and successful literacy campaigns in history took place shortly after the Reformation in Sweden under the auspices of the government and Lutheran church. Many places experiencing intensely pious religious fervor—Scotland, New England, and Protestant areas in France, Germany, and Switzerland—reached "near universal literacy" by 1800. None of the litany of "higher cognitive functions," "modernization," or "progress" happened in these places. It was literacy for domestication and that's what they got—domestication—not a riot of intellectual inquiry and progress.

Of course we don't need to go into the past to find examples of literacy that has not triggered an interest in science, logic, and so on. We need only to look at Anyon's working-class fifth graders, the lads, the Freeway high schoolers, the Irish, Italian, and Puerto Rican children in the Brownstoners' school, and the people from Roadville. They were all literate, but none of them were in the early stages of a process that would inevitably lead to the Ivy League.

There's literacy, and then there's literacy. The children from all of Anyon's schools (the working-class, middle-class, affluent professionals, and executive elite) were literate, but this fact obscures more than it reveals. The children from Anyon's schools demonstrated different *levels* of literacy.[3] The lowest level is simply the ability to "sound out" words and turn sentences that are typical of informal face-to-face conversation into writing. It is referred to as the "performative level." Quite obviously, fifth graders in all four schools were literate at the performative level.

The next level is the "functional level." It is the ability to meet the reading and writing demands of an average day of an average person. Reading *USA Today*, filling out a job application, understanding directions for using a household gadget, and writing a note to leave on the kitchen table for your spouse are some examples of functional literacy. The children in Anyon's working-class school were learning functional literacy. Work for them was following step-by-step directions. When asked, "What do you think of when I say the word *knowledge*?" no one used the word *think*; only one child used the word *mind*.

The third level is the "informational level." This is the ability to read and absorb the kind of knowledge that is associated with the school and to write examinations and reports based on such knowledge. The children in Anyon's middle-class school seemed to be working toward informational literacy. Work for them was getting the right answers; it rarely involved creativity. Knowledge for them was remembering facts. When asked, "Can you make knowledge?" they answered that they would look it up.

The fourth level is "powerful literacy." Powerful literacy involves creativity and reason—the ability to evaluate, analyze, and synthesize what is read.

───ɯ───

James Gee[4] traces the powerful literacy of the present to seventeenth century England, where literacy combined with political, economic, and cultural forces to produce an *invention* that was to be developed over the next hundred years. This invention is one we were all introduced to in school—the essay.

The British essayists, Sir Francis Bacon and that crowd, devised ways to exploit writing for the purpose of formulating original knowledge. Essayists took an assertion (what we all learned in school as the "thesis" or "topic sentence") and examined it, ferreted out the assumptions upon which it was based, and stated them as explicitly as possible. Explicit, explicit, explicit. When the essayist was through, unstated and frequently unconscious assumptions and implications had been made explicit; inconsistent assumptions and implications had been confronted and resolved. New knowledge was therefore created.

The essay is public rather than private. It is not addressed to any individual and the identity of the author is unimportant. The focus is on the content. It is accurate. Writers and editors check facts and reformulate statements after reflecting on their accuracy, precision, and consistency. It is intended for a large audience with whom the author is not intimately acquainted. Facts are stated explicitly; descriptions and explanations are detailed, and arguments are spelled out precisely. It is revised and edited to eliminate redundancy.[5]

The essay became a powerful tool in the hands of an already powerful class. Institutions associated with the most highly developed physical, natural, and social sciences, government, politics, economics, literature, art, and language in the West were developed using powerful literacy and these institutions continue to depend on it in their day-to-day operations and development.

The children in Anyon's affluent professional and executive elite schools were learning forms of powerful literacy. The affluent professional school stressed using literacy to *create* while the executive elite school emphasized using literacy to *understand and control.*

I often ask my students, most of them school teachers, to write their definitions of literacy and to share them in small groups. They nearly always write a definition like the following: Literacy is the ability to read a paragraph and understand the meaning the author intended. It is also the ability to write one's ideas so that another person can understand them.

Then I introduce the concept of levels of literacy—performative, functional, informational, and powerful literacy, and I ask them to decide where their definitions fall. They nearly always classify their definitions as informational, and sometimes even powerful. When I tell them that I don't agree, that I would classify their definitions as functional at best, they argue their definition implies informational and powerful literacy because these levels are based on the ability to understand the meaning an author intends and to write ideas so others can understand. They see schooling as allowing children to progress naturally from the lower forms of literacy to the higher. They admit that some students or whole groups of students get stuck along the way, but they don't know why or what to do about it.

My students are not unique. Informational and powerful literacy seem to have flowed naturally from performative and functional literacy in their experience. Powerful literacy is so intimately connected with the way powerful Americans think that it seems like the natural, inevitable outcome of learning to read and write. It's not so. Nothing happens automatically when a person learns to read and write at a performative or functional level, certainly not powerful literacy. It is especially unlikely that anything will happen when performative and functional literacy are taught for domestication as it was in Protestant Europe or New England in the seventeenth-century or in Anyon's working-class or middle-class schools, for that matter.

Children of the gentry learn to read and write in classrooms whose discourse mirrors that of their own communities. They continue to make progress toward powerful literacy, which is, of course, the literacy of their homes and community. The children of the working class learn to read and write in classrooms whose discourse mirrors that of their own communities, but they do not make progress toward informational and powerful literacy. Their progress ends with functional or perhaps informational literacy, which is, of course, the literacy of their homes and community.

Do we instill in working-class children the understanding that the purpose of literacy is to create new knowledge that is relevant to their lives? Do we teach them procedures and invite them to create their own procedures or make our procedures more congenial to themselves or more useful to themselves? No. We say, "Do it my way or it's wrong." We say, "What we're trying to do here is get some notes for the end of the year [state] exams."

Do we run classrooms in such a way that working-class children will learn the attitudes and behaviors of powerful people regarding authority, conformity, isolation, and power, which in turn make the use of explicit language sensible and necessary? No. Instead we replicate the attitudes and behaviors of powerless people regarding these matters in our classrooms.

Power [handwritten margin note]

Both the Brownstoners and the Freeway parents wanted the kind of literacy for their children that would get them into the better four-year colleges—powerful literacy. The Brownstone parents understood the connection between progressive classrooms and acquiring higher levels of literacy, and they had moderate success. The Freeway parents did not understand the connection between higher levels of literacy and progressive classrooms, and they had no success.

We are mystified when working-class children learn to read and write but do not progress to informational and powerful literacy, and so we try to teach them the basics of reading and writing *better*—back to basics again and again in the vain hope that if we make them literate *enough* they will do what's natural and become logical, scientific, technological, explicit, and on and on.

The older they get the harder we try to give them the basics and the more frustrated we become. We blame them for being so lacking in intelligence that they cannot do what's natural or so perverse that they will not do what's natural. By this time, their oppositional identity is making itself felt, school's over, and the war is on.

Giving children more and more drills in phonics and basic skills never has and never will lead to powerful forms of literacy. In fact, directive, domesticating teaching styles such as those we observed at Freeway, which invariably accompany the skills and drills "solution," replicate the authoritarian, conformist, powerless societies of intimates that make implicit, context-dependent language and communication inevitable and explicit, context-independent language unnecessary. When forms of powerful literacy and the ability to operate as powerful persons in powerful institutions are seen as the ultimate objective of the schools, the teaching methods we saw in Anyon's working-class schools and at Freeway High School are not the solution. They only exacerbate the problem.

Chapter 11

LITERACY WITH AN ATTITUDE

The history of American schools between the Civil War and World War I shows that public education of the poor in this country was motivated by the recognition that democracy requires a literate electorate on the one hand and by rapidly growing cities and child labor laws that resulted in hordes of unemployed youths on the other hand. But the beginnings of government involvement in the education of the poor in England appear to have been motivated by fear of an unruly working class that was becoming literate in ways that the ruling class found dangerous. There are important lessons to be learned from this history.

In the middle ages, the few books that existed were in Latin rather than in the languages of the people. Popular literacy was simply nonexistent. But with the invention of the printing press around 1450, printing shops spread throughout Europe, and books in modern language began to appear. The availability of such books gave rise to considerable self-taught literacy. Less than one hundred years after the invention of the printing press a law was passed in England forbidding all women and men under the rank of yeoman from reading the Bible.

By 1600, one of ten agricultural laborers (the lowest on the economic scale) in England could read. Those who could read were "exposed to a steady hail of printed pamphlets of news, political and religious propaganda, astrological prediction and advice, songs, sensation, sex and fantasy."[1] "This literacy was a political and social force . . . , a constant bit player in revolution."[2]

In a single year, 1642, there were some two thousand different pamphlets published in England. In an effort to control the flow of information and opinion, laws were passed requiring that books and papers be licensed. In 1712, taxes were imposed to make pamphlets too expensive for the poor. Soon, groups began to chip in to buy single copies and read them together. Owners of taverns where this activity went on were sometimes threatened with arrest on charges of sedition.[3]

This type of popular literacy reached its height at the end of the eighteenth century, 1790 to 1810. This is the period E. P. Thompson describes in his classic *The Making of the English Working Class*.[4] There was enormous social upheaval in Europe and America. The Industrial Revolution was well under way in Britain. The American colonies had rebelled against British rule and had ratified a Constitution and Bill of Rights guaranteeing freedom of speech, freedom of the press, freedom of religion, freedom of assembly, and the right to bear arms. In France the monarchy was overthrown, Louis XIV and Marie Antoinette were beheaded, the aristocracy was decimated in public executions, and there was mob rule referred to as "The Terror" from June 1793 to July 1794.

In 1791, Thomas Paine's *Rights of Man* was published asserting the rights of all Englishmen. It was "republican, democratic, and fiercely anti-aristocratic."[5] During a civil disturbance in 1792, a local worthy, General Lambton, was accosted by a mob with these words: "Have you read this little work of Tom Paine's? No? Then read it—we like it much. You have a great estate, General; we shall soon divide it amongst us."[6]

In 1793, when a portion of *Rights of Man* was published in pamphlet form, 200,000 copies sold in one year—one for every fifty people in England, a nation of ten million. Paine's book was not the initial cause of the unrest, but it gave fuel to a revolutionary spirit already awake in England. One manifestation of this spirit was the "corresponding" societies that sprang up all over England.

The most famous of these societies was the London Corresponding Society, which was formed in 1792 when nine "well-meaning, sober and industrious men" met in London to discuss politics and reform. They formed themselves into a society and collected dues to buy paper for the purpose of corresponding with other like-minded groups. For admission, members were asked to agree that "the welfare of these kingdoms require that every adult person, in possession of his reason, and not incapacitated by crimes, should have a vote for a member of Parliament."

Society membership was unlimited, that is, no one was to be excluded. This was a radical step because it overturned the centuries-old identification of involvement in politics (political rights) with property rights. It opened the door for self-activating and self-organizing processes among the common people. By 1795, The London Corresponding Society is believed to have had five thousand active dues-paying members and another five thousand enrolled but not fully active.[7]

Similar societies appeared throughout England. Many of their prominent members were skilled artisans, shopkeepers, and physicians. There is no doubt, however, that those on the very lowest level of the economic ladder were represented. A government spy reported of the membership in London:

> There are some of decent tradesmanlike appearance, who possess strong, but unimproved faculties, and tho' bold, yet cautious. The delegates of this description are but few. There are others of an apparent lower order—no doubt journeymen, who though they seem to possess no abilities and say nothing, yet they appear resolute . . . and regularly vote for every motion which carries with it a degree of boldness. The last description . . . and which is the most numerous, consist of the very lowest order of society—few are even decent in appearance, some of them are filthy and ragged, and others such wretched looking blackguards that it requires some mastery over that innate pride, which every well-educated man must necessarily possess, even to sit down in their company. . . . These appear very violent & seem ready to adopt every thing tending [to] Confusion & Anarchy.[8]

The reason these were called "corresponding societies" was of course that they corresponded with one another. After debating a question or reading and discussing a tract they would summarize their findings in writing and send them off to other societies and letters from other societies would also be read and discussed. A government agent wrote that in Sheffield, 2,500 of the "lowest mechanics" were enrolled in a "Constitutional Society" where

> they read the most violent publications, and comment on them, as well as on their correspondence not only with the dependent Societies in the towns and villages of the vicinity, but with those . . . in other parts of the kingdom.[9]

The purpose of the societies was eloquently stated by a witness giving testimony at a trial (for treason, of course) of Thomas Hardy, one of the London leaders:

> To enlighten the people, to show the people the reason, the ground of all their sufferings; when a man works hard for thirteen or fourteen hours of the day, the week through, and is not able to maintain his family; that is what I understood of it; to show the people the ground of this; why they were not able.[10]

And, of course, the societies came to the conclusion that "the ground of this; why they were not able" was *not* that it was the will of God, or the natural order of things, but the result of the way society was organized. They further concluded that this organization of society continued with the cooperation of working men and that it could be changed if working men no longer cooperated.[11] This kind of talk led to charges of high treason—the penalty for which was to be hanged by the neck, cut down while still alive, disembowelled, beheaded, and quartered. The gentry was not amused by this kind of talk among "persons of the lowest order."

Meetings were described by some members as being very sociably egalitarian, and orderly.

> The usual mode of proceeding at these weekly meetings was this. The chairman (each man was chairman in rotation) read from some book . . . and the persons present were invited to make remarks thereon, as many as chose did so, but without rising. Then another portion was read and a second invitation given. Then the remainder was read and a third invitation was

given when they who had not before spoken were expected to say something. Then there was a general discussion.[12]

Government spies, on the other hand, paint a somewhat rowdier picture.

Almost everybody speaks, and there is always a very great noise, till the delegate gets up. People grow very outrageous and won't wait, then the delegate gets up and tries to soften them.[13]

In poorer neighborhoods, meetings were held in taverns with "songs, in which the clergy were a standing subject of abuse," where there were "pipes and tobacco," and where "the tables strewed with penny, two-penny, and three-penny publications."

The Corresponding Societies encouraged people from different walks of life to come together in a "society of strangers," to question authority and exercise power. Their whole point was for members to reflect on society and their place in it, to learn what others were thinking, to discuss it, evaluate it, come to conclusions, formulate new ideas and opinions, and exchange those conclusions, opinions, and ideas with others in the form of correspondence. If this doesn't remind you of powerful literacy, it should.

The literacy of the Corresponding Societies was literacy *with an attitude*—not the self- defeating attitude of the lads or the sulkers and steppers, but the attitude of critical agents who recognized the potential power of literacy combined with civic courage.

The reaction of the British government was panic and repression. Leaders of the London Corresponding Society were tried for treason in 1792, but acquitted by their juries. *The Rights of Man* was banned as seditious libel in 1793 and Paine was driven into exile. Leaders of Corresponding Societies in Scotland were tried and transported to penal colonies. Public meetings were outlawed. Corresponding Societies were no longer welcomed by tavern keepers who feared being charged with sedition, and the societies began to disband. In 1799, Corresponding Societies were outlawed and strict controls were imposed on the printing trade.

At the same time, other measures were taken to *use* literacy to counter the dangerous ideas of the literate masses. Pamphlets attacking Paine's ideas, and more often his character, were widely distributed. Other tracts appeared condemning the violence and ideals of the French Revolution. Among the pamphleteers was Hannah More, a Quaker who characterized British supporters of the French Revolution as "the friends of insurrections, infidelity and vice."[14] She also organized Sunday schools where poor children were taught to read.

When criticized by those who saw literacy among the poor as a threat, More replied "My object is not to make them fanatics, but to train up the lower classes in habits of industry and piety."[15] She and many of her cohorts saw schooling, not as a threat to political stability, but as a new means of regulation and discipline, a new way to shape the habits and character of the people.[16]

In 1806, Patrick Colquhoun, wrote in his book, *New and Appropriate Systems of Education for the Laboring People:*

> The prosperity of every state depends on the good habits, and the religious and moral instruction of the labouring people. By shielding the minds of youth against the vices that are most likely to beset them, much is gained to society in the prevention of crimes, and in lessening the demand for punishment. . . .
> It is not, however, proposed by this institution, that the children of the poor should be educated in a manner to elevate their minds above the rank they are destined to fill in society, or that an expense should be incurred beyond the lowest rate ever paid for instruction. Utopian schemes for an extensive diffusion of knowledge would be injurious and absurd.[17]

Colquhoun had a full agenda. He argued for an organized police force, amassed lurid statistics to demonstrate the threat posed by the laboring classes, and is one of the first to comment on a correlation between criminal behavior and illiteracy. He favored a monitorial system of schooling where older children taught younger ones, and where the brightest among the eldest were appointed "monitors" who reported to a headmaster. One of the chief attractions of this system was that it was cheap. One teacher could oversee the training of scores of children. It also imposed a regime of constant surveillance, inspection, and regulation.

Colquhoun, More, and others like them had the insight that would carry the day. Literacy is only dangerous among the working class when it is used to further working-class interests, as it had been used in the Corresponding Societies. However, schooling could be used by the upper class to get control of the children of the poor; they could turn working-class literacy into a tool to protect the status quo. Literacy could domesticate the poor rather than rile them up.

Although the beginnings of public support for church schools in Great Britain between the years 1780 and 1850 were undoubtedly motivated by philanthropy to some degree, they also served the purpose of steering the poor away from radical ideas. At the same time it was becoming clear that a work force with functional literacy was advantageous, if not essential, for continued industrialization and that only the state had the resources to school large numbers of children.

The Corresponding Societies of the 1790s where working men learned to read and write were replaced fifty years later by state-supported schools for children. By the 1830s, working class literature saw a marked shift away from the educational and political toward sensational periodicals and fiction. This was the beginning of the commercial entertainment and information industry.[18]

Since 1800, violence or the threat of violence has never really disappeared in the struggle against ideas that threaten political and economic privilege, but as tactics, violence and threats of violence have been replaced by domesticating education, which has become the bedrock of class relations. Nearly two centuries later Paulo Freire observed that education is never neutral. It either liberates or domesticates. The Corresponding Societies represented education for liberation. Soon after 1800, when the first feeble attempts at state-supported education for the poor appeared in Great Britain, it was education for domestication.

Chapter 12

NOT QUITE MAKING LITERACY DANGEROUS AGAIN

There are certain kinds of contemporary classrooms that have a lot in common with the Corresponding Societies of England in the 1790s. This leads some observers to wonder whether we are in for some interesting times. First, let's have a look at a couple of these classrooms.

Marla McCurdy[1] gathers her first graders around her and asks them how they would spell some words. Soon she has the sentence "The dog chased the cat" written on the board in the following way:

a dg sd a ct

After writing a few such sentences as a class project, McCurdy suggests to the children that in the future, when they are writing, they should try to write their own words without asking her how to spell them. She reminds them to put a space or dash between words and to write from left to right.

At first she is a little discouraged, but soon finds that if she gets to the children as soon as they finish, many of them can read back what they have written. For example, a nonreader writes something such as what you see in Box 12.1 and reads back to her, "This is my imaginary friend, Bgooga." The writing of other children is more easily understood, as in Box 12.2.[2]

MP 9Z

BGGB FNS   IMINar

Box 12.1

AND I SAW A LION HE ASK ME
ME NAM WS ABBY

Box 12.2

By the end of the year, McCurdy's writing program incorporates the following features:

Children are expected to write every day. Blank books made from lined paper and with construction-paper covers are always available in the storybook corner. Children's works in progress also are kept there.

McCurdy talks individually with the children on a regular basis. She helps them decide what to write about. She listens as they read their books to her. She reads their books as they listen and then asks them questions. For the "story," *When I go home, I play with my dog.* she might ask, "What kind of dog is it? What color? What games do you play? How old is the dog? How is the dog special?" Sometimes, as a result of these conferences, the children add to their stories or revise them. Sometimes they do not. Their choice.

When children are satisfied that their stories are finished, McCurdy or an aide types them, using conventional spelling, punctuation, and capitalization. Covers are made and books are created that are added to the classroom library of children's works. Children often read works in progress aloud to other students, and they borrow ideas from one another. They read one another's published books from the library and show a great deal of interest in them.

Nancie Atwell[3] is a middle school teacher. She teaches writing in a workshop format. She begins each workshop with a short lesson introducing writing techniques as students in the class appear to need them. These lessons are kept short because they are not the most important part of the workshop. The most important and effective teaching happens during Atwell's personal responses to students writing—conversations in which students begin to discover what they really want to say.

After the short lesson Atwell calls on each student and asks what he or she will be working on that day and where the student is in the process. Students respond with, "A story, I'm writing the first draft," "Editing a poem," "Working on the letter I started yesterday."

Once every student has committed himself or herself and begins working, Atwell takes a primary grade chair and carries it to the side of the desk of a child where she sits down and asks, "How is it going?" This signals the beginning of a brief teacher-student conference. During these conferences Atwell responds to the students' writing. She listens, tells what she hears, summarizes, paraphrases, restates, asks questions about things she does not understand or would like to know more about, and asks what the writer might do next. She makes suggestions, but she does not write them down or indicate that they are more than suggestions. This underscores a central tenant of Atwell's method: ownership. The students have control over their writing. The teacher does not.

The four corners of the room are designated conference areas. When students need a response to something they have written or to an idea, they are free to ask one or two other students to join them in a conference area where they consult in quiet voices.

Seven or eight minutes before the end of each workshop, "group share" begins. Students sit together in a circle on the floor, and one or two read a paper or part of a paper. Atwell models productive ways of listening and responding, and the group discusses useful and not very useful responses.

When a student is satisfied that his or her paper is finished—it says what he or she wants to say, the way he or she wants to say it, the piece is submitted to Atwell for final editing. She makes any editorial changes necessary to bring the piece up to minimal standards. She records the skills that the student seems to have mastered plus one or two skills that need attention. The next day, Atwell has an editing conference with the student, where she teaches the one or two skills she has identified from the paper as needing work and makes note of what she has taught. She continues to work on those skills in future editing conferences with the student.

Sharing in conferences and during group share is the easiest and most frequently used form of publishing. A few of the other publication opportunities Atwell recommends to her students are photocopying papers to share with family and friends; posting writing on bulletin boards; submitting writing to contests, school newspapers, local newspapers, and magazines; tape-recording radio plays; and videotaping commercials.

Atwell also teaches reading in a workshop format. Students choose their own reading material from the library, bookstores, or home. Each student has a notebook called a "dialog journal." Students are required to write one letter a week to Atwell or to another student in their journals. In these letters students tell why they chose a particular book and what they liked or did not like and why. The person addressed responds to these letters in the student's journal, and the journals are returned. Through reading and responding to the students' journals, Atwell learns where students need guidance and exposure to new ideas. She teaches short lessons at the beginning of each reading workshop that grow out of what she learns from students' literature logs.

John Willinsky refers to the methods used in McCurdy's and Atwell's classrooms and the assumptions that underlie them as "New Literacy," which he defines as "strategies in the teaching of reading and writing which attempt to shift the control of literacy from the teacher to the student."[4]

New Literacy has some important similarities with the Corresponding Societies. The "steady hail" of pamphlets to which members of the Corresponding Societies had access is reflected in the wide range of reading materials introduced into New Literacy classrooms. In McCurdy's first grade, children read their stories to each other and borrow ideas from one another, and McCurdy reads their stories to them. In Atwell's reading workshop, the students bring books of their choice. Students' writings on topics of their choice become reading material for other students as well.

In New Literacy classrooms, as in the Corresponding Societies, the line between oral and written communication is indistinct. Writing is not on the model of the solitary writer and the anonymous audience. Talking is encouraged. Students frequently read what they have written as a form of publication. They discuss what they have read. But in terms of empowering students, the most important characteristic that New Literacy shares with the Corresponding Societies is that expression is emphasized over correctness. In the Corresponding Societies, ideas were not rejected if they were not expressed in standard received English. In the New Literacy classroom, children's ideas are not rejected if they are not expressed in standard English or written "correctly."

The Bgooga story is certainly an example of accepting expression in a most unconventional style rather than insisting on conventionality first. McCurdy's habit of typing the children' stories using conventional spelling, punctuation, and capitalization is a real sticking point with many traditional teachers who see this as a form of cheating. But McCurdy sees it as a way of accepting the child's expression rather than waiting for the child to master the conventions—to achieve correctness. And, of course, as a result, in McCurdy's class everyone publishes.

In Atwell's class, where students are older, students share ideas and help one another with their stories and essays. Atwell brings the students' writing up to acceptable standards in terms of mechanics and conventions in the proofreading or editing phase, and everyone publishes. Of course, in both classes the teachers' responsibility to teach standard English usage and conventions of writing is taken seriously, but expression and publication are not put off until the students have mastered the canons of correctness.

In the traditional, teacher-directed classroom the paper that gets "published" is first of all correct by the standards of school literacy, and it is assumed standards have been met largely through the individual student's knowledge of conventions and her or his solitary efforts. Group editing and teacher editing are seen as "cheating" and dishonest. Students whose knowledge of conventions fails to produce writing that meets the standards of schooled literacy are effectively silenced. Whether they have anything to say in their writing is not an issue. In a traditional classroom, a principal, if unconscious, function of teachers is gatekeeping—prohibiting expression on the part of students until they have conformed to school standards of "correctness."

Gatekeeping has an immediate and lasting effect on children. Donald Graves[5] and others asked primary grade students to tell him what you have to do when you write. Children who are identified by their teachers as "good writers" (ones who pass muster and produce conventional "stories" written legibly and correctly) say that you must tell a good story, make it exciting, give details, and so on. Children who are identified by their teachers as poor writers (those who do not pass muster) answer that you must make your letters right, spell correctly, know where to put commas, and so on. Even college students describe writing in a similar fashion. Good writers talk about quality of expression; poor writers talk about mechanics and conventions—that is, "correctness."[6]

The gatekeeping function of the school starts early. The following transcript records two first grade children making contributions during "sharing time."[7] Mindy is from a middle-class community. Deena is not.

Mindy: When I was in day camp we made these candles.

Teacher: You made them?

Mindy: And, uh, I tried it with different colors with both of them, but one just came out. This one came out blue and I don't know what this color is.

Teacher: That's neat-o. Tell the kids how you do it from the very start. Pretend we don't know a thing about candles. Okay. What did you do first? What did you use? Flour?

Mindy: Um. Here's some hot wax, some real hot wax that you just take a string, and tie a knot in it, and dip the string in the wax.

Teacher: What makes it have a shape?

Mindy: Uh. You just shape it.

Teacher: Oh. You shape it with your hand. Mmm.

Mindy: But you have . . . first you have to stick it into the wax and then water, and then keep doing that until it gets to the size you want it.

Teacher: Okay! Who knows what the string is for?[8]

Mindy has in effect "published" with the enthusiastic support of her teacher.

Same teacher, different child:

Deena: I went to the beach Sunday and to McDonalds and to the park and I got this for my birthday. My mother bought it for me and I had two dollars for my birthday and I put it in here and I went to where my friend named Gigi—I went over to my grandmother's house with her and she was on my back and we was walking around by my house and, um, she was heavy. She was in sixth or seventh grade . . .

Teacher: Okay. I'm going to stop you. I want to talk about things that are very important. That's important to you, but tell us things that are sort of different. Can you do that? And tell us what beach you went to.[9]

Deena was cut off by a well-meaning teacher who had a pretty clear idea of what successful "sharing" is like. It's like Mindy's. It's not like Deena's. A year and a half later, a researcher asked Deena what she thought of sharing time in first grade. Deena replied "Sharing time got on my nerves. She was always interrupting me, saying, 'That's not important enough,' and I hadn't hardly started talking!"[10]

Gatekeeping appears in reading instruction as well. James Collins[11] cites three examples of teachers interrupting students' oral reading when their word recognition and understanding of the text is flawless. In one example, the child correctly reads "What did the little duck see?" but the teacher interrupts to insist that the child pronounce the *t* in *what* distinctly. Collins points out that most speakers of English would *not* pronounce the *t* in *what* distinctly (if at all) when followed by the *d* in *did*. The problem is that the teacher has identified this child as one who speaks a dialect where the final sounds are "dropped," and so she is unwittingly overprecise. Another teacher interrupts a child to insist that he pronounce *I'll* as she did rather than "Ah'll" as he did. In another case, a teacher interrupts a child who reads "'... for goodness sake why?' axed Olive." The teacher says, "Asked." The child re-reads the phrase, stressing the word *asked* but still pronouncing it "axed."

Children whose dialect and pronunciation are similar to the teacher's are given the opportunity in oral reading to exhibit their word recognition ability and their comprehension and feel affirmed. But when insistence on correctness before expression is the *modus operandi* of the school, and it is typically the *modus operandi* of the school, children whose word recognition skills and comprehension are equally as good, but whose dialect and pronunciation differ from the teacher's are not permitted to exhibit their accomplishments.[12]

Gatekeeping continues in many forms throughout students' school careers. Researchers in a junior high school in an East Harlem Puerto Rican community observed the following lesson in a United States History and Civics class.[13] The teacher, whom the researchers referred to as Ms. S, was teaching a lesson supplied by the New York City Board of Education on vandalism. Each student had a copy of a text that defined vandalism and discussed its negative outcomes. There were pictures and questions for discussion accompanied by a fill-in-the-blanks test. If Ms. S had followed the lesson as it was designed she would have tied the discussion to the test, thereby focusing and controlling the flow of ideas. However, Ms. S was a very competent teacher who was well in tune with the economic and political realities of her students lives and was committed to "empowering" them. She rephrased and repeated questions and topics and called on students to answer and contribute.

Things were going quite well in this question-answer format. She was soliciting more and more student opinions on wider and wider topics until a student suggested that he might commit an act of vandalism if his friends asked him to and she asked, "Would you break the law for a friend? What do you owe them?" All hell broke loose. The students became very animated leaning out of their desks, waving their hands for recognition. One shouted out "I'd help my friend cheat on a test," and another shouted, "I don't owe them anything. Like I didn't ask my mother to bring me into this world. It depends on the situation." This last rather puzzling contribution came from a student named Ellie.

The researchers report goes on as follows.

At this point, the discussion gets very animated and proceeds much faster. Several students are talking at once. The teacher is trying to call on those with hands raised, and for a while she tries to summarize, and mediate between, points made by different students. For example, she says more than once, "Wait a minute, wait a minute! There's not as much difference between what Ellie is saying and the rest of you as you think," following this (when the students allow her) with an explanation and summary of points different students have offered. But more and more students shout out short responses to Ellie, who sticks to her original point (which may not be well understood by everyone, but it is an open question of how much the precise argument mattered to each of the students). Students confer with each other in loud overtones, giving each other their own viewpoints. They give the impression that they are too eager to say something to wait to be called on. Some bang hands or books on desks when someone else makes a particularly funny joke or a salient or controversial point. They sometimes mimic disgust with someone's expressed view, sometimes support it with a nod and a "right on!"

The students are clearly excited about the argument and are very eager to participate. But this is no longer a performance *for* the teacher, but a real exchange of views between the students. Ms. S finally stops attempting to intervene (it is difficult to get the floor in all the uproar), and lets the students compete freely for turns at talk, which results in a lot of simultaneous turn-taking and use of both verbal and non-verbal strategies for getting a chance to be heard by others.

When the bell signals the end of the period, the students continue to argue, shout, and laugh as they file out of the room, still focused on the issue of what one owes one's friends.[14]

The teacher's observations about this incident are what mine would have been 25 years ago. She felt it was all right to "let them go" like that once in a while, but not too often. She used to do it more often when she started teaching but she worried that they were not learning enough "skills" when she did, and that too much of this was "touchy-feely." When the researcher asked if she could not make a connection between this excitement and these skills, she explained that she would give them a writing assignment the next day on the question, "What responsibility does the President have?"

I haven't the slightest idea what Ms. S thought the connection was between the assignment and the ideas expressed in the free-for-all. One thing was certain. Their expression during the discussion was not "received" as valid. Discussion was rare in Ms. S's classroom, and when it happened it was considered touchy-feely, not the real stuff of the classroom. Consider how the same lesson might have played itself out in Anyon's executive elite school, but here the discussion would have conformed to school discourse, and the gateway to expression would have been open. In East Harlem, the discussion did not conform to school discourse, and the gate was slammed shut.

In another case, a sixth grade class in Boston had been to see the circus. The following day the teacher told them that their assignment was to write two or three paragraphs about their favorite act at the circus. Elliot, a boy in the class, produced the following text:

The Pink Panther Act

I liked the Pink Panther Act very much. Because he is my favorite character. I've seen him on T. V. cartoons and movies. Where he is not on. But there a man named Inspector Clooseau. Who is trying to catch the Pink Panther. The movies are in color as a cartoon. When he's in the circus the best act is when hes on a three wheeler and two men are chasing him on motor cycles. And they are chasing him all around the areana. I really liked the circus a lot. It was amazing.[15]

When Elliot brought his draft to the teacher, she was very puzzled by the line "I've seen him on T.V. cartoons and the movies. Where he is not on." Elliot tried to explain (not very clearly) that Pink Panther Movies open with a cartoon of Inspector Clouseau chasing the Pink Panther, but the movies themselves were not about the Pink Panther; they are about Inspector Clouseau. The Pink Panther is not in the movies; he's only in the opening credits. The teacher still could not understand and became exasperated, when a researcher who was observing the class intervened and explained what Elliot was trying to say.

The teacher decided that all the business about the movies was irrelevant—it wasn't about the circus act—and she directed Elliot to leave it out. She made some further suggestions, and Elliot's third and final draft read.

The Pink Panther Act
On October 19, 1984, our classroom went to see the Barnum and Bailey Circus. It was lots of fun. I liked the Pink Panther Act very much, he was my favorite character. The best part I think is when the Pink Panther is on a three wheeler and two men are chasing him on dirt bikes. They are chasing him all around the arena. I've seen the Pink Panther on T.V. cartoons, and in the movies. I really liked the Circus a lot. It was amazing.[16]

When the researcher interviewed Elliot, she discovered that Elliot had seen all the Pink Panther movies and watched Pink Panther cartoons on Saturday mornings. The Pink Panther was in fact Elliot's "favorite character." When asked whether he liked his piece better with or without the reference to Inspector Clouseau, he responded:

The teacher knows best. Miss Stone said for me to take it out 'cause it wasn't, it was like changing the subject. She's the teacher and I have to listen to her. But I think it would have made the story more interesting.[17]

Although the paragraph is vastly improved in terms of correctness, what Elliot wanted to say got edited out. That's gatekeeping.

Gatekeeping effectively silences many people for life. English teachers like myself often would rather not say what they do for a living in a group of strangers, particularly among working-class strangers. If you do, you can be certain that a number of them, the more confident ones, will make lighthearted but apologetic references to their "English" despite the fact that in most cases there is nothing remarkable about their English—either good or bad. Working-class people's experience of English teachers is that they are not interested in what people have to say; they are interested in judging the correctness of the way they say it.

But what if that were to change? What if the teacher's role as gatekeeper were severely curtailed? What if New Literacy became widespread and expression were put first—before correctness? Might we have at the turn of the twenty-first century in America what they had at the turn of the nineteenth-century in England—a lot of have-nots who have found their voice and who begin to use democratic processes the way they are designed to be used, while becoming more and more literate in the process?

That's not likely, for several reasons. First, there is nothing inherent in New Literacy that leads to challenging the status quo.[18] There are classrooms on the cutting edge of New Literacy where students never write anything other than fictional narratives and "reports" of the most bland nature. You can scour the several books and articles on the topic by Nancie Atwell, for example, and not find a hint that she sees challenges to the status quo as a desirable, likely, or even possible outcome of her approach.

Second, New Literacy tends to demand more resources, more teachers, and harder work than traditional methods, especially in working-class classrooms where some degree of oppositional identity has been established. Contrast the resources and effort necessary on the part of the teacher in a class like Atwell's to those things in a classroom at Freeway, where the chief "method" is having students copy notes from the blackboard to be memorized for a test.

So, although there is a growing movement toward collaborative approaches in education, these approaches still are found in only a minority of American schools. They appear in executive elite and affluent professional schools and in "gifted" programs in middle-class schools. They are rare in "average" classes in middle-class schools and they are nearly nonexistent in working-class schools, where traditional methods are nearly universal even in the "top" classes.[19] I would be very surprised, for example, if the Academics Plus program that the sulkers and steppers were excluded from did not employ very traditional methods.

In most cases, progressive methods such as New Literacy will not be employed unless parents demand it. Anyon reported that the methods employed in her middle-class school were very much like those in her working-class schools. It has been my experience that most middle-class students and parents are willing to endure traditional methods because it gives them what they want—preparation for well-paid middle-class work. This may change as middle-class, as well as blue-collar jobs, disappear. Middle-class parents may come to want a better education for their children, but it is an open question whether they will know what to demand any more than blue-collar parents in Freeway did.

What happens when New Literacy is introduced into the classrooms of gentry children? Nothing. The Brownstoners were after something like New Literacy classrooms. To the extent they succeeded, and even if they had succeeded more, these classrooms were not to become hotbeds of political unrest like the Corresponding Societies. They were to become, rather, bulwarks of the status quo.

That is not to say that progressive education never appears in working-class schools. Shirley Brice Heath acted as a consultant to schools in the area where she did her study. She asked teachers who were familiar with her findings to observe in their classrooms and school communities as she had done in Maintown and Roadville. Previous to this experience, teachers seemed to think that children from communities like Roadville were trying to engage in school discourse and failing. Under Heath's tutelage the teachers began to realize that these children were engaging in the discourse of their own communities. They were not trying to learn or engage in any other discourse. The teachers began to realize that they had been *expecting* school discourse; they were not teaching it. Through Heath's work the teachers began to learn some of the precise differences between working-class and school discourse, and they began to think about how they could teach school discourse since it is necessary for school success.

In one school, teachers in grades one through five began to have their students dictate stories into tape recorders. The teacher typed these stories and made copies for the entire class. Each story was discussed by the entire class and among smaller groups of students and revised and rewritten by the author. Even in first grade, all the children's stories began to take on the characteristics of conventional Maintown stories. They became more explicit as others asked questions and writers became aware that there were details that people from other communities could not know. By the sixth grade, children were comparing tape recorded oral versions, written transcripts, and revised written versions, and they were discovering ways of communicating meaning in writing with punctuation, choice of words, sequencing events, building complex sentences, and supporting ideas with facts. In teaching history, the sixth grade teacher used the children's accounts of events in their lives as starting points for writing fictional accounts of events from the point of view of characters in history.

One teacher seized on the opportunity presented when a blind student joined her class in mid-year. She asked students to take the boy on tours of the classroom and the school and tape record their talk as they toured. At the end of each tour the students spoke a summary of their tour into the recorder. Later, the entire class listened to the tapes, paying special attention to the questions the blind boy asked. They then wrote descriptions of parts of the school based on the tapes, starting with a general description of the area, followed by details and concluding comments. These activities went on for several weeks and concluded with students writing reports on topics they chose, starting with generalizations followed by supporting details and conclusions.

In another class, students brought in documents their parents were faced with every day such as traffic tickets, housing regulations, warranties, directions for appliances, and income tax forms. They tried to make sense of these documents in small groups and wrote lists of questions as they arose. Finally they rewrote the documents in more easily understood language.

In one fifth grade classroom of nearly all boys, the teacher started an eight-week science unit on growing vegetables by having Heath talk about her work as an anthropologist and show a film of a Latin American village where she had worked. She suggested that the class study the food of their own community and how it was grown as if they were anthropologists. They decided they would try to discover the farming techniques of the "best farmers" for growing "the most common foods." They would present their findings in writing, photographs, charts, and diagrams in a book that the students in fifth grade next year would use for a textbook.

They discussed the idea of "reliability of sources" and decided that they would need to find at least two sources—one spoken and one written—for each fact they discovered. They decided they needed to define "best farmers" and "most common vegetables." They decided that farmers who were mentioned for special accomplishments in the gardening columns of the local newspapers, such as growing a one hundred-pound watermelon, were the best farmers. They examined cookbooks published by local churches with recipes for preparing local produce to determine the most common vegetables.

They interviewed the best farmers to get their life stories and to get answers to specific questions. They listened to the tapes over and over until they could write a brief summary of each life story. The teacher typed the summary and placed it in the book along with a photograph of the farmer. They gathered "folk concepts" and explained them with scientific reasons found in science books and commercially prepared booklets for farmers. For example, it was a folk concept that seed store potatoes are better for planting than potatoes bought for the table. The scientific reason is that seed store potatoes are treated with pesticides, and therefore produce healthier plants.

Under the guidance of the teacher these students learned to take the implicit, context-dependent knowledge of home and community and translate it into explicit, context-independent categories and abstractions valued in schools. For example, they all knew greens are eaten more than any other vegetable in their community. Through their investigation, they began to wonder *why*? They discovered that it's because there is only one growing season for other vegetables while there are two growing seasons for greens, and some greens grow wild all year round. The important thing is that the children thought of this question and answered it for themselves. It was not dictated to them in the following way

Write *why, question mark*. And then on the next line write *two growing seasons, dash, wild greens grow all year*.

—as it might have been at Freeway High School.

By the end of eight weeks, these students were using words like *source, check out* (verify), *summarize,* and *translate.* They had not only inquired, compiled, sorted, and refined information; they understood these processes. Although many of them were from communities where questions were usually answered indirectly with a story, they had been forced to formulate specific questions to get at specific bits of information or definitions, and they began to understand why "story" answers are problematic for science. They laughed together about the fact that they could not get "old Mr. Feld" to answer a direct question. They remarked as the unit test drew near that they would be asked direct questions and would have to give detailed answers—no stories.

These fifth grade students had learned to engage in school discourse. They were able to translate personalized, context-dependent, orally expressed knowledge into the depersonalized, context-independent, primarily written knowledge of the classroom, and they understood some of the values, attitudes, behaviors, beliefs, ways of learning, and ways of expressing what one knows that make up school discourse.

In this class of twenty-three students, twelve scored in the 90s, eight in the 80s, three in the 70s on the standardized unit test accompanying the science text book. None failed. None of these children had ever passed one of these tests before.

In another school, during the first weeks of school a second grade teacher asked community members, parents, lunch room workers, the school custodian, and the principal to come into her class and talk to the students about the way they talked, what they read and wrote, and why. They brought in samples of what they read and wrote as well.

Before these visits, the teacher prepared the students to become "language detectives." For each guest they answered the questions: What sounds did I hear when she/he spoke? What did she/he say about how she/he speaks? What did she/he read? What did she/he write?

Based on these talks, the children talked about formal and informal speech of local visitors as compared with television newscasters. They talked about words they heard in casual local speech that they did not hear on network news, such as *ain't* and *yonder.* Throughout this study the students were doing their regular phonics and reading skills lessons as usual, and they talked about sounds they learned in their phonics lessons that they did not hear in local casual speech, such as the -*ng* and -*s* endings on many words. The teacher had a tenth grade art student come in and draw stick figure cartoons of different people reading and writing in different settings. Soon the second graders were creating such cartoons of their own. By the end of the year these second graders were able to notice that the principal talked one way when reading morning announcements on the loud speaker and another way when he was kidding around with the older children in the hall, and they could say what the differences were and the reasons for them.

These stories would be interesting and even heartening if they were told about affluent professional or executive elite schools, but they would not be amazing. Teaching such as this is more or less expected in such schools. What makes these stories amazing is that they happened in working-class schools.

Ten years later, however, the lessons that had worked so well with Heath's input had disappeared from these schools. Some of the teachers had left. Those that remained spoke of the period when these methods were being used as the high point of their careers. But things change. The teachers pointed to "a lack of faith in schools," resulting in increased bureaucratic interference and more testing dictated from the state capital and Washington. The most outspoken of them said that teachers had become "lackeys in a system over which we have no control." [20]

They also reported that Heath's presence in the schools had been responsible for a great deal of what they did. They viewed her as both an insider and an outsider. As a former teacher who acted as an aide and co-teacher in the classroom, she was a "member of the club." Yet she was an outsider who had useful knowledge, but had no power within the school. She made suggestions and helped implement them; she didn't give orders and blame teachers when things didn't work out. She was collaborative, not directive.

If you're not a teacher you probably do not realize what hard work I've described on these last few pages. Isolated occurrences of this kind of teaching appear quite regularly in working-class schools, usually as the result of the know-how and energy of a single teacher or principal. These bright spots tend to remain isolated and to soon disappear. To sustain them, teachers need support of one another, administrators, parents, the community, and the nation, and they don't get it. There is no powerful constituency insisting on such schooling for working-class (and, to some extent middle-class)[21] children, as there is for affluent professional and executive elite children. The Brownstoners knew what they wanted and they knew how to make it happen. The Freeway parents didn't. Until a powerful coalition is built of working-class parents, teachers in working-class schools, *and their allies* we will not mobilize resources or give teachers the support they need to make such schooling work across the board. It's going to take organization and muscle to afford powerful literacy to all our children. We're talking politics here, friends, with a capital *P*.

What would happen if working-class students had political motives for acquiring literacy? What would happen if the schools encouraged working-class students to view education as the means to furthering a working-class agenda and create a truly democratic society?

The answer proposed by some is that we would get classrooms populated by working-class children that would really resemble the Corresponding Societies. These classrooms would look like New Literacy classrooms, but with an attitude. That might make literacy dangerous again.

Chapter 13

MAKING LITERACY DANGEROUS AGAIN

A ronowitz and Giroux[1] suggest that we must view teachers not primarily as technicians equipped to accomplish goals set for them by curriculum experts and administrators but as intellectuals, free women and men with special dedication to the values of the intellect and the enhancement of the critical powers of the young.

Aronowitz and Giroux discuss three kinds of intellectuals: hegemonic, critical, and transforming.[2] Hegemonic intellectuals identify with the gentry and work to maintain the existing order. They are often consultants to major foundations, members of university faculties, managers of the culture industry, teachers, and school administrators. Hannah More and Patrick Colquhoun from chapter 11 were hegemonic intellectuals.

Critical intellectuals imagine themselves to be critics of society and the existing order who stand outside society. They believe themselves to be apolitical, to take no sides, to have no agenda, to be free of bias, to be free-floating. But in fact they often represent the interests of the dominant group and the status quo. They imagine themselves to be apolitical because maintaining the status quo appears to be natural—not politics at all. I believe this to be true of all of Anyon's teachers, the lads' teachers, and the Freeway teachers. In fact, I would argue, this is true of nearly all American teachers and school administrators.

Transforming intellectuals, on the other hand, are self-consciously critical of inequities in our society. They see the schools as sites of struggle between competing groups that have distinct histories, contexts, and cultures. They see their mission as helping students "develop a deep faith in struggle to overcome injustices and change themselves." They aim to help their students become "critical agents" by providing conditions where students can "speak, write, and assert their own histories, voices, and learning experiences." They view their students, not as individuals, but as "collective actors" within culture, class, racial, historical, and gender settings and with particular problems, hopes, and dreams. They try to help these collective actors become "agents of civic courage"—that is, to help them acquire the knowledge and courage that will make "despair unconvincing and hope practical."[3]

One of the most famous transforming intellectuals was Paulo Freire, a Brazilian educator who attracted worldwide attention in the 1960s and 70s for his ideas concerning teaching literacy to poor adults.[4] Freire was a professor of philosophy and education at the University of Recife, a city where there were eighty thousand children between the ages of seven and fourteen who did not attend schools, where adult literacy was estimated at 30 to 40 percent, and where literacy campaigns had been repeatedly mounted with no effect.

Freire saw that literacy campaigns were bound to fail as long as the "students" viewed literacy as part of a culture that was alien to them. To translate this into the vocabulary that I have been using in this book, Freire understood the concept of oppositional identity and resistance. He understood that for the poor in the slums of Recife, literacy was seen as part of the identity of the "other"—a hated "other" in a society where the gap between the rich and poor is ever so much more obvious than it is in the United States.

Freire understood that if they thought about it, the poor of Recife would have concluded that any effort they put into adopting the culture of the rich, including literacy, would be in vain, since they would not be accepted among the rich, and would not get the benefits that literacy gave the rich. The only result would be that they would become alienated from their own people.

I say "if they thought about it" because Freire understood an even more fundamental fact about the lives of the illiterate Third World poor: they don't think about it. They are so submerged in their daily lives that they have little or no awareness of the possibility for change, much less what they might do to bring about change. They view their condition as natural, the will of God, or determined by fate.

Freire developed an approach to adult literacy that gave a whole new meaning to the old-fashioned concept of "student motivation." In initiating a literacy campaign in an area, he first sent in investigators to find the people to whom others turned for help. He invited them to become the first members of his "class," which he referred to as a "culture circle."

The first step in a culture circle was to help members think about the differences between nature and culture. "Coordinators" introduced the following pictures or "codifications" and led discussion about them, an activity referred to as "decoding."[5]

For the first picture, the coordinator asked, "Who made the well?" "Why?" "What material did he use?" "Who made the tree?"

Picture 13.1

Picture 13.2

"How is the tree different from the well?" "Who made the pigs, the bird, the man?" "Who made the house, the hoe, the book?"

The discussion was not designed to teach the people that there is a difference between nature and culture and that culture is created when people use natural materials to create and change their environment. They already knew these things. The discussion (decodifying) was designed to encourage the participants to talk about these things, something that in their submerged state they rarely did, something, in fact, that their culture did not encourage. Freire referred to the culture of Brazil's illiterate poor as a "culture of silence."

The discussion surrounding the second picture is designed to elicit the following ideas: People can make culture; animals cannot. People can communicate both orally and graphically. *The proper role of people is to be active and to communicate with others—not to be passive or to be used by others. Proper communication between people is dialogue between equals.*

Is this getting into an ideology? Does Freire have a point of view? Is it a democratic ideology? Does it come into conflict with the reality of the lives of the poor people of Recife? Does it come into conflict with the reality of the lives of Shirley Brice Heath's Roadvillers, of Ogbu's involuntary immigrants, of Anyon's working-class school children (or her middle-class school children, for that matter), of Willis's lads or Weis's Freeway high school students? It sure does.

The next three pictures facilitate a further discussion of culture and how it is transmitted to the young. In picture 13.3 the bow and arrow represent culture. The Indian teaches his son to make a bow and arrow and to hunt with it through direct experience. In picture 13.4 the gun represents culture. This tool is so complex that the

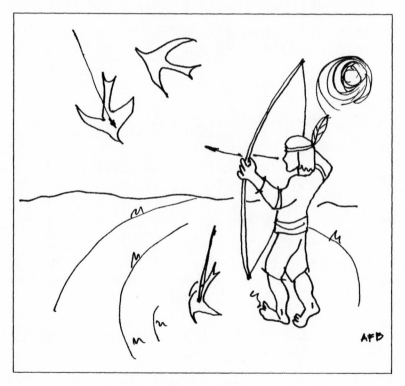

Picture 13.3

Picture 13.4

Picture 13.5

technology for making it must be written down. Only those who can read can learn to make it. The more advanced a people's technology is, the greater the power they have to transform the world. Education, technology, and power are closely related.

In the fifth picture we have another hunter, but since cats cannot make tools (cannot make culture) this hunter can never modify her hunting activities. She is limited by nature. The hunters in pictures 13.3 and 13.4 are not. These observations lead to a discussion of instinct, intelligence, liberty, and education.

Picture 13.6 shows people whom those in the culture circle recognize as their peers making clay pots. The message: You too are creators of culture. Picture 13.7 shows a pot from picture 13.6 with flowers in it. People in the circle see another way that they make culture—by arranging flowers. Also, in picture 13.7 there are representations of flowers on the vase put there by the workers. These flowers are symbols, graphic representations that stand for

Picture 13.6

Picture 13.7

something else. Symbols are created by people as part of their culture. They have something in common with writing. Picture 13.8 shows a popular song written in a book. The people in the circle discuss the possibility of learning to read these words—words to a song which they already know.

Picture 13.8

Picture 13.9 shows two cowboys, one from the south of Brazil dressed in wool and the other from the northeast dressed in leather. The concepts developed from this codification are that clothing is part of culture. Availability of material, climate, and the work people do have an effect on clothing. Culture responds to necessity, but sometimes culture remains the same after the conditions that influence it change. Tradition has an effect on culture.

Picture 13.9

Picture 13.10

Picture 13.10 shows a culture circle. Participants are asked to think about themselves and what they are doing—to reflect. The phrase *democratization of culture* is introduced by the coordinator. The group's culture is its own. It is created by them. It is engaged in by them. It can be modified by them. They can step back and think about it and how they create it and engage in it.

By now Freire hoped the people would see literacy in a new light, not exclusively as part of the culture of the rich, but as something that might be part of their culture. If they can make pots and symbols, they can make books.

In case you missed the introduction of the concept of class struggle in relation to pictures 13.3, 13.4 and 13.5, let me point it out to you. Power is partly derived from advanced technology, and advanced technology relies on literacy. The lesson for participants in the circle was hard to miss: The literate are powerful and you're not. What are you going to do about it?

This theme was continued as the circle turned its attention to "generative words." Generative words were words with two qualities. First, they would generate impassioned discussions of the social and political realities of the lives of the people in the district. Secondly, they had spelling-sound relationships that could be learned and recombined to form other Portuguese words. The Portugese words for *plow, slum, land, food, work, salary, government, brick,* and *wealth* were generative words chosen for one community.

Just imagine the discussion that words such as *slum, land, food, work, salary, government, brick,* and *wealth* would engender in the slums of cities like Recife or Rio de Janeiro. *Plow* might prompt a discussion of the value of human labor, the process of transforming nature, and relations between labor and capital. *Food* might prompt a discussion of malnutrition, hunger, infant mortality, and disease. *Work* might prompt a discussion of people's value in relation to their work, and the relationship between manual, technological, and mental work. *Slum* might prompt a discussion of housing, food, clothing, health, and education in the slums, and these might be seen as problems that needed solutions rather than conditions that must be silently accepted.

Under these circumstances it doesn't matter what "method" you use to teach reading. The "students" want what the teacher has, and so you've got the real-school model operating. The students will cooperate and work in exchange for the teacher's knowledge.

After the discussion of each word the coordinator would focus on the written form of the word. He would write it in syllables and teach the sounds of the letters in the syllables. Then he would combine the consonant letters in the syllables they had learned with vowel letters and teach them to pronounce these invented syllables.

For example, the word *tijola* (brick) would appear under a drawing (a codification) showing the use of bricks on a construction site. The circle would discuss the concept of "brick." What is it? How do we relate to it through work? How is it used in our lives and in the lives of other people? The coordinator would then focus on the written word *tijola*.

The word *tijola* has three syllables: *ti, jo, la*. The coordinator would arranged the syllables as follows:

ti	ta	te	*ti*	to	tu
jo	ja	je	ji	*jo*	ju
la	*la*	le	li	lo	lu

and teach the participants the idea that consonants followed by vowels form syllables, and once you know how these syllables are spelled and how they are pronounced, you can read and write many words such as *luta* (struggle), *loja* (stove), *lula* (squid), and *lata* (tin can).

By learning a small number of well-chosen words and the syllables you can make from these words with vowel substitutions, a Portuguese-speaking Brazilian can learn to read and write many words.

Before Freire agreed to bring his literacy program into an area, he insisted that all the authorities understood that he was educating for liberation and that they agreed not to interfere. Meetings were held every weeknight for one hour for six to eight weeks. As soon as generative words were introduced participants began to write their ideas. Soon they were examining local newspapers and discussing local issues. Those who finished (about three-fourths of those who started) could read and write simple texts, could get some understanding from local newspapers, and could discuss political and social problems.

The heart of Freire's program was its basic method—*dialogue*. Think back to the ten codifications and the discussion that might ensue from viewing them. One idea the second codification is designed to elicit is that "proper communication among people is *always* dialogue between equals." But culture circle participants might not agree. Should communication between parents and children always be dialogue between equals? Between men and women? Husbands and wives? Landlords and tenants? Police and people apprehended in the act of committing a violent crime? Prisoners and prison guards? Teachers and students? Culture circle coordinators attempted to engage in dialogue rather than debate on these issues, or, in Freirean terms, they tried to engage in dialogue rather than anti-dialogue.

Teachers in regular schools introduce discussions all the time, and they sometimes use similar discussion starters as Freire's codifications. I can imagine myself twenty-five years ago introducing such a topic for discussion in my eighth grade social studies class. While planning the lesson I would have listed the "understandings" that would result from the discussion, for example, *Proper communication between adults in a democracy is dialogue between equals.* I would have thought about the kinds of exceptions to such a generalization that I found acceptable. For example, its okay for people such as police officers, who are put in a position of authority through democratic procedures, to sometimes give orders to others and enforce them without any discussion. I would also anticipate exceptions that children might raise but which I found objectionable. For example, it's okay for men to give their wives orders because the man is the head of the house. (This was twenty-five years ago, remember.)

In fact, my objectives might have been to help the students think through acceptable and unacceptable exceptions to the rule. I would have thought the lesson was successful if we had dealt with several acceptable and unacceptable exceptions. If there were one or two students who insisted on upholding an "unacceptable" exception, I would chastise them, probably in a fairly lighthearted way, and imply that their position was morally inferior to mine and I could only hope that they would see the light. I might even have taken a vote—a favorite trick of persons in authority when they know the vote will be in their favor. That would be the end of the lesson. Mission accomplished. On to the next lesson.

This is not dialogue. It's a lesson where the topic is controlled by the teacher. It's successful if the teacher's objectives are fulfilled—

if his or her predetermined conclusions are agreed to. It's a clear-cut case of hegemony—influence over others without the apparent use of force. It goes on in schools all the time and I am not categorically opposed to it. It's a way of helping students consider questions, formulate opinions, and back up their opinions with facts, expert opinions, and so on. There's nothing inherently evil about that. It's what teachers are trained to do. But there is an unequal power relationship between the teacher and the students from the start and there are all sorts of sanctions (grades, for example) hanging in the air that the teacher can manipulate to have the discussion come out "right."

Coordinators in Freire's culture circles were trained to engage in honest dialogue with the participants. The entire enterprise depended on it. Freire was not interested in propaganda. He was not interested in replacing one set of slogans (the oppressor's) with another (the angry left's). Box 13.1 lists characteristics of dialogue as contrasted with anti-dialogue as suggested by Study Circles, an organization dedicated to promoting dialogue.[6]

Dialogue in a culture circle meant that the participants could express opinions different from the coordinators and the coordinator resisted using his or her position of authority to carry the day. This is not easy to do. In several attempts to use Freirean methods in Third World literacy campaigns, the weakest link in the process has been that coordinators have engaged in "anti-dialogue."[7] We've seen several examples of anti-dialogue, blatant ones such as the teacher who said, "Do it my way, or it's wrong," and subtle ones such as the way I would have conducted the "proper communication among people" lesson twenty-five years ago.

The closest thing to a dialogue in the descriptions of classrooms I've presented in this book was the discussion between the teacher and her students in Anyon's affluent professional school regarding a teacher's strike. The teacher was clearly outgunned by her fifth graders, who were children of affluent professionals, but Anyon observed that she "may have made some impression on them." Here, we had something like dialogue between equals. It's no accident that it happened in the affluent professional school. Teachers in gentry schools often engage in dialogue with their students, not because the teachers "empower" the students, but because the students are already powerful.[8]

Dialogue	Anti-Dialogue
I search for basic agreement.	I search for glaring differences.
I search for strengths in your position.	I search for weaknesses in your position.
I reflect on my position.	I attack your position.
I consider the possibility of finding a better solution than mine or yours.	I defend my solution and exclude yours.
I temporarily suspend my beliefs.	I am invested wholeheartedly in my beliefs.
I assume that many people have a piece of the answer.	I assume there is one right answer and I have it.
I want to find common ground.	I want to win.
I submit my best thinking hoping your reflections will improve it.	I submit my best thinking and defend it to show it is right.
I remain open to talk about the subject later on.	I expect to settle this here and now.

Box 13.1 Characteristics of Dialogue and Anti-dialogue

I do an exercise in two of my courses to introduce the idea of dialogue to my students. It's called "The Discipline Game."[9] The players are *a teacher*, *students*, and *a jury*. The teacher or a student chooses a card with a "situation." For example, a student makes the following request to the teacher: "The class is tired after lunch and wants to talk instead of work."[10] The teacher and student(s) negotiate for three minutes. The jury decides whether there was a successful negotiation, and awards points to the teacher, the students, or both.

The game has endless variations and possibilities. The teacher can have advisors and take time out to consult with them. Negotiations can be followed by discussions of how realistic the situations and solutions are, of the advisability of negotiating with students, and categories of situations that are negotiable and that are not. Students can bring in situations from their classroom experience to use in playing the game. The author of the game suggests that playing it gives teachers and students a vocabulary for negotiation—something that is notably lacking on the part of teachers and students in schools such as Anyon's working-class school and Freeway high school.

At the outset, almost all my students playing the part of teachers totally capitulate. "Okay, I'll give you fifteen minutes to talk quietly and then we'll begin class." In the discussion following, my students fall into two categories. Those in the first category say this is great; it would work in their classrooms, and they can't wait to try. Students in the second category express grave reservations. They say this would never work in their classrooms. They insist that if you gave their students fifteen minutes they'd want thirty minutes next time. If you negotiated a short "rest," they'd start arguing about homework and tests. There'd be chaos.

They are all surprised when I tell them that in my opinion giving the students fifteen minutes is not good negotiating. The teacher has needs. Presumably there was something planned for those fifteen minutes that needed to be done. How can the teacher's work get accomplished and the students' need for rest be met? Negotiate that! Once they get the idea that negotiation is not giving in and expecting students to cooperate because the teacher was nice to them (a very big mistake as any experienced teacher in any school can tell you), and it does not mean the teacher will automatically be taken for a patsy, my students begin to get into some interesting dialogues.

The best student I ever saw in the teacher's part was, not surprisingly, a teacher in the most upscale Catholic high school in the Buffalo area. On the first day of playing the game, in response to the "rest request," he answered without skipping a beat, "Okay, take fifteen minutes and during that time I'll put a homework assignment on the board that will cover part of the lesson so we can cover everything I planned for today." This was greeted with shocked dismay on the part of the "students." His next offer was, "Okay, look at the headings in today's chapter and write a single sentence that states what the chapter is about. I'll give you ten minutes so you can catch your breath while you're doing it. I'll collect it and grade it." There was some interest in this offer. I don't remember how the negotiation came out, but I do remember that this student understood that *negotiate* does not mean *capitulate*, and I'll never forget the stunned expressions on the "students'" (all teachers in real life) faces when he made the homework offer.

As the semester progresses and we play the game for about twenty minutes each week, most of the students become pretty good at negotiating. They acknowledge that teachers cannot accommodate students' requests without having their own needs met, and those who have insisted that any negotiation will lead to chaos (those who I suspect are authoritarian in their own classrooms) at least express some understanding of the concept and agree that collaborative discipline (and perhaps even teaching) has some possibilities. And of course, I keep reminding students of the parallels between good negotiating and dialogue and bad negotiating and anti-dialogue.

If the heart of Freire's program was its method—dialogue—the soul of his program was its objective—consciousness raising, what he referred to as "conscientization." His aim was to help participants in the culture circles think about culture, how they create it and engage in it and how, since it is something they create, it is something they can change. He tried to help them reflect on the connections among culture, literacy, technology, and power. He believed that when he accomplished these objectives, the participants would be burning to learn to read and write and the real-school model would kick in. They would want what the teacher had, and they would cooperate and work to get it.

Now we have something teachers understand. It's the old concept of *motivation*—not only leading a horse to water, but fixing it so she wants to drink! But that's only part of what Freire meant by the concept of conscientization. What comes next is what separates real Freireans from old-fashioned school teachers who simply see Freire as someone with a terrific idea for motivating a particularly troublesome segment of the school population to become better students and get better jobs and join the middle class.

Freire had a different outcome in mind. His culture circles had more in common with the Corresponding Societies among working men in nineteenth-century England than with the "alternative high schools" of twentieth-century America.

Freire was not interested in helping border crossers make it over safely. He was interested in helping the poor recognize the social and economic interests that bind them together as a group, to take strength from their group identity and begin to struggle to further their interests through democratic means, and to recognize that they confront, not *individuals* outside their group, but other *groups* whose interests are often antagonistic to theirs. He envisioned a government and economy where there would be smaller differences between the rich and poor, not only in terms of wealth and income but in terms of quality of life.

Freire's vision was one of class struggle. It was about empowering the powerless *as a class* so they can stand up for themselves. This is what made him a transforming intellectual.

So this was Freire's program—dialogue, conscientization, literacy, and collective struggle pursued simultaneously. In 1963, Freire was asked to direct a national literacy project by a newly elected president of Brazil. In one province the number of registered voters increased by more than 150 percent. Freire and his colleagues expected to have 200,000 culture circles operating throughout the country by 1964, but there was a military coup and the program was abruptly ended. Freire was placed under house arrest, imprisoned for ten weeks, and finally sought refuge in Chile. Seems to me the program must have been working.

Because the United States at the close of the twentieth century is not Brazil in the early '60s, Freire's program cannot simply be transplanted. But many American educators who consider themselves to be transforming intellectuals have instituted programs in elementary and high schools and adult literacy programs, and, as we shall see, concepts that Freire worked out thirty years ago are still crucial to these efforts.

Chapter 14

TAKING SIDES

I love the class where my students read Robert Peterson's "How to Read the World and Change It."[1] They come in with their eyes as round as saucers. "What did you think of it?" I ask innocently. "You can't do that!" they reply, almost in unison. "It's too political!" "I'd never get away with it."

Peterson is a self-proclaimed Freirean teacher in a fourth and fifth grade inner city classroom in Milwaukee, Wisconsin, where most of his students are Latino. He starts off the school year with a unit on the students' families and backgrounds, starting with a time line showing their birth dates and those of their parents and grandparents. They then put pins in a world map showing places of birth and each child talks to older relatives to collect one story, joke, or memory from their family to write or tell orally.

Peterson teaches "cultural journalism" of the sort that produced the *Foxfire*[2] books and made Eliot Wiggington famous. Wiggington had his Georgia high school students interview old-timers to discover and preserve for future generations folk skills that were disappearing such as broom making, quilting, and even moonshining. The result was a series of best-selling books published by Doubleday. The proceeds were plowed back into the writing program, which is still operating.

Great! My students love this. It's creative, child centered, and progressive. But then Peterson tells us that

Freire assumes that what will most inspire the learners is discussion and reflection on his or her own experiences, particularly his or her own oppression. In my eyes, many children in urban America are oppressed by a few key institutions: school, family, and community.[3]

Whoa! Warning bells sound! But Peterson goes on calmly to discuss the "difficult problems" he has addressed in focusing on such oppression. The first way he does this is to bring the world into the classroom, so that children start reflecting on their own lives. For example, one year during a boycott against grapes he showed a tape produced by the United Farm Workers and followed it up by taking students to hear Cesar Chavez, then president of the United Farm Workers, speak at a nearby college. By chance there was a strike at a local factory a few days later, and Peterson took six students armed with a tape recorder to the factory to interview the strikers.

He believed these six students learned more in that half-hour than they had in years of social studies lessons. His class began to discuss their parents' jobs—where they worked and whether they belonged to a union. *Grievance* became a spelling word and soon there were grievances about all sorts of things in the students' lives. The essence of his approach, says Peterson, "lies in the connections it builds between the topic at hand, the students' lives and the broader world around them." By this criterion the union episode worked well.

Another way Peterson focuses on oppression in the lives of his students is to deal with power relations in his classroom. This seems as if it should be easy enough to handle. If your students are oppressed, stop oppressing them. Just go in tomorrow and say, "You decide what we'll learn, how we'll learn it, and how grades will be determined. I am no longer your oppressor." Unfortunately, this approach is tried with some regularity by new teachers, followed uniformly by one of Willis's "horrific breakdowns."[4]

At the time he wrote this article, Peterson worked in a working-class school similar to the one described by Anyon, where students were allowed little autonomy. The dominant theme was control on the part of the teachers and resistance on the part of the students. Teachers who wanted to deal with such students in anything but an authoritarian manner had to, in Peterson's words, "be prepared for an enormous struggle."[5] But still he realized that as long as he ran his classroom in a despotic manner his students would not learn to make decisions, to be responsible, or to take charge of their learning and their lives. His aim was to construct "a classroom in which students have the maximum amount of power that is legally permitted and that they can socially handle."[6] He engaged in the "enormous struggle" on several fronts.

First he created a positive atmosphere in the classroom through activities that stressed self-affirmation, mutual respect, communication, group decision making, and cooperation because he knew that these values and skills are associated with the gentry. Many middle-class teachers think these values and skills are "natural," and when children do not possess them, they throw up their hands and revert to an authoritarian style. Peterson took a different approach. He believed that if his students didn't have these values and skills, it was his job to teach them. And so he used lessons and activities such as the following.

He did circle activities where each student was asked to share a personal fact or opinion and he insisted on the following ground rules. No put-downs. Listen. Don't interrupt. Everyone gets a turn (including the teacher). Everyone gets equal time. Everyone has the right to pass. Once they were understood, these ground rules became classroom rules for the entire school day—for the teacher as well as the students.[7]

He did small-group problem solving sessions with four or five students and himself in front of the class. He talked about the sessions afterward with the entire class. Did everyone understand the problem right away? Who helped others understand? Who asked helpful questions? Who suggested solutions? When the problem was solved, did someone sum up? Were there any put-downs? Did everyone listen? Did anyone interrupt?

The point is that you don't give a bunch of fifth graders a topic to discuss and throw up your hands when it turns into a free-for-all, as Ms. S. did in the vandalism "discussion."[8] Teachers are supposed to teach, not blame children for what they don't know how to do. But when the make-believe school model is in effect and resistance is the dominant theme, don't expect this to be easy. Get ready for the "enormous struggle."

On other fronts, Peterson teaches history lessons designed to engage his students and improve their self-esteem. The history of the education of girls and women's fight for the vote, for example, helps girls see that people have fought for their rights and perhaps they should take advantage of those they have and fight for others. I wish someone had shown me and my fifth grade classmates a documentary such as "Out of Ireland,"[9] which recently ran on PBS. There were struggles in the history of my own ancestors that I never really understood. It sure gave my self-esteem a lift when I saw it about a year ago, a lift I could have used when I was twelve.

Peterson has a method for dialoguing with his students. He shows them a drawing, photograph, or cartoon, or he reads them a poem or story, and he asks:

What do you see?

What's happening to your feelings?

Relate it to your life.

Why do we face these problems?

What can we do about it?

And when I say Peterson dialogues, I mean he dialogues; he doesn't demagogue. His aim is not simply to incite students but to help them think through possible and productive responses to injustice. When his students don't like something that the president has said or done, their solution is to kill him. They want to solve the problem of gangs in their neighborhoods by machine gunning gang members or sending them to the electric chair. He challenges these "solutions" (which he believes, incidentally, are the result of media saturation) and tries to get the children to think about why they think the way they do, and he tries to bring these topics up in other contexts for further dialogue. The thing about dialogue is that it's never over.

He helps students question the truth of print. He gives them a story from a third grade reader crediting an anonymous policeman for the invention of the traffic light and a short piece from a book on African American inventors that credits a black scientist with inventing the traffic light,[10] and he asks, "Is everything you read in books true? Which of these do you believe? Is there a way to find out which is true?"

He asks his students to count the number of pages in their five-hundred-page history textbook that are devoted to the history of labor in the United States. It turns out the number is five. He asks what that means. Why might it be so? He teaches some of the history of labor strife in Milwaukee and asks students to question their parents about it. When they discover that their parents, who are working people, don't know the history of labor strife in their own city he asks why that might be so.

He uses controversial posters and quotations to encourage writing and discussion. For example, the following comes from Desmond Tutu.

> When the missionaries first came to Africa they had bibles and we had the land. They said, "Let us pray." We closed our eyes. When we opened them we had the bibles and they had the land.[11]

Peterson models social responsibility. He believes it's important to understand the world and when injustices are uncovered to act, not simply complain. He attends meetings, goes to marches, lobbies politicians, and belongs to social justice organizations. He is, in fact, an editor of one of the most progressive educational publications in America, *Rethinking Schools*.[12]

On another front he teaches—not only about the history of injustices suffered, but about victories over injustice. Women's suffrage and the civil rights struggle are examples of people coming together and getting positive results. Peterson believes such histories "nurture civic courage."[13] Notice that Peterson does not valorize "rugged individuals" who rose to gentry status through their own monumental efforts, but groups of people who through collective efforts changed the system and became better off as a group.

On one occasion, a number of years ago, he invited a speaker to address his class on the "sanctuary movement," in which Americans were openly harboring illegal aliens from Central America who they believed were political refugees from dictatorships that our government supported. The speaker described government

bombings of villages with weapons supplied by the United States. The
upshot of this was that Peterson took twelve students after school on
public transportation with parental consent to a protest rally at the
federal building with signs they made saying such things as

*Support the poor! Not the "freedom fighters" They're the rich.
Give Nicaragua Some Food Instead of Weapons.*[14]

Since they were the only visible Latino group at the rally, the other
demonstrators gave them a great reception and a prominent place
in the proceedings.

And so, in come my students, bug-eyed, saying, "You can't do
that; it's too political," or "I'd never get away with it." Of course,
taking sides is political. It reflects a position—a point of view. When
you make a big fuss over Valentines Day and Mother's Day and
ignore International Women's Day, it's political.

A widely used United States history book appears to give Abraham
Lincoln and John Brown (both white men) exclusive credit for the
abolition of slavery. There is no mention of grass-roots abolitionists,
many of them women, of slave revolts, or even of runaway slaves as
contributing to the abolition of slavery. That's political.

"Isn't it political," I ask, "to teach the history of European
missionaries bringing 'civilization' to Africa and never mention
Bishop Tutu's assertion that in the end the Europeans had the land
and the Africans had the bibles?

"Isn't it political to teach the history of women's suffrage or the
abolition of slavery or the civil rights struggle as the work of larger-
than-life heroes rather than as the accomplishment of common
people who organized and took collective action?

"Isn't it political to justify American foreign policy because it
brings the benefits of industrialization to the Third World rather
than suggest that our foreign policy exploits the people of the Third
World and supports dictators?"

I point out that what shocks them about Peterson is not that
he's political; it's that he's controversial. We engage in dozens of
political acts and make dozens of political statements in our classrooms every day that support the status quo. We don't think of
them as political because they are not controversial.

My students' next reason why they cannot follow Peterson's lead is, "It's not in the curriculum." Piffle! I've taught in public school at every level from elementary through graduate school and no principal or chair or supervisor ever asked me whether what I was teaching on a particular day was in the curriculum. Furthermore, curricula always have broad objectives such as "learning to participate in a democracy," so that you'd have a pretty sorry command of logic and language if you couldn't justify everything Peterson did as meeting stated objectives.

What "I'd never get away with it" really means is, "If I tried it, I'd get into trouble." I'll go along with that 100 percent, but "I'd get into trouble" is not an ethical reason why a professional does not make a professional decision. I'll agree it is the reason millions of professional decisions are made every day—that's why the status quo is the status quo—but we're talking justice here, not go-along, get-along.

"But," they insist, "why should I get into trouble over strikers and war protesters. It's not my job." That's where they and Peterson part company. As a follower of Freire, Peterson believes that it's his job to teach powerful literacy to his students, and if he is going to succeed, he must get the real-school model working in his classroom. The students must want the knowledge he is offering badly enough to cooperate and work hard to get it. He believes he must make his students aware of what's at stake on a conscious, political level, and therefore, he must relate literacy to his students' lives and the lives of their parents. He believes he must run his classroom in a way that gives his students a reason to engage in explicit, context-independent language and school discourse. Visiting picket lines, joining war protesters, and facilitating cooperative, small-group learning are as much a part of his literacy curriculum as the spelling rule, "*i* before *e* except after *c*." He believes there's no point, in fact, of teaching "*i* before *e* except after *c*" unless he does the rest. Why should they listen?

William Bigelow and Linda Christensen are two high school teachers at Jefferson High School in Portland, Oregon, who have also determined to be on their students' side.[15] They too understand the concept that dialogue is something other than more conversation in the classroom. One of their objectives in the Literature in

U.S. History course that they co-teach is "to involve students in probing the social factors that make and limit who they are and ... help them reflect on what they could be."[16]

Students studied the forced Cherokee Indian removal from the South to west of the Mississippi River during the Andrew Jackson administration. Following reading and role playing the parts of the Indians, plantation owners, bankers, and the Jackson administration, Bigelow and Christensen asked the students to write about a time when they had their rights violated, telling what they felt and what they did in response. They then shared their stories in a "read-around" format, and the students were asked to take notes on the kinds of rights people felt they had and what action they took when their rights had been violated.

Here are a few examples: A girl wet her pants in class because the teacher would not let her leave the room to go to the bathroom. A girl encountered a lecherous teacher in middle school. Another was sexually harassed on her way to school, and she felt that she was mistreated by the school administration when she reported the incident. A boy was hassled by the school administration because he was wearing a political symbol on his jacket. A black boy was watched more closely by clerks at a convenience store than his companions who were white.

The students then spent time examining the "collective text." Almost half the violations of their rights took place in school. There were a surprising number of stories of sexual harassment.[17] A number of white students were surprised by the varieties of racism black students encountered.

Most students did not respond to these violations of their rights at all. Those who did respond, responded as individuals. One student complained to a counsellor; another told her mother; others told friends. No one they told followed through on their behalf.

Bigelow and Christensen felt this activity covered several of their objectives. It connected the curriculum (the Cherokee removal) to the students' lives. It helped them see that they can create knowledge from their own lives. It helped them reflect not only on their individual lives, but on their society and how society "makes and limits who they are." It helped the students shift their focus from themselves as individuals with individual problems to themselves as members of groups who had problems in common that demanded collective solutions.

In another instance, Bigelow and Christensen had students read a novel, *Radcliffe*, wherein an upper-class boy (Radcliffe) begins to attend a predominantly working-class school in England. In one episode the teacher humiliates a boy who cannot answer a question by saying, "There's no reason for Victor to think at all. We all know where he is going to end up, don't we [pointing out the window at the factory chimneys.]? There are places out there waiting for him already."[18]

"What are the boys in this classroom learning?" Bigelow and Christensen asked their students. The answer was that the teacher expected children of laborers to be laborers and children of bosses to be bosses, that students had no power to respond to insults directed at one of them but intended for all of them, and that the school endorsed the social hierarchy and the status quo.

Most teachers, even those who consider themselves transforming intellectuals, would probably be satisfied with these responses from their students, but Bigelow and Christensen were just getting warm. They asked their students, who were predominantly working class, to observe what went on in their classes similar to what they read about in Radcliffe's class. Did the teachers promote questions and critiques or obedience and conformity? What kind of knowledge and understanding was valued? What kind of relationships among students were encouraged? Here is one student's response.

> In both biology and government, I noticed that not only do boys get more complete explanations to questions, they get asked more questions by the teacher than girls do. In government, even though our teacher is a feminist, boys are asked to define a word or to list the different parts of the legislative branch more often than the girls are. . . . I sat in on an advanced sophomore English class that was doing research in the library. The teacher, a male, was teaching the boys how to find research on their topic, while he was finding the research himself for the girls. Now, I know chivalry isn't dead, but we are competent of finding a book.[19]

When Bigelow and Christensen asked students to reflect on who benefited from the methods of education to which they were subjected, Connie wrote the following.

I think that not only is it the teacher, but more importantly, it's the system. They purposely teach you using the "boring method." Just accept what they tell you, learn it and go on, no questions asked. It seems to me that the rich, powerful people benefit from it, because we don't want to think, we're kept ignorant, keeping them rich.[20]

Bigelow and Christensen comment that Connie's hunch that her classes benefited the rich and powerful was incomplete, but it did put her on the road to understanding that the character of her education was not simply accidental.

Were Bigelow and Christensen content? Not at all. They gave the students a short excerpt from a classic in the sociology of education,[21] which states that there is differential schooling in America such that poor children are prepared to become poor adults and rich children are prepared to become rich adults, and that although this is done to a certain extent through different content being taught in different schools and "high" and "low" classes in the same schools, it is accomplished largely through *the way classes are conducted*.[22] This is, of course, what Anyon's study was all about.

After introducing this "theory," Bigelow and Christensen provided an opportunity for their students to test it. They arranged for students in a high school (which they refer to as "Ridgewood High") in a wealthy community to host the students from Jefferson High School for a day.

Bigelow confesses to being disappointed that his students noticed differences in atmosphere rather than differences in classroom dynamics, but they did make some eye-opening observations: More money is spent per pupil at Ridgewood. The cafeteria food is better. Students are allowed to eat outside and anywhere in the building. They are permitted to wear hats and listen to Walkmen (all violations at Jefferson). Teachers at Ridgewood ask students, "What college are you going to?" Teachers at Jefferson ask, "Are you going to college?" Students at Jefferson are more highly supervised and rule governed.

Were Bigelow and Christensen ecstatic at their success? No, instead they noted a failure. They had encouraged their students to see themselves as victims. Although the theory they offered their students gave them an analytical framework with greater power to interpret their school lives than anything they had ever encountered, ultimately, it suggested hopelessness. The students' sociological detective work had only underscored their powerlessness.

But Bigelow and Christensen did not leave it there. They include in their curriculum times when people built alliances to challenge injustice. They teach the history of abolition, the labor movement, women's suffrage, and the civil rights movement, not as the story of heroic individuals such as John L. Lewis, Elizabeth Cady Stanton, and Martin Luther King Jr., but as the history of people who got together and took the collective action that made the contributions of these heroes and heroines possible.

Bigelow and Christensen are not likely to teach the Rosa Parks myth, that she was a seamstress who was too tired to give her seat to a white man, and so she was arrested, and so the black people boycotted the bus and got the law changed—one heroic act done almost by accident by an individual acting alone, and an easy victory over essentially kindhearted whites. They are more likely to teach the history of the Montgomery bus boycott as a victory of rank and file people acting collectively.

Rosa Parks was not a tired old seamstress. She was an activist, the secretary of the local NAACP chapter. She and many other black people had been discussing discrimination against them and ways they might fight against it in churches and organizations for some time. When she was arrested (she had been ejected from buses before for refusing to give up her seat, but never arrested), the people were ready to act. They organized the boycott. They organized meetings and rallies and alternative transportation. They fought off lawsuits and dirty tricks such as having insurance cancelled on church vehicles used as alternative transportation. They kept each other's spirits up until their demand for the end of bus segregation was met—381 difficult days after the boycott began.[23]

Sure, leaders arose. Martin Luther King Jr. emerged as a national leader out of the boycott. But he was a newcomer to Montgomery when the boycott erupted. It began as the collective action of rank and file people.

Bigelow and Christensen go back to the "collective text" exercise and remind students that they can learn to understand seemingly personal problems as societal problems and act with others to solve them. And like Peterson, Bigelow and Christensen are active in political movements outside the classroom. This demonstrates to students that they believe fundamental change is possible and desirable.

Bigelow concedes that because of the unequal power of teacher and student, the classroom can never truly mirror the democratic society that he works toward. He does not hold "a plebiscite on every homework assignment,"[24] nor does he pretend that he has no more expertise and knowledge than his students. He does not abdicate his authority. But he does try to employ dialogue and work for conscientization and he attempts to enable his students to become "collective actors" and "agents of civic courage," and to make "despair unconvincing and hope practical."[25]

The editors of *Rethinking Our Classrooms*,[26] Peterson, Bigelow, and Christensen among them, describe what they refer to as "classrooms for equity and justice" as follows.

Curriculum and methods are grounded in the lives of the students. The teacher does not lecture about the removal of Cherokee Indians to west of the Mississippi and tell the students to read about it and give them a multiple choice test on Friday. The students in Bigelow's classroom relate this colossal act of oppression to the oppression they feel in their own lives as young people, as females, and as minorities, through "collective narratives."

Curriculum and methods are "critical"; they are designed to enable students to ask critical questions. Who makes decisions and who's left out? Who benefits and who suffers? What are the origins of unfair practices and situations? How could things be different? How could we bring about change? Instead of teaching history in chronological order— from war to war—it can be taught thematically—

How has social change come about in the United States?
How has conflict between groups in the United States been resolved, or not resolved?
What processes have been used to bring about change?
What is the history of dissent?

Howard Zinn suggests teaching the history of the Mexican War from the standpoint of the United States government and its generals, from the standpoint of the foot soldier, and from the standpoint of the Mexicans. Of course there is controversy. Of course this raises questions of right and wrong, and the answers are not all that easy. Zinn cautions against teaching that some believe this and some believe that—take your choice. He suggests that teachers take sides, but present opposing points of view as fairly as possible.[27]

Curriculum and methods are activist.   If we teach children to critique the world but fail to teach them to act, we instill cynicism and despair. In classrooms for equity and social justice, campaigns that successfully increased equity and justice such as abolition, universal suffrage, and civil rights are taught as grass-roots movements, not miracles wrought by superheros. Teachers serve as models of activists against injustice.

The curriculum and methods are rigorous.   A social justice classroom offers more to students and expects more from them. It operates on the real-school model. The teacher has high-status knowledge and the students cooperate because they want what the teacher has. Students are expected to pass tests, even standardized tests.

If you're dealing with working-class children, there are all kinds of reasons why they are not as likely to excel on standardized tests as executive elite children. For example, to correctly answer one item on the Scholastic Aptitude Test (the SAT, used for many colleges as an entrance exam) the student would need to know the meaning of the word *regatta*. I don't think anyone would deny that this item favors rich people. You can find numerous examples of this kind of bias in any standardized test. For this reason there are many educators and others who are opposed to standardized testing.

That is not my position (and here I think I probably part company with Peterson and company). My position is that standardized tests ought to be as free of class bias as possible (the *regatta* item certainly ought to go), but in the meantime I think the appropriate response of working-class parents to poor standardized test scores should be dissatisfaction with the education their children are getting, not a desire to see the testing stop.

However, until standardized tests can be devised that are free of class bias (probably never), it's unfair to use working-class students' performance on them as a measure of the success of school reform—whether it be social justice classrooms or any other reform. The fair criterion would be, do they do as well or a little better than they do now. After all, they're getting a lot in social justice classrooms that they are not getting in domesticating classrooms, and that is not measured on standardized tests.

If they are doing as well or a little better, we need not worry on that score. In time, when the empowering education for working-class children is better established, we should expect the gap in average performance on standardized tests between rich children and working-class children to narrow, but until then, bring on your standardized tests. If students in my Freirean classroom can't do as well or better than they did when they were in a domesticating classroom, something's wrong; and it may be that the curriculum is not rigorous enough.

Curriculum and methods are participatory and experiential.   Concepts need to be experienced firsthand, not just listened to, read about, written about, and tested. Peterson's students talked about the grape boycott and the issues involved, but they also went to hear Cesar Chavez. The experience of attending such an event is far greater than reading or even listening to a speech. They visited a picket line, and they attended a protest rally at the federal building. Bigelow and Christensen's students didn't just read about "economic reproduction of society" theory. They visited another school and consciously observed and took notes on teaching practices in their own school.

The curriculum and classroom practices are hopeful, kind, and visionary.   Children should feel that the teacher and other students care about them and find them significant. To the greatest extent possible, the classroom should prefigure the kind of democratic and just society we envision.

But I'm not quite finished. It seems to me that there needs to be an additional component in the classroom for equity and justice. And so I'd add an item.

Powerful literacy and school discourse are taught explicitly. In chapter 12,
I described the teachers in schools where Shirley Brice Heath acted
as a consultant. They had children in grades 1 through 5 working
with their own stories in the form of voice recordings, exact transcripts of these recordings, and edited written transcripts that
resulted from questions and feedback from the teacher and other
students. The stories of all the children, even the youngest, began
to conform more to the linear, explicit, topic-centered stories of
school discourse, and the older children began to discover that in
school discourse, writing is not simply talk written down. Instead,
they were learning that school-based writing (the writing of powerful literacy) conveys meaning through word choice, sequencing
events, using complex sentences, and supporting ideas with facts
and details. They learned that these are not just highfalutin', pain
in the neck, pointless characteristics of rich people's writing (and
talk); they are really useful and necessary for conveying information in the discourse community in which they were learning to
operate.

The fifth graders who wrote the "textbook" to be used for next
year's fifth graders learned that defining terms and formulating
explicit questions and seeking explicit answers is not just useless
teacher talk. They are necessary for writing science. They learned
that folk concepts and science often address the same questions
and provide answers that do not conflict with one another; they
simply reflect different ways of knowing things and of saying things.
One works well in a community of intimates; the other is necessary
in a community of strangers. One can be translated to the other,
and they are both Okay in their place.

The second graders were beginning to learn that there are
different ways of using language when they became language detectives and made observations about the principal's use of language when he read the morning announcements over the intercom
and when he was kidding around with an older student in the hall.
With this beginning, they might learn later that some ways of
using language express power and some don't. And they might see
the utility of learning to use the ones that do.

In the works I've cited, Peterson, Bigelow, and Christensen
emphasize Freirean dialogue and conscientization, but say little

about explicitly teaching the language of school discourse and powerful literacy. Heath's teachers, on the other hand, emphasize methods of teaching the language of the school, but say nothing about power issues. Freire's offering without Heath's offering can lead to a lot of attitude, but can be a little short on literacy. Heath's offering, on the other hand, without Freire's offering can lead to border crossing without any challenge to the status quo. And very few border crossers make it. All the subtle mechanisms detailed in this book militate against would-be border crossers and their teachers. Heath's teachers, in fact, gave up these projects soon after she left.

If teachers who are transforming intellectuals are successful, the real-school model is established because the students want what the teacher has and teachers are prepared to teach it. The bastardized progressivism that separates students on the basis of scholastic achievement tests (which correlate highly with socioeconomic status) and "attitude" (which also correlates highly with socioeconomic status) and differentiates the curriculum and *method* of teaching (as we saw in Anyon and elsewhere) gives way to education for liberation across the board. Phony democracy and easy work in working-class schools give way to real democracy and hard work.

When this happens, progressive, collaborative methods begin to emerge because traditional, directive methods are inherently domesticating, not liberating. "Do it my way or it's wrong," is not liberating. "What we're trying to do here is get some notes for Friday's test," is not liberating. Progressive, collaborative methods can be liberating, but for many children they are not possible without simultaneous conscientization and dialogue.

Transforming intellectuals take sides. They are on the side of democracy and social justice.

Chapter 15

MAD AS HELL, AND NOT GOING TO TAKE IT ANY MORE

The *least* we can do is face facts. Our schools liberate and empower children of the gentry and domesticate the children of the working class, and to a large extent the middle class as well. You may want to argue that that's all right, or at least it's all that's possible—fine. But let's stop denying it.

The *next least* thing we can do is help teachers become better gatekeepers on the lookout for border crossers by enabling them to understand the subtle mechanisms that make border crossing so difficult. For example:

> Students from the Roadvilles of America may view what the teacher regards as "creativity" as telling lies, cooperative learning as cheating, and "discovery learning" as wasting time when they should be learning facts.

> Teachers expect students to possess the assumptions, values, and behaviors associated with school discourse, and they blame them when they do not.

> Teachers teach performative and functional literacy and think it leads naturally to powerful literacy. They are baffled and blame their students when it does not.

> Teachers do not understand that authoritarian, directive methods exacerbate the problem of powerlessness of their

students and hamper the acquisition of school discourse and powerful literacy.

But nothing short of dialogue, conscientization, and explicitly teaching school discourse and powerful literacy will give all students a chance at an empowering, liberating education, the kind of education Anyon found in the affluent professional and executive elite schools. That's the *most* we could do. And since the American ideal is that every child should have a chance at the best education, nothing short of conscientization, dialogue, and explicitly teaching school discourse and powerful literacy is acceptable.

If the authors reviewed in this book have demonstrated anything, they have demonstrated that the savage inequalities in schools are not the result of a conscious conspiracy to oppress the working class. These inequalities are the result of system-wide subtle mechanisms of which most of us are completely unaware and that can only be addressed through organized collective effort.

There are numerous organizations within the professional education community whose self-proclaimed goal is to bring democracy and equity to our nation's schools. They tend to take the position that as Americans with American democratic ideals and as professional educators they must take up the enormous struggle and improve matters through increased effort and mutual support. There are also numerous organizations outside the professional education community whose self-proclaimed goal is to bring democracy and equity to our nation's schools. They tend to take the position that they're mad as hell and they're not going to take it any more. I'll discuss organizations within the professional education community first.

Jean Anyon,[1] whose groundbreaking work I have referred to throughout this book, now heads up a teacher education program, which she describes as an example of a "best effort" for preparing teachers for working-class schools. It is based on an understanding of how an urban system works and an explicit intention to add "working for equity and justice" to the job description of teachers. Its goals include:

> Sensitivity to the moral, economic, and political right of working-class children to an education equal to that routinely offered to children of affluent professionals and executive elites;

Respect for cultural and social diversity and for the contributions of all groups to the development and functioning of society;

"Intelligent" utilization of progressive methods.[2]

In this program students:

Learn to take a reflective and critical stance regarding schools, city systems, and the ability of students and teachers to perform well in city schools;

Learn United States history as the history of ordinary people who have contributed to progress and fought against injustice;

Learn about the political and bureaucratic nature of school systems through firsthand study in local school districts;

Undertake extensive study of urban and suburban classrooms (à la Anyon's study of the four levels of schooling reported in chapter 2) and reflect on their own experiences as schoolchildren (as in the two "journal responses" I reported from my students in chapter 2);

Study and observe reforms currently being tried in urban schools;

Practice teach in clusters in schools where reforms are being tried and where they can support one another in resisting the negativity of other adults in the setting.

Anyon expresses the hope that this program will produce teachers who can "perform well under the most adverse conditions."[3]

There are numerous other college and university programs dedicated to producing teachers who will implement progressive, democratic ideals in their classrooms. Some examples are The Teacher Education Program at John Carroll University in Cleveland,[4] The Teacher Education for Civic Responsibility program at Ohio University,[5] The Master of Arts in Teaching program at Oregon State University,[6] and The Institute for Democracy in Education at Western Carolina University.[7]

College and university outreach programs are another kind of organized effort within the professional education community that address issues of democracy and equity in schooling. For example, in 1990 faculty in the department of education at the California State University at Dominguez Hills[8] found conditions in schools in neighboring communities to be much the same as those Anyon described in the working-class schools in her study a decade earlier. They applied for a grant from the federal government's Drug Free Schools and Community Fund arguing that domesticating schooling is responsible for high levels of drug use among students. They proposed training school personnel in ways of creating more progressive classrooms as a way of fighting drug use. They got the grant. Two grants, in fact.

They presented eighty-five teachers, principals, police officers, and counsellors with the theory[9] that humans can choose how they wish to behave, and that, unless forced to do otherwise, they choose behavior to meet one of four psychological needs: fun, freedom, power, and love and belonging.

This theory was then applied to "cooperative adventures"—increasingly difficult and complex tasks that required communication and cooperation. After completing the cooperative adventures the groups studied models of community.[10] Finally, participants were challenged to create communities in their schools and classrooms consistent with what they had learned and experienced.

The trainees reported mixed results. One sixth grade teacher decided that the training only would work with children who already had self-control and creative problem-solving skills. This is not, as incidents reported in this book have shown, an atypical response from teachers in working-class schools. She seems somehow to have missed in her training that teachers need to learn new skills to operate in a different kind of classroom community, and they need to teach new skills to their students.

On the other hand, there were successes. After a teacher worked on community building in her third grade class for several weeks, a student asked to have a class discussion about recess. The playground was not a safe place during recess and in their discussion the students decided to stay in their room and work on cooperative adventures of the sort the teacher had learned at her training. Soon other students began to drop in for recess and eventually there was a separate "adventure recess" for anyone who wanted to join and follow the rules.

College and university outreach programs such as the one at the University of California at Dominguez Hills have had limited impact. Although they typically address the most resistant populations, they offer little support after the program is concluded. As we saw with Heath's teachers, who abandoned the exciting and effective methods she helped them develop, it is simply asking too much of teachers to carry on without continuing support.

Teachers' networks are a third kind of organized effort within the professional education community dedicated to bringing education for empowerment to all the nation's classrooms. The Institute for Democracy in Education, the Foxfire Networks, and Educators for Social Responsibility are three examples.

The Institute for Democracy in Education[11] began during the Reagan years, when teacher bashing became a national pastime. A small group of Ohio teachers got together to discuss two trends: First, there was a call for greater and greater control of classrooms from the state capital in the form of more standardized testing, mandated curricula, and tighter control of the daily schedule. Second, virtually every proposal for reform was expressly motivated by the need for a more productive work force. The primary function of the schools as envisioned by Jefferson—to produce citizens for a democracy—was forgotten.

Teachers' concerns were summed up by a kindergarten teacher who helped form The Institute for Democracy in Education:

My goal is to help my kids become active, involved members of their community. I try to teach this by having them be active, involved members of our classroom and school and neighborhood. But what I'm being told now is that what we are really to do is just get kids ready to take tests so we can make better cars than the Japanese. So I'm told to drill and sort and measure; and whether or not my kids can think, cooperate, be creative, or work for a common goal is irrelevant.[12]

This small group of Ohio teachers learned that there are a great many other teachers who feel themselves under siege, who see their oppression linked to the oppression of their students, and who are ready to work to empower themselves and their students. What they lack is the vision that something different is possible. The Institute for Democracy in Education helps teachers formulate that vision.

The Institute soon learned that democratic educational reform is more difficult than most reformers seem to understand. Therefore, it does not offer inspirational speakers who provide teachers with easy steps to solving their problems—alone in their own classrooms with nothing needed but a little inspiration and extra individual effort. Instead, it offers a forum for teachers to come together, bring their problems to the table, and seek one another's support in solving them. Presently, The Institute for Democracy in Education has groups in every state and in every province of Canada. There are fourteen regional offices. It publishes a quarterly journal, *Democracy in Education*, and holds a national conference annually.

Foxfire Networks[13] are named after the Foxfire books,[14] which grew out of the teaching approach started by Eliot Wigginton with his high school English students in rural Georgia. The Foxfire "approach" is based on the belief that the goal of schooling is a more effective, humane, and democratic society, and that that goal should be reflected in every teaching strategy and classroom activity. The Foxfire approach can be defined by its "core practices":

> The teacher is a collaborator, team leader, and guide rather than boss.
>
> Schoolwork is infused with student choice.
>
> Peer teaching, small group work, cooperative learning, and teamwork are preferred methods.
>
> Schoolwork engages students in reflecting on their communities and connections between their communities and the world.
>
> Mistakes are not the occasion for chastisement, but opportunities to learn.
>
> There is an audience beyond the teacher for students' work.
>
> Academic integrity is demanded.
>
> Mastering state and locally mandated "skills lists" is expected. The Foxfire approach demands more.

In 1986, Foxfire Fund, Inc. initiated an effort to promote the Foxfire approach in schools around the country. It arranged to have a graduate-level course in the Foxfire approach offered in cooperating colleges and universities and organized the teachers who took the courses into "networks" or support groups. At present there are more than eleven networks and more are pending.

Educators for Social Responsibility[15] was started in the early 1980s by educators who believed that the great movements of the twentieth century—labor, civil rights, and women's rights, for example—have taught us that it is the informed and responsible participation of average citizens that will determine our political, social, and economic future.

Educators for Social Responsibility believes that tomorrow's citizens must be conscious of others and how they are related to others. They must be open-minded, but at the same time able to analyze and criticize positions. They must be able to take others' perspectives. They must be able to appreciate the complexity of social relationships and to look for root causes rather than simplistic solutions. They must assume responsibility for errors in their own thinking. And finally, they must have the vision and courage to act.

Teachers who embrace these beliefs soon find themselves in troubled waters. They are adding to an already demanding work load and experimenting in an unfamiliar terrain. They are often teaching skills and attitudes that are "not affirmed by the administrative or instructional climate of the school."[16] Educators for Social Responsibility acts as a support group for such teachers and as a network for sharing ideas. It presently has twenty-five chapters and reaches more than 10,000 educators each year through workshops, institutes, and conference presentations.[17]

However, the problem of education for domestication for working-class students cannot be solved *solely* by initiatives from inside the education establishment. Asking new teachers, even those from excellent teacher preparation programs, to bring about change in schools like Anyon's working-class school or Weis's Freeway High School is asking too much. Almost always, what happens instead is that the new teacher is socialized into the existing culture of the school. Teacher networks, especially in combination with teacher education programs, have been the mainstay of efforts to bring democratic, just, and equitable education to our schools. However, the teachers who belong to such organizations as Educators for Social Responsibility probably make up less than 1 percent of teachers in the country.

In order for there to be significant progress, those ultimately injured by the problem, the working class themselves, must take a hand. That's not as novel an idea as it may seem.

Since nearly the beginning of the Industrial Revolution there have been what we have all come to know as "labor organizers." In Freirean terms, labor organizers conscientize individuals and urge them to use their talents and passions to further their self-interest. They create collectives, committees, and organizations that function in a disciplined, focused, and strategic manner. They guide these organizations to influence political and economic decisions that affect the lives of their members.

In 1938, Saul Alinsky, a professor of sociology at the University of Chicago, applied the art and science of labor organizing to community problems such as inferior public services in working-class neighborhoods. Over the years he helped form the Industrial Areas Foundation, a nationwide network that took on such issues as civil rights, job discrimination, and education. Alinsky created a new role in the public arena, that of "community organizer."

The missing piece in the effort to "make despair unconvincing and hope practical"[18] in the fight for decent education for working-class children emerged when parents began organizing around school issues using an Alinsky model.

In their 1998 report[19] The Annenberg Institute on Public Engagement for Public Education asserted that there is a quiet revolution taking place in public education. It is the beginning of a fundamental shift in the kind of behavior Americans engage in on behalf of their children. It signals a change in the structures of power in education. It is referred to as public conversation, parent involvement, school/community partnerships, citizens action, neighborhood improvement, community organizing, and even standards setting. It has the following characteristics: it focuses on improving teaching and learning; it brings to the table those who are typically excluded; and it facilitates training and dissemination of information that prepares communities to make tough decisions.

Kate Poe,[20] a community and labor organizer who concentrates on school issues, starts with the assumptions that schools reflect inequalities found in society at large. We can't get power to fix schools without organizing and putting pressure on those who have power.

The problem, as Poe sees it, is that too many of us buy into the social service model of education where professionals treat parents and community members as clients rather than as partners. Such educators are often kind, respectful, and helpful, but they tend to discount what parents and community members know and what they can do.

Unlike adults in communities with schools like Anyon's affluent professional and executive elite schools, working-class people, in large part because of the way they were educated, do not feel a sense of entitlement; they tend to be intimidated by school staff.

Under such circumstances, using Alinsky's model, parents, community members, and older students are organized into democratic and participatory associations staffed by paid, trained organizers who are accountable to the membership. Such associations are led by parents or community members, not school personnel; it doesn't work to put people whose jobs depend on an institution in charge of reforming it.

Community organizers have discovered, as labor organizers discovered long before them, that people will not organize over problems that seem insurmountable, but they will organize around winnable issues. For example, domesticating education is a problem that is too overwhelming to organize around, but issues can be identified surrounding domesticating education that are concrete, understandable, and manageable. A list of such issues developed in this book appears in Box 15.1.

These issues are derived from an analysis of the subtle mechanisms that make the teachers' job of teaching and the students' job of learning so difficult. If parents and teachers understand them, they will understand too that there is no point in name calling or blaming teachers, students, or parents. It's the mechanisms that need to be addressed. Parents, teachers, and students play roles and observe rules in keeping these mechanisms operating. Overcoming these destructive mechanisms will call for changes in everyone's roles and the rules they observe.[21]

For example, an issue that is often related to domesticating education is that teachers make derogatory remarks to and about

What We Have and Don't Want *Domesticating Education*	What We Need and Don't Have *Liberating Education*
— Knowledge is presented as facts isolated from wider bodies of knowledge.	— Knowledge is *rarely* presented as facts isolated from wider bodies of knowledge.
— Knowledge taught is not related to the lives and experiences of the students.	— Knowledge taught is always related to the lives and experiences of the students.
— Teachers do not make a practice of explaining how assignments are related to one another.	— Teachers make a practice of explaining how assignments are related to one another.
— Work is easy.	— Work is challenging.
— Knowledge from textbooks is valued more highly than knowledge gained from experience.	— Textbook knowledge is validated or challenged in terms of knowledge gained from experience.
— Knowing the answers and knowing where to find the answers are valued over creativity, expression, and analysis.	— Creativity, expression, and analysis are essential beyond knowing the answers or knowing where to find the answers.
— Discussion of challenges to the status quo, past and present, rarely occurs.	— Discussion of challenges to the status quo, past and present, frequently occurs.
— History of labor unions, civil rights, women's suffrage, and other victories for justice and equity are taught as the accomplishments of "heroes" and "heroines" not as the result of grass roots struggles.	— History of labor unions, civil rights, women's suffrage, and other victories for justice and equity are taught as collective action taken by common people.
— Instruction is typically copying notes and writing answers to factual questions.	— Instruction is *rarely* copying notes and writing answers to factual questions.

Box 15.1 Issues Surrounding Domesticating Education

What We Have and Don't Want	What We Need and Don't Have
Domesticating Education	*Liberating Education*
— Work is evaluated in terms of following steps. A satisfactory answer does not suffice. "Do it my way or it's wrong."	— "Work" is sometimes presented as following steps in procedures, but students are given choices and rewarded for original solutions.
— "Writing" consists of filling in blanks or lines on teacher-constructed handouts or workbook pages.	— "Writing" is taught in a workshop format as described in chapter 12.
— Both teachers and students focus on good grades and a diploma as the objective of schooling.	— Neither teachers nor students focus on good grades and a diploma as the objective of schooling.
— Students' access to materials is tightly controlled.	— Students have access to materials.
— Movement of students is tightly controlled.	— Students have considerable freedom of movement.
— Students are rewarded for passivity and obedience, not for initiative and inquisitiveness.	— Students are rewarded for initiative and inquisitiveness, not passivity and obedience.
— Students are rarely given an opportunity to express their own ideas.	— Students are frequently given an opportunity to express their own ideas.
— Teachers are gatekeepers. They focus on correctness before expression.	— Teachers focus on expression before correctness.
— Teachers make derogatory remarks to and about students.	— Teachers never make derogatory remarks to or about students.

Box 15.1 Issues Surrounding Domesticating Education *(continued)*

students. No one thinks this is a good idea,[22] but it happens. This is the kind of thing people will come out to a meeting about, and it's winnable. When the dialogue begins, teachers will undoubtedly want to discuss the role students often play in this issue. That is, students make derogatory remarks to teachers and wantonly (from the teachers' point of view) provoke such remarks from teachers. But everyone can probably agree that these remarks are not useful and a system for addressing them when they occur in the future can probably be agreed upon.

Building on this small victory, the organizer helps parents to formulate other issues and to further organize around them. In this process, the organizer's job is to help parents learn leadership skills and how to function in a disciplined, focused, and strategic manner.

Frequently, teachers and other staff in troubled working-class schools agree that it is desirable to involve parents and community members, but they are quick to claim that parent mobilization is impossible and that if it were possible, parents and community members would only oppose progressive reforms. Community organizers have found that it is true that many parents only become involved during times of crisis such as a violent incident or a vote on school uniforms, and it is also true that parents often oppose reforms (including progressive reforms) that are implemented without their involvement or consent.[23]

However, community organizers can point to successes in all kinds of neighborhoods with all kinds of parents.

The Alliance Schools Project Of the Interfaith Education Fund[24] in Austin, Texas, is the outgrowth of the work of the Industrial Areas Foundation, the national network started by Alinsky. It now has more than forty umbrella groups working to improve life in low-income communities.

The Alliance begins working in communities at the invitation of community groups, schools, school districts, or religious congregations. Alliance organizers start by talking one-on-one to parents, teachers and principals. This is followed up by meetings where parents and teachers are encouraged to tell their stories, to answer the questions, "What's important to me?" and "What needs to change?" There are also grade-level meetings for teachers, parent coffees, and house meetings bringing together parents and community members.

All this person-to-person communication explodes myths, identifies potential leaders, and builds relationships that serve to develop a core leadership team of parents, teachers, and administrators. Drawing on their conversations with others, this leadership group crafts an action plan. This is a two- or three-year process that ensures that the management team will be truly representative and will serve as a formal mechanism through which all concerned parties can share power, decision making, and responsibility for their school.

In the late 1980s, the Morningside Middle School District in Fort Worth was the worst-performing middle school in the district. Through Alliance efforts there has been greater parent involvement in the parent-teacher organization and in the school's policy committees. The school now ranks third among the city's twenty-two middle schools in student achievement.

The Alliance-sponsored San Antonio Education Partnership responded to community concerns about the future of high school students. They created new jobs and scholarships. In just a few years the number of seniors maintaining a B average went from 19 percent to 61 percent and the graduation rate went from 81 percent to 92 percent.

Organizers from near and far have attended the Industrial Areas Foundation's intensive ten-day training sessions, hoping to emulate the Alliance's success. The Alliance now serves 145 schools in Texas, New Mexico, Louisiana, and Arizona, and currently more schools want to join the Alliance network than there are organizers to serve them.

Mothers on the Move (MOM)[25] started in 1992 when a group of women in the South Bronx visited a fourth grade classroom as part of an adult literacy class sponsored by the non-profit Bronx Educational Services. The purpose of the visit was to convince the children to stay in school and work hard so they wouldn't need to attend adult literacy classes when they grew up. Instead, the women were outraged by a school culture that was blatantly disrespectful to children. Their anger prompted them to action and with the help of Bronx Educational Services they organized.

They visited tenaments and apartment buildings and talked face to face with residents. They listened to concerns about the schools, and these concerns became their agenda. They organized regular meetings in a storefront headquarters and with the help of community organizers they developed plans for action. They have worked with school principals to implement new reading programs and to move drug activity away from school grounds. They have lobbied district administrators to get their fair share of textbook funds. They played an active role in forcing out a district superintendent whom they accused of allowing South Bronx schools to deteriorate over twenty years, and they played an active role in choosing a replacement.

MOM has developed productive relationships with a few of the area's principals. However, in 1998 a MOM co-director was quoted as saying, "We hope we can work collaboratively with the new superintendent and that there will be a different attitude from the principals. There needs to be some type of cultural change in the way they view parents. In the meantime, we try to take the high road and keep doing the work we're doing."[26]

In 1998 MOM had a membership of seven hundred moms (and some dads). Part of its broader strategy is to build leaders from among its own ranks. It provides training sessions in public speaking and meeting facilitation. It sponsors workshops on New York City's complex policies and programs. As a result it has developed powerful parent-driven leadership. Two of its members have been elected to the District Community School Board and one is on New York State's Visiting Committee for Lower-Performing Schools.

In Milwaukee, parents and teachers in one of the city's few integrated neighborhoods organized independently to save a school scheduled for closing. They organized broad support, developed a solid plan, and convinced the board of education to let them establish a bilingual whole language school managed by parents and staff. The school employs a full-time community organizer who is paid the equivalent of a teacher's salary.[27]

In New York City, a parent organization won school board approval for a mini-school to serve a housing project and two community-designed high schools. These victories followed years of working on smaller scale school-level issues and the election of twelve school board members who share the group's interests.

In Chicago, the Cross City Campaign for Urban School Reform, among others, has pressed for and won community-based management for schools, with real power. By law parents must make up a majority of members on local school councils which have the final say in hiring and firing principals! To a large degree, authority and control of funds have been shifted to local schools. The central administration has lost much of its regulatory authority; its function is now to support locally determined school policies. Those who make decisions are accountable for their implementation.

Educators committed to justice and equity have also devised ways of mobilizing parents who are reluctant to get involved. The University of Wisconsin, Milwaukee sponsors an ongoing action-learning seminar where participants—parents, teachers, administrators, and community members—come together to design "pathways to parental involvement in school work." This involves "the home, school and community working together as partners for the benefit of the children."[28]

The seminar began by identifying some of the significant barriers to effective parent, school, and community collaboration, and action plans were created to address and overcome the barriers. One example of the many strategies that have been recommended is providing classes in schools for parents in literacy, English language, and computers, math, science, and social studies.

Many aspects of the Milwaukee program are similar to Anyon's vision of "full service schools," that is, schools as community centers "where the economic and political disenfranchisement of parents is addressed through a wide variety of services that include housing assistance, job training and career opportunities, preparation for the GED certificate and college assistance." Parents, according to Anyon, are more likely to get involved in their children's education (and in educational reform) "if they see meaningful results for themselves from involvement at the school."[29]

There are signs too that the working class may find heretofore unlikely allies in the struggle for equity and justice and education for liberation—the middle class. Since the post–World War II suburban population explosion, the terms *middle class* and *suburban* have been almost synonymous. As the middle class abandoned cities, city residents lost their clout. Today only 29 percent of the nation's people and 12 percent of our voters live in cities.[30] Most of our state and federal elected officials represent suburban constituencies. However, things change.

The problems of the city are rapidly becoming the problems of the suburbs. Crowding, traffic congestion, poverty, and slashes in funding for services and education are all on the rise in suburbia. Upscale suburbs are experiencing serious problems of drugs and violence in their high schools. Students in middle-class schools are receiving instruction in broom closets and hallways, sports programs are being eliminated, and slashing of state funding is making further cuts necessary. At the same time, middle-class work is disappearing through downsizing and exporting of jobs,[31] and children of middle-class people are finding it increasingly difficult to find traditional middle-class work with traditional middle-class pay. The choice is to slip into the working class at a time when working-class fortunes are in serious decline or compete with the affluent professionals and executive elites for "symbolic analyst"[32] jobs.

Possibility, the dominant theme that Anyon found in her middle-class school in 1980 has been replaced with *angst*. Cooperating with an education system that offers informational literacy only and withholds powerful literacy is making less and less sense to middle-class parents and children.

We may be coming into a period of cultural and social ferment. Anyon points out that such periods historically follow periods of savage capitalism. There is a resurgence of grass-roots movements rooted in labor unions, neighborhoods, religious congregations, and consumer and environmental groups.

It is an open question whether the middle class whose fortunes are diminishing will join the working class in the struggle for justice and equity in schooling. It is an open question whether the middle class will be any more successful in getting the kind of education necessary for their children to compete in a changing economic environment than the working-class Freeway parents were. In any case, I believe (and fervently hope) we are in for some interesting times.

I hope I have been successful in developing five themes in this book, which I will draw together in these last paragraphs. I don't have much hope for a lot of progress if any one of these five themes is ignored.

1. Traditional, directive methods are nearly always found in working-class schools and are often found in middle-class schools. To acquire powerful literacy, one must feel powerful.

Traditional, directive methods are inherently domesticating. They rarely lead to powerful literacy. Progressive, collaborative methods are liberating and empowering, and can lead to powerful literacy, but they rely on a certain amount of cooperation and good will on the part of students. Resistance of working-class children to schooling makes the use of progressive, collaborative methods difficult to impossible.

2. Language and literacy are always parts of broader systems known as discourses. The discourses of some communities are different from and sometimes in conflict with school discourse. Children from such communities need to be taught school discourse. Where there are conflicts between home and school discourse, children need to learn school discourse as part of a strategy in the struggle for justice. They do not need to be forced to concede that school discourse is "right" and their discourse is "wrong."

3. There are different levels of literacy, and children whose discourse communities do not engage habitually in informational and powerful literacy must be taught these levels of literacy and the discourses that underlie them. Such children do not acquire these things "naturally."

4. Conscientization and dialogue (the work of community organizers and teachers who take the side of their working-class students) can lead working-class students and parents to see that powerful literacy and school discourse are necessary and desirable to further their self-interest. When organized around this realization, working-class adults and older students can bring pressure on the schools to deliver higher forms of literacy. Conscientizing people who are getting shortchanged and organizing them to use their talents and passions in their own self-interest is what Freire was all about. It's what Alinsky was all about. It opens the way for dialogue and negotiation between the schools and empowered working-class organizations. Based on efforts to find a win-win solution and on an understanding of the subtle mechanisms that undermine good education for working-class students, this process offers hope— at long last—for a good education for working-class children.

5. When self-defeating working-class resistance gives way to working-class demands for powerful literacy, the other subtle mechanisms that impede working-class children's education will not go away by themselves. Teachers will need to turn to the curriculum and methods pioneered by Freirean teachers such as Peterson, Bigelow, and Christensen, the knowledge, attitudes, and skills taught in "equity and justice" oriented college and university teacher preparation programs, outreach programs like the one offered by the University of California at Dominguez Hills, and teacher support groups such as The Institute for Democracy in Education, the Foxfire networks, and Educators for Social Responsibility.

These themes can be also looked at another way: What do working-class parents and older working-class students need to do, and what do teachers of working-class children need to do?

Working-class parents and older working-class students must realize that they must master school discourse and powerful literacy in order to struggle for justice and equity. They must organize and pressure the schools to teach their children school discourse and powerful literacy. They need to work with their children to cooperate as the schools begin to deliver.

The National Coalition of Education Activists,[33] The Cross City Campaign,[34] The Gamaliel Foundation,[35] and the Industrial Areas Foundation[36] are four organizations available to individuals and groups of working-class people and their allies who want assistance in organizing. The Annenberg Institute on Public Engagement for Public Education maintains a list of "public engagement sites." The list, which included 174 sites in 1998, will be expanded as the Institute's research continues. It can be accessed on the Institute's web site (www.aisr.brown.edu).

Teachers of working-class children need to learn how to teach school discourse and powerful literacy to working-class children. They need to stop teaching performative and functional literacy and waiting for the children to acquire school discourse and powerful literacy "naturally." They need to understand that traditional, directive methods are antithetical to the acquisition of powerful literacy, and that progressive, collaborative methods are necessary for the acquisition of powerful literacy.

They need to become Freirean educators like Peterson, Bigelow, and Christensen. They need to support the efforts of college and university teacher preparation programs that produce teachers for whom equity and justice are primary objectives in their classrooms; they need to welcome these young teachers into their midst and support them. They need to take part in outreach programs like the one offered by the University of California. They need to join teacher support groups like The Institute for Democracy in Education, the Foxfire networks, and Educators for Social Responsibility. In short, they need to engage in the enormous struggle.

There have been many valiant tries by a lot of courageous and energetic teachers and principals, but in the face of resistance from students and apathy from colleagues, these efforts wither and die. If working-class (and middle-class) children are to get a decent education, the working class (and middle class) is going to have to demand it, and that means "get an attitude" and "get organized."

Notes

Chapter 1. Title, Author, and Hard-bitten School Teachers

1. Maurice Levitas. *Perspectives in the Sociology of Education* (Boston: Routledge & Kegan Paul, 1974).

2. Jonathan Kozol. *Savage Inequalities: Children in America's Schools* (New York: Harper Perennial, 1992).

3. I've fictionalized the name of the school. In fact, I taught at two Chicago elementary schools and refer to incidents that occurred in both of them later in the book.

4. John Stewart Carter. *Full Fathom Five* (Boston: Houghton Mifflin Co., 1965).

5. But it's thirty years later now, and we no longer refer to teachers as hard-bitten; we refer to them as "hard-assed." Let's admit it. Language lost a certain elegance in the sixties, and it has not recovered.

Chapter 2. A Distinctly Un-American Idea: An Education Appropriate to their Station

1. Jean Anyon, "Social Class and the Hidden Curriculum of Work," *Journal of Education* (1980): pp. 67–92 and "Social Class and School Knowledge," *Curriculum Inquiry* (1981): pp.3–42.

2. A rebus story is one where pictures and letters are brought together to form words. For example, a cartoon picture of a hand, a plus sign, and the letters *some* make up the word *handsome*.

209

3. S. Bowles and H. Gintis, *Schooling in Capitalist America: Educational Reform and Contradictions of Economic Life* (New York: Basic Books, 1976); M. W. Apple, *Ideology and Curriculum* (Boston: Routledge and Kegan Paul, 1979); P. Bourdieu and J. Passeron, *Reproduction in Education, Society, and Culture* (Beverly Hills: Sage, 1977).

4. Robert B. Reich, *The Work of Nations: Preparing Ourselves for 21st Century Capitalism* (New York: Vintage Books, 1991. See also Thomas W. Fraser, *Reading, Writing, and Justice: School Reform as if Democracy Matters* (Albany: State University of New York Press, 1997).

5. The grant proposal is described in J. Cynthia McDermott, "An Institute for Independence through Action, Process, and Theory." In John M. Novak, ed. *Democratic Teacher Education: Programs, Processes, Problems, and Prospects* (Albany: State University of New York Press, 1994).

6. Jonathan Kozol, *Savage Inequalities: Children in America's Schools* (New York: Harper Perennial, 1992).

7. Megan Elizabeth Connolly, Paper 1, LAI 563 Language, Society, and Language Arts Instruction (Photocopied, Department of Learning and Instruction, State University of New York at Buffalo, 1998).

8. Susan Marie Sampson, Paper 1, LAI 563 Language, Society, and Language Arts Instruction (Photocopied, Department of Learning and Instruction, State University of New York at Buffalo, 1998).

Chapter 3.   Harsh Schools, Big Boys, and the Progression Solution

1. Daniel P. Resnick, "Historical Perspectives on Literacy and Schooling," *Daedalus* (1990): pp. 15–32.

2. *Baltimore Catechism: A catechism of Christian doctrine, prepared and enjoined by order of the Third Plenary Council Baltimore; with explanations in the form of short notes and of sections in simple question and answer. Published by ecclesiastical authority* (Chicago: The John P. Daleiden Company, 1918)

3. David W. Swift, *Ideology and Change in the Public Schools: Latent Functions of Progressive Education* (Columbus: Charles E. Merrill Publishing Company, 1971). The argument that progressive ideals were instrumental in developing our present, arguably unjust school system is taken almost entirely from Swift.

4. Ellwood P. Cubberly, *Public Education in the United States* (Boston: Houghton-Mifflin Company, 1919), p. 328 rev. ed. Quoted in David W.

Swift, *Ideology and Change in the Public Schools: Latent Functions of Progressive Education*, p. 35.

5. Clifton Johnson, *The Country School in New England* (New York: D. Appleton and Company, 1893), pp. 47–52. Quoted in David W. Swift, *Ideology and Change in the Public Schools: Latent Functions of Progressive Education*, p. 36–37.

6. Clifton Johnson, *Old Time Schools and School Books* (New York: The Macmillian Co., 1904), pp. 123–126. Quoted in David W. Swift, *Ideology and Change in the Public Schools: Latent Functions of Progressive Education,* pp. 33.

7. Ruth Freeman, *Yesterday's Schools* (Watkin's Glen, N.Y.: Century House, 1962), p. 77. Quoted in David W. Swift, *Ideology and Change in the Public Schools: Latent Functions of Progressive Education*, p. 34.

8. Ruth S. Freeman, *Yesterday's Schools,* pp. 78–79. Quoted in David W. Swift, *Ideology and Change in the Public Schools: Latent Functions of Progressive Education,* p. 34.

9. U. S. Commissioner of Education, *Annual Report of the Commissioner of Education Made to the Secretary of the Interior for the Year 1870* (Washington, D. C.: 1875), p 273. Quoted in David W. Swift, *Ideology and Change in the Public Schools: Latent Functions of Progressive Education,* p. 42.

10. Lawrence A. Cremin, *The Transformation of the School* (New York: Random House, Inc, Vintage Books, 1964), p. 22. Quoted in David W. Swift, *Ideology and Change in the Public Schools: Latent Functions of Progressive Education.* p. 19.

11. John Willinsky, *The New Literacy: Redefining Reading and Writing in the Schools* (New York: Routledge, Chapman and Hall, Inc. 1990), p. 8.

Chapter 4. Oppositional Identity: Identifying "Us" as "Not Them"

1. The concepts of "involuntary minorities," "oppositional identity," and the details supporting these concepts are taken from John U. Ogbu, "Cultural Diversity and School Experience," in Catherine E. Walsh, *Literacy as Praxis: Culture, Language, and Pedagogy* (Norwood, N.J.: Ablex Publishing Corporation, 1991), pp.25–50.

2. In fact, West Indian blacks who immigrate to the United States outperform American-born blacks in terms of levels of education, income,

and occupational status. See Thomas Sowell, ed., *Essays and Data on American Ethnic Groups* (Washington, D. C.: Urban Institute, 1978), pp. 41–49.

3. John U. Ogbu, "Cultural Diversity and School Experience."

4. Kerby Miller and Paul Wagner, *Out of Ireland: The Story of Irish Immigration to America* (Washington, D. C.:Elliott & Clark Publishers, 1994).

5. Perry Gilmore, "'Gimme Room': School Resistance, Attitude, and Access to Literacy," in Candice Mitchell and Kathleen Weiler, eds., *Rewriting Literacy: Culture and the Discourse of the Other* (New York: Bergin & Garvey, 1991), pp. 57–76.

6. Perry Gilmore, p. 66.

7. Perry Gilmore, p. 67.

8. Robert Coles, *The Spiritual Life of Children* (Boston: Houghton Mifflin, 1990).

9. Robert Coles, p. 24.

10. R. Scollon and S. B. K. Scollon, Narrative, *Literacy and Face in Interethnic Communication* (Norwood, N.J.: Ablex Publishing Corporation, 1981).

11. Bob Herbert, "In America: Workaday Racism" (New York: The New York Times Company, 1996). http//www.dorsai.org/~jdadd/texaco3.html. See also Jim Fitzgerald, "Jury Hears Tapes in Texaco Case," (Associated Press: April 29, 1998). http://www.blackvoices.com/news/98/04/29/story07.html.

12. Gary Natriello, Edward L. McDill, and Aaron M. Pallas, *Schooling Disadvantaged Children, Racing Against Catastrophe* (New York, Teachers College Press: 1990).

Chapter 5. The Lads

1. Paul E. Willis, *Learning to Labor: How Working Class Kids Get Working Class Jobs* (Westmead, England: Saxon House, 1977).

2. Willis, p. 1.

3. Recall the discussion of my black eighth graders on Chicago's south side with high reading scores in 1965 and a group of eighth graders in Winnetka, Illinois, with the same scores and where they probably are in terms of socioeconomic status today.

4. Willis, pp. 11–12.

5. Willis, p. 12.

6. Willis, p. 29.

7. Willis, p. 54.

8. Willis, p. 57.

9. Willis, p. 62.

10. Kozol, Jonathan, *Savage Inequalities: Children in America's Schools* (New York: Harper Perennial, 1992).

11. Samuel Bowles and Herbert Gintis, *Schooling in Capitalist America: Educational Reform and the Contradictions of Economic Life* (New York: Basic Books. 1976). Perry Gilmore, "'Gimme Room': School Resistance, Attitude, and Access to Literacy," in Candice Mitchell and Kathleen Weiler, eds., *Rewriting Literacy: Culture and the Discourse of the Other* (New York, Bergin & Garvey: 1991), pp. 57–76. S. Hamilton, "The Social Side of Schooling," *Elementary School Journal* 83 (1983): pp. 313–334. E. Leacock, *Teaching and Learning in City Schools* (New York: Basic Books, 1969).

12. Willis, p. 77.

13. Willis, p. 78.

14. Willis, p. 70.

15. Willis, p. 80.

16. Willis, p. 74.

17. Willis, p. 59. Labov and Robbins observed that among black and Puerto Rican boys in New York a high level of acceptance on the street was a good predictor of poor school performance and reading score. W. Labov and C. Robbins, "A note on the Relation of Reading Failure to Peer-Group Status in Urban Ghettos," *The Record—Teacher's College* (1969), 70 pp. 395–405.

Chapter 6.   Changing Conditions—Entrenched Schools

1. Lois Weis, *Working Class without Work: High School Students in a De-industrializing Economy* (New York: Routledge, 1990).

2. Weis, p. 19.

3. Weis, p. 23.

4. Weis, p. 27.

5. Weis, p. 68.

6. Weis, pp. 28–29.

7. Weis, p. 29.

8. Weis, p. 29.

9. Weis, p. 28.

10. Weis, p. 28.

11. Weis, p. 28.

12. Weis, p. 30.

13. Weis, p. 82.

14. Weis, p. 82.

15. Weis, p. 84.

16. Weis, p. 86.

17. Weis, pp. 88–89.

18. David Bensman and Roberta Lynch, *Rusted Dreams: Hard Times in a Steel Community* (New York: McGraw Hill, 1987), p. 28.

19. Weis, p. 170.

20. Weis, p. 171.

21. Weis, p. 171.

22. Weis, p.173.

23. Weis, p. 173.

24. Weis, p. 174.

25. Weis, p.

26. I have been told by friends who taught in western New York when the mills were still open that a number of full-time male teachers in Freeway schools worked full-time jobs in the mills on the 4–12 shift and that this was well-known to the administration and school board.

27. R. T. Sieber, "The Politics of Middle-Class Success in an Inner City Public School," *Journal of Education* 164 (1981): pp. 30–47.

28. Sieber was studying the differences between an Episcopal, Catholic, and Public school in this ethnically mixed neighborhood in New York

City. He did not anticipate finding the situation that had developed in the public school.

29. Recall that teachers in Anyon's working-class schools were often rude to students. One teacher remarked that she would not teach in the suburbs because the kids "thought they had rights." Insulting remarks by teachers to students were observed in both the lads' school and at Freeway high school. I recently met an upper-middle-class African American woman who lives in an affluent suburb of Atlanta. She told me she was sending her twin boys to a private school because, although she was committed to public education, she would not have her boys spoken to in the manner that both teachers and staff spoke to black boys in the local public elementary school.

Chapter 7. Class, Control, Language, and Literacy

This chapter is based largely on the observations of Basil Bernstein. Basil Bernstein, *Theoretical Studies Towards a Sociology of Education* (London: Routledge and Kegan Paul. 1971), *Applied Studies Towards a Sociology of Education* (London: Routledge and Kegan Paul, 1973), *Towards a Theory of Educational Transmission* (London: Routledge and Kegan Paul, 1973), and *The Structuring of Pedagogic Discourse* (London: Routledge and Kegan Paul, 1990).

1. Sociologists, particularly British sociologists, are thinking of a rather more affluent group of people than the average American when they refer to the middle class. Identifying class is a very complicated matter, but they are usually referring to people such as doctors and lawyers rather than policemen and white collar workers. In America, we all think we're middle-class. I'm certain the people in Freeway would think of themselves as middle-class, but sociologists would probably identify them, even most of the teachers at Freeway high school, as working-class.

2. L. Schatzman and A. Strauss, "Social class and communication," *American Journal of Sociology* 60 (1955): pp. 329–339.

3. T. Givon, *On Understanding Grammar* (New York: Academic Press, 1979), p. 287.

4. T. Givon, p. 297.

5. Students in Anyon's working-class school are a good example of a group of people who feel powerless. They resisted the school's authority, but their actions were implicit—mostly nonlinguistic, in fact. The reasons for their resistence were never stated. Contrast this with the affluent professional and executive elite students who routinely engaged in negotiations with their teachers, explicitly stating grievance and reasons for change.

6. Jeanne Chall and Vicki Jacobs, "Writing and Reading in the Elementary Grades: Developmental Trends Among Low SES Children," in Julie M. Jensen, *Composing and Comprehending* (Urbana, Ill.: ERIC Clearing House on Reading and Communication Skills, 1984), pp. 93–104.

Chapter 8.   Where Literacy Emerges

1. J. Buckhalt, R. Rutherford, and K. Goldberg, "Verbal and Nonverbal Interactions of Mothers and their Down's Syndrome and Nonretarded Infants," *American Journal of Mental Deficiency* 82 (1978): pp. 337–343. T. Cross, "Mothers' Speech Adjustment: The Contribution of Selected Child Listener Variables," in C. A. Snow and C. A. Ferguson, eds., *Talking to Children: Language Input and Acquisition* (Cambridge: Cambridge University Press, 1977), pp. 151–188. C. E. Snow, "The Development of Conversation between Mothers and Babies," *Journal of Child Development* 4 (1977): pp. 1–22.

2. Gordon Wells, "Language as Interaction," in Gordon Wells, *Language through Interaction* (Cambridge: Cambridge University Press, 1981), pp. 22–72, 102.

3. Wells, p. 107.

4. Wells, pp. 24–25.

5. M. A. K. Halliday, *Learning How to Mean: Explorations in the Study of Language* (London: Edward Arnold Publishers, 1975), pp. 111–112.

6. M. King, "Speech to Writing: Children's Growth in Writing Potential," in J. Mason, ed., *Reading and Writing Connections* (Boston: Allyn and Bacon, 1989), pp. 7–30, 14.

7. M. King, p. 15.

8. J. C. Harste, V. A. Woodward, and C. L. Burke, *Language Stories and Literacy Lessons* (Portsmouth, N.H.: Heinemann, 1984).

9. Ashley Hartfield, "The Runaway Elephant," in Patrick J. Finn, *Helping Children Learn to Read* (New York: Longman, 1990), p. 175.

10. Shirley Brice Heath, *Ways with Words* (Cambridge: Cambridge University Press, 1983).

11. In fact, Heath studied three communities. I refer to only two of them in this discussion.

12. James Paul Gee, "What Is Literacy," in *Rewriting Literacy: Culture and the Discourse of the Other.* Ed. C. Mitchell and K. Weiler. New York: Bergin & Garvey, 1991, p. 3.

13. The typical discourse of affluent professional and executive elite homes is inconsistent with the discourse of traditional, directive class-rooms—which explains the entire Brownstone episode.

Chapter 9. Where Children Are Taught to Sit Still and Listen

1. Shirley Brice Heath, *Ways with Words* (Cambridge: Cambridge University Press, 1986).

2. Heath, p. 143. The woman quoted actually said, " . . . we was cut from the same pattern. We all knowed what to expect." Such usages as "we was" and "we knowed" are commonly identified as dialect and are actually classified as "illiteracies" by some authors. My experience is that "dialect" is too often blamed for the educational, economic, and social woes of those who engage in it. Rather than focus on what she is saying about her community's attitude toward conformity, which is the real issue here, teachers too often want to go right to work to teach such women subject-verb agreement and the standard form of the past tense for the irregular verb *to know*, thinking that she, now "literate," would march unwaveringly toward mainstream values, behaviors, and status. For that reason, I've edited the woman's remarks.

3. Shirley Brice Heath, "Separating 'Things of the Imagination' from Life: Learning to Read and Write," in W. H. Teale and E. Sulzby, *Emergent Literacy* (Norwood, N.J.: Ablex Publishing Corporation, 1986), pp. 156–172, 161–162.

4. Jean Anyon, "Social Class and the Hidden Curriculum of Work," *Journal of Education* (1980): pp. 67–92 and "Social Class and School Knowledge," *Curriculum Inquiry* (1981): pp.3–42. David W. Swift, *Ideology and Change in the Public Schools: Latent Functions of Progressive Education* (Columbus, Ohio: Charles E. Merrill Publishing Company, 1971). Paul E. Willis, *Learning to Labor: How Working Class Kids Get Working Class Jobs* (Westmead, England: Saxon House, 1977). Lois Weis, *Working Class without Work: High School Students in a De-industrializing Economy* (New York: Routledge, 1990).

Chapter 10. The Last Straw—There's Literacy and Then There's Literacy

1. E. A. Havelock, *Preface to Plato* (Cambridge, Mass.: Harvard University Press, 1963).

2. From the earliest literacy campaigns, the idea was to teach the poor to read, not to write. Teaching writing to the poor implies that they

might have something to say, an idea that does not often occur to domesticating educators, and if it does, it frightens them. Hannah More, a late-eighteenth-century advocate of literacy for the poor, asserted, "I allow of no writing for the poor. My object is not to make them fanatics, but to train up the lower classes in habits of industry and piety." More is quoted in B. Simon, *Studies in the History of Education: The Two Nations and the Educational Structure 1780–1870* (London: Lawrence and Wishart, 1960), p. 133.

3. The concept of four levels of literacy is taken from Gordon Wells, "Apprenticeship in Literacy," in C. E. Walsh, *Language, as Praxis: Culture, Language, and Pedagogy* (Norwood, N.J.: Ablex Publishing Corporation, 1991). Wells calls the highest level of literacy "epistemic literacy." Gee discusses levels of literacy as well and refers to the highest level as "essay-text literacy." James Gee, "Orality and Literacy: From *The Savage Mind* to *Ways with Words*," in J. Mabin, *Language and Literacy in Social Practice* (Clevedon, England: Multilingual Matters Limited, The Open University, 1994).

4. James Gee, "Orality and Literacy."

5. Wells suggests that levels of literacy are associated with levels of social class. Performative and functional literacy are associated with discourse communities such as that of Roadville. Informational and powerful literacy are associated with discourse communities such as that of Maintown.

Chapter 11.   Literacy with an Attitude

1. M. Spufford, *Small Books and Pleasant Histories: Popular Fiction and Its Readership in Seventeenth-century England* (Cambridge: Cambridge University Press, 1981).

2. J. Willinsky, *The New Literacy: Redefining Reading and Writing in the Schools* (New York: Routledge, 1990), p. 177.

3. Willinsky, p. 184.

4. E. P. Thompson, *The Making of the English Working Class* (New York: Vintage Books, 1963).

5. J. Donald, "How Illiteracy Became a Problem (and Literacy Stopped Being One)," in C. Mitchell and K. Weiler, eds., *Rewriting Literacy: Culture and the Discourse of the Other* (New York: Bergin & Harvey, 1991), pp. 211–228, 212.

6. E. P. Thompson, p. 103.

7. E. P. Thompson, p. 154.

8. E. P. Thompson, p. 156.

9. E. P. Thompson, p. 103

10. E. P. Thompson, p. 151.

11. An idea promulgated by Paine and continued by Thoreau, Gandhi, Martin Luther King, Jr., and Paulo Freire.

12. E. P. Thompson, p. 155.

13. E. P. Thompson, p. 155.

14. E. P. Thompson, p. 108.

15. B. Simon, *Studies in the History of Education,* p. 133.

16. J. Donald, 214.

17. P. Colquhoun, *A New and Appropriate System of Education for the Labouring People.* (London: J. Hatchard, 1806), pp. 11–12.

18. J. Donald, p. 220.

Chapter 12.   Not Quite Making Literacy Dangerous Again

1. M. McCurdy, "Writing on Their Own: Kindergarten and First Grade," in N. Gordon, ed., *Classroom Experiences: The Writing Process in Action* ((Portsmouth, N.H.: Heinemann, 1984).

2. Note similarity to Ashley's Runaway Elephant Story in chapter 8. These writers are a little further along than Ashley.

3. N. Atwell, *In the Middle: Reading, Writing, and Learning with Adolescents* (Portsmouth, N.H.: Heinemann, 1987).

4. J. Willinsky, *The New Literacy: Redefining Reading and Writing in the Schools* (New York: Routledge, 1990), p. 8.

5. D. Graves, *Writing: Teachers and Children at Work* (Portsmouth, N.H.: Heinemann, 1983).

6. J. Bechtel, "Videotape Analysis of the Composing Process of Six Male College Freshman Writers." Paper presented at the Annual Meeting of the Midwest Regional Conference on English in the Two Year College (ERIC Document ED 177 558) and S. H. Pianco, "A Description of the Composing Process of College Freshmen Writers," *Research in College Teaching 13*: pp. 5–22.

7. S. Michaels, "Narrative Presentations: An Oral Preparation for Literacy with First Graders," in J. Cook-Gumperz, ed., *The Social Construction of Literacy* (Cambridge: Cambridge University Press, 1986), pp. 94–116.

8. S. Michaels, 1986, p. 105.

9. S. Michaels, 1986, pp. 108–109.

10. S. Michaels, 1986, p. 110.

11. J. Collins, "Hegemonic Practices: Literacy and Standard Language in Public Education," in C. Mitchell and K. Weiler, *Rewriting Literacy: Culture and the Discourse of the Other* (New York: Bergin & Garvey, 1991), pp. 229–254, 239.

12. For a review of the research on the relationships between social class and ability grouping, teacher expectations, and unequal treatment in reading groups see Patrick Shannon, "Reading Instruction and Social Class," in Patrick Shannon ed., *Becoming Political: Readings and Writings in the Politics of Literacy Education* (Portsmouth, N.H.: Heinemann, 1992), pp. 128–138.

13. M. Sola and A. Bennett, "The Struggle for Voice: Narrative, Literacy, and Consciousness in an East Harlem High School," in C. Mitchell and K. Weiler, eds., *Rewriting Literacy,* pp. 35–56.

14. M. Sola and A. Bennett, pp. 44–45

15. S. Michaels, "Hearing the Connections in Children's Oral and Written Discourse," in C. Mitchell and K. Weiler, eds., *Rewriting Literacy*, pp. 103–122, 110.

16. S. Michaels, 1991, p. 114.

17. S. Michaels, 1991, p. 116.

18. Willinsky and Hunniford discovered a group of young adolescent girls in two new literacy classrooms who read nothing but "young adult romance novels." J. M. Willinsky and J. O. Hunniford, "Reading the Romance Younger: The Mirrors and Fears of a Preparatory Literature," *Reading- Canada-Lecture* 4(1): pp. 16–31.

19. The 1 classes in the Brownstoners school were very traditional and directive when the Brownstoners arrived. That was the cause of the consternation of the Brownstoners.

20. Shirley Brice Heath, *Ways with Words* (Cambridge: Cambridge University Press, 1983).

21. Recall that Anyon found the middle-class school more like the working-class school than the affluent professional or executive elite school.

Chapter 13. Making Literacy Dangerous Again

1. S. Aronowitz and H. Giroux, *Education Still Under Siege, Second Edition* (Westport, Conn.: Bergin and Harvey, 1993).

2. Actually, Aronowitz and Giroux have four categories, but I don't find the fourth, accommodating intellectuals, very helpful.

3. Aronowitz and Giroux, 1993, p. 46.

4. P. Freire, *Cultural Action for Freedom* (Cambridge: Harvard Education Review, 1970); *Pedagogy of the Heart* (New York: Continuum, 1997); *Pedagogy of the Oppressed* (New York: Seabury Press, 1970); *Pedagogy of the Oppressed: New, Revised 20th-anniversary Edition* (New York: Continuum, 1993); *Teachers as Cultural Workers: Letters to Those Who Dare to Teach* (Boulder: Westview Press, 1998).

5. C. Brown, *Literacy in 30 Hours: Paulo Freire's Process in North East Brazil* (London: Centre for Open Learning and Teaching, Writers and Readers Publishing Cooperative, 1975).

6. Study Circles Resource Center, P. O. Box 203, Pomfret, CT, 006258; scrc@neca.com.

7. R. F. Arnove, "The Nicaraguan National Literacy Crusade of 1980" in E. R. Kintgen, B. M. Kroll, and M. Rose, *Perspectives on Literacy* (Carbondale, Ill.: Southern Illinois University Press, 1988).

8. A second grade teacher in Anyon's working-class school said, "I would *never* teach in the suburbs. Parents there think their kids are God's gift. Although, some parents *here* are beginning to think their kids have rights, too." J. Anyon, "Social Class and School Knowledge," *Curriculum Inquiry* (1981): pp.3–42, 7. Teachers of the Brownstoners' children displayed considerably more deference toward them than toward other children in the school. Teachers boasted about how many of their students were doctors, lawyers, writers, and architects. They clipped occasional items about their students' parents from society columns and passed them around the teachers room. At the same time they complained that the Brownstone children were spoiled, lacking in discipline and respect, and overprivileged and that their parents were pushy, overbearing, and interfering. Some teachers with enough seniority to have the right to teach "top" classes, declined to teach 1 classes at the Brownstoners' school to avoid parental

pressure and interference. R. T. Sieber, "The Politics of Middle-Class Success in an Inner City Public School," *Journal of Education* 164 (1981): pp. 30–47.

9. Alfred S. Alschuler, "The Discipline Game Manual," in A. S. Alschuler, *School Discipline: A Socially Literate Solution* (New York: McGraw-Hill Book Company, 1980), pp. 177–204.

10. Alschuler, p. 185.

Chapter 14. Taking Sides

1. R. E. Peterson, "Teaching How to Read the World and Change It: Critical Pedagogy in the Intermediate Grades," in C. E. Walsh, *Literacy as Praxis: Culture, Language, and Pedagogy* (Norwood, N.J.: Ablex Publishing Corporation, 1991), pp. 156–182.

2. E. Wigginton, editor, *The Foxfire book: hog dressing; log cabin building; mountain crafts and foods; planting by the signs; snake lore, hunting tales, faith healing; moonshining; and other affairs of plain living* (Garden City, New York: Doubleday, 1972); *Foxfire 2: ghost stories, spring wild plant foods, spinning and weaving, midwifing, burial customs, corn shuckin's wagon making and more affairs of plain living* (Garden City, New York: Anchor Press, 1973); *Foxfire 3: Animal Care, Banjos and Dulcimers, Wild Plant Foods, Butter Churns, Ginseng, and Still More Affairs of Plain Living* (New York: Doubleday, 1975); *Foxfire 4: fiddle making, springhouses, horse trading, sassafras tea, berry buckets, gardening, and further affairs of plain living* (Garden City, New York: Anchor Press/Doubleday, 1977); *Foxfire 5: ironmaking, blacksmithing, flintlock rifles, bear hunting, and other affairs of plain living* (Garden City, New York: Anchor Press/Doubleday, 1979); *Foxfire 6: shoemaking, gourd banjos, and songbows, one hundred toys and games, wooden locks, a water powered sawmill, and other affairs of just plain living* (Garden City, New York: Anchor Press/Doubleday, 1980).

3. Peterson, p.161.

4. In her 1995 book, *Other People's Children*, Lisa Delpit discusses the dilemma of educators of black children who want to use progressive methods because of their benefits but who are also aware that many black parents are very directive with their children, and so the children misunderstand teachers' orders stated in a nondirective manner. A progressive teacher is likely to say, "Do you want to put the paints away now?" Children who are not accustomed to such orders erroneously think that not

putting away their paints is an option. Given choices, "Do A, B, or C," such children often think "Do nothing at all" is a choice as well.

Peterson, like all progressive teachers of working-class children, understands the struggle that ensues when you try to share responsibility for learning with working-class students who are used to being given direct orders both at home and at school; he understands as well that directive methods "work" as far as keeping the lid on a classroom full of working-class children, but that they are antithetical to empowering education.

5. Peterson, p. 164.

6. Peterson, p. 158. Compare this with Willinsky's definition of New Literacy: Those strategies in the teaching of reading and writing that attempt to shift control of literacy from the teacher to the student.

7. There are a growing number of violence prevention programs in schools that teach these skills. One, the Alternatives to Violence Program was started in the New York State prison system. It is now offered in schools and communities throughout the country and abroad. In western New York it is called AViS (Alternatives to Violence in Schools). Western New York Peace Center, 2123 Bailey, Buffalo, NY, 14211.

8. M. Sola and A. Bennett, "The Struggle for Voice: Narrative, Literacy, and Consciousness in an East Harlem High School," in C. Mitchell and K. Weiler, eds., *Rewriting Literacy: Culture and the Discourse of the Other* (New York: Bergin & Garvey, 1991), pp. 35–56.

9. Kerby Miller and Paul Wagner, *Out of Ireland: The Story of Irish Immigration to America* (Washington, D. C.:Elliott & Clark Publishers, 1994).

10. R. Adams, *Great Negroes: Past and Present*, (Chicago: Afro-Am Publishing Company, 1969). Scott Foresman, *Golden Streets* (Glenview, Ill.: Scott Foresman, 1980).

11. Peterson, p. 172.

12. Rethinking Schools, 1001 East Keefe Ave., Milwaukee, WI, 53212.

13. Peterson, p. 170.

14. Peterson, p. 179.

15. W. Bigelow, "Inside the Classroom: Social Vision and Critical Pedagogy," in P. Shannon, *Becoming Political: Readings and Writings in the Politics of Literacy Education* (Portsmouth N.H.: Heinemann, 1992), pp. 72–82.

16. Bigelow, p. 72.

17. Bigelow, p. 73. Weis made the same observation about Freeway High School.

18. Bigelow, p. 75. A teacher at Freeway High School made almost the identical comment.

19. Bigelow, pp. 75–76.

20. Bigelow, p. 76.

21. S. Bowles and H. Gintis, *Schooling in Capitalist America: Educational Reform and Contradictions of Economic Life* (New York: Basic Books, 1976).

22. Bowles and Gintis, 1976; Jean Anyon, "Social Class and the Hidden Curriculum of Work," *Journal of Education* (1980): pp. 67–92 and "Social Class and School Knowledge," *Curriculum Inquiry* (1981): pp. 3–42.

23. Herbert Kohl, "The Politics of Children's Literature: What's Wrong with the Rosa Parks Myth," in B. Bigelow, L. Christensen, S. Karp, B. Miner, and B. Peterson, *Rethinking Our Classrooms: Teaching for Equity and Justice* (Milwaukee: Rethinking Schools, Ltd., 1994), pp. 137–140.

24. Bigelow, p. 72.

25. S. Aronowitz and H. Giroux, *Education Still Under Siege*, Second Edition (Westport, Conn.: Bergin and Harvey, 1993), p. 46.

26. B. Bigelow, et al., pp. 137–140.

27. H. Zinn, "Why Students Should Study History: An Interview with Howard Zinn," in B. Bigelow, et al., pp. 137–140.

Chapter 15. Mad as Hell, and Not Going to Take It Any More

1. Jean Anyon, *Ghetto Schooling: A Political Economy of Urban Educational Reform* (New York: Teachers College Press, 1997).

2. *"Intelligent* utilization of progressive methods" refers to the struggle that ensues when you try to share responsibility for learning with working-class students who are used to being given direct orders both at home and at school. See Note 4, chapter 14. Hilton Smith, "Foxfire Teachers' Networks (Viewed Through Maxine Greene's *The Dialectic of Freedom),*" in John M. Novak, ed., *Democratic Teacher Education: Programs, Processes, Problems, and Prospects* (Albany: State University of New York Press, 1994), pp. 21–46.

3. Anyon, 1997, p. 178.

4. Thomas E. Kelly, "Democratic Empowerment and Secondary Teacher Education," in John M. Novak, ed., *Democratic Teacher Education* pp. 63–98.

5. Keith Hillkirk, "Teaching for Democracy: Preparing Teachers to Teach Democracy," in John M. Novak, ed., *Democratic Teacher Education,* pp. 89–102.

6. Barbara McEwan, "Deliberately Developing Democratic Teachers in a Year," in John M. Novak, ed., *Democratic Teacher Education,* pp. 103–124.

7. Lisa A. Bloom and Mary Jean Ronan Herzog, "The Democratic Process in Teacher Education: Two Case Studies," in John M. Novak, ed., *Democratic Teacher Education,* pp. 199–214.

8. J. Cynthia McDermott, "An Institute for Independence through Action, Process, and Theory," in John M. Novak, ed., *Democratic Teacher Education,* pp. 125–142.

9. W. Glasser, *Control Theory* (New York: Harper Row, 1984) and *The Quality School* (New York: Harper Row, 1990). Hillkirk, 1994.

10. One model of community comes from M. S. Peck, *The Different Drum: Community Making and Peace* (New York: Simon and Schuster, 1987). The second comes from R. Morrison, *We Build the Road as We Travel* (Philadelphia: New Society Publishers, 1991). It involves the concept of "equilibrio," a process that harmonizes and balances a diverse and growing community of interests such as those of the individual (both students and teachers) and the classroom community; between the classroom and the school; and between the school and the community. Equilibrio requires practice, time, and reflection. It requires commitment and willingness to release our own control to that of the group.

11. George Wood, "The Institute for Democracy in Education: Supporting Democratic Teachers," in John M. Novak, ed., *Democratic Teacher Education,* pp. 21–46.

12. Wood, 1994, p. 13.

13. Hilton Smith, "Foxfire Teachers' Networks," pp. 21–46.

14. See Note 2, chapter 14.

15. Sheldon Berman, "Introduction," in S. Berman and P. LaFarge, eds., *Promising Practices in Teaching Social Responsibility* (Albany: State University of New York Press, 1993).

16. Berman, 1993, p. 10.

17. Good Works Job Listing, Educators for Social Responsibility (http//www.tripod.com, 1998).

18. S. Aronowitz and H. Giroux, *Education Still Under Siege*, p. 46.

19. Annenberg Institute on Public Engagement for Public Education, *Reasons for Hope, Voices for Change: A Report of the Annenberg Institute on Public Engagement for Public Education* (Providence: Annenberg Institute on Public Engagement for Public Education, Brown University, 1998)(http//www.aisr.brown.edu).

20. National Coalition of Education Activists, *Action for Better Schools: The Newsletter of the National Coalition of Education Activists*, "Community Organizing: The Missing Piece in School Reform?" 5, 3 (Fall/Winter 97): p. 1, 2, and 6 (P. O. Box 679, Rhinebeck, NY, 12572).

21. For a discussion of seeking solutions to problems by examining roles and rules that foster conflict rather than blaming individual "players," see A. S. Alschuler, *School Discipline: A Socially Literate Solution* (New York: McGraw-Hill Book Company, 1980).

22. There is sometimes quibbling over whether teachers' directives to working-class children are abusive or simply "language they understand." However, there are examples of abusive language directed at students that are simply nondebatable. In her 1997 study Anyon heard the following remarks addressed to students:

(A teacher to a first grade class) You're disgusting; you remind me of children I would see in a jail or something.

(A teacher to a sixth grade class) Shut up and push those pencils. Push those pencils, you borderline people!

(A teacher to a fifth grade class) If I had a gun, I'd kill you. You're all hoodlums.

(A teacher to a fourth grade girl) You're mother's pussy smells like fish. That's what stinks around here. (29)

The teacher who addressed the "pussy" remark to a fifth grade girl was "recognized and discussed by the [school] staff as someone who " 'hated the kids and let them know it.' " Parents routinely protested when their children were assigned to him. During the year this remark was made the principal tried to deny him tenure, but was overruled by higher-ups in the board of education.

23. This is true in upscale communities as well as working-class ones. A huge amount of energy was expended during the heyday of the whole language movement in upscale communities, explaining the method, the reasons for it, its benefits, and its successes. In a few working-class communities of which I'm aware, teachers tried a few whole language lessons and when parents asked questions, the same questions their rich counterparts asked, the teachers decided the parents were opposed, and that therefore change was impossible.

24. Annenberg Institute on Public Engagement for Public Education, 1998, p. 36.

25. Annenberg Institute on Public Engagement for Public Education, 1998, p. 22.

26. Annenberg Institute on Public Engagement for Public Education, 1998, p. 22.

27. National Coalition of Education Activists, *Action for Better Schools,* p. 1. Robert Peterson, who was discussed at length in chapter 14, was involved in these struggles and now teaches at this school.

28. University of Wisconsin, Milwaukee, Center for Urban Community Development, "Designing Pathways to Parental Involvement in School to Work: A Template for Planning and Action," by Participants in a Milwaukee Public Schools' Action Learning Seminar, facilitated by P. Bangura, D. Folkman and K. Rai.

29. Anyon, 1997, p. 180.

30. Anyon, 1997, p. 4. See also D. R. Judd and T. Swanstrom, *City Politics: Private Power and Public Policy* (New York: Harper Collins, 1994) and B. G. Salmore and S. A. Salmore *New Jersey Politics and Government: Suburban Politics Comes of Age* (Lincoln: University of Nebraska, 1993).

31. Anyon, 1997, pp. 182–183. See also J. Persky, E. Sklar, and W. Wiewel, *Does America Need Cities: An Urban Investment Strategy for National Prosperity* (Washington, D.C.: Economic Policy Institute and the National Conference of Mayors, 1992).

32. "Symbolic Analyst" refers to Robert Reich's top category of employment. See note 4 chapter 2.

33. National Coalition of Education Activists, P. O. Box 679, Rhinebeck, NY 12572–0679.

34. Cross City Campaign for Urban School Reform, 407 S. Dearborn St. #1725, Chicago, IL 60605–1119.

35. Gamaliel Foundation, 203 N. Wabash, Chicago, IL 60601–2406.

36. Industrial Areas Foundation, 165 W. 86th St. New York, NY 10024–3412.

References

Adams, R. *Great Negroes: Past and Present*. Chicago: Afro-Am Publishing Company, 1969.

Alschuler, A. S. *School Discipline: A Socially Literate Solution*. New York: McGraw-Hill Book Company, 1980.

Annenberg Institute on Public Engagement for Public Education. *Reasons for Hope, Voices for Change: A Report of the Annenberg Institute on Public Engagement for Public Education*. Providence, R.I.: Annenberg Institute on Public Engagement for Public Education, Brown University, 1998. (http//www.aisr.brown.edu)

Anyon, Jean. *Ghetto Schooling: A Political Economy of Urban Educational Reform*. New York: Teachers College Press, 1997.

———. "Social Class and School Knowledge." *Curriculum Inquiry* 11,1 (1981).

———. "Social Class and the Hidden Curriculum of Work." *Journal of Education* 162, 2 (1980).

Apple, M. W. *Ideology and Curriculum*. Boston: Routledge and Kegan Paul, 1979.

Arnov, R. F. "The Nicaraguan National Literacy Crusade of 1980." In *Perspectives on Literacy*. Ed. E. R. Kintgen, B. M. Kroll, and M. Rose. Carbondale, Ill.: Southern Illinois University Press, 1988.

Aronowitz, S., and H. Giroux. *Education Still Under Siege* Second Edition. Westport, Conn.: Bergin and Harvey, 1993.

Atwell, N. *In the Middle: Reading, Writing, and Learning with Adolescents*. Portsmouth, N.H.: Heinemann, 1987.

229

Baltimore Catechism: A catechism of Christian doctrine, prepared and enjoined by order of the Third Plenary Council Baltimore; with explanations in the form of short notes and of sections in simple question and answer. Published by ecclesiastical authority. Chicago: The John P. Daleiden Company, 1918.

Bechtel, J. "Videotape Analysis of the Composing Process of Six Male College Freshman Writers." Paper presented at the Annual Meeting of the Midwest Regional Conference on English in the Two Year College. ERIC Document ED 177 558.

Bensman, David, and Roberta Lynch. *Rusted Dreams: Hard Times in a Steel Community.* New York: McGraw Hill, 1987.

Berman, Sheldon. "Introduction." In *Promising Practices in Teaching Social Responsibility.* Ed. S. Berman and P. LaFarge. Albany: State University of New York Press, 1993.

Bernstein, Basil. *Theoretical Studies Towards a Sociology of Education.* London: Routledge and Kegan Paul, 1971.

_____. *Applied Studies Towards a Sociology of Education.* London: Routledge and Kegan Paul, 1973.

_____. *Towards a Theory of Educational Transmission.* London: Routledge and Kegan Paul, 1973.

_____. *The Structuring of Pedagogic Discourse.* London: Routledge and Kegan Paul, 1990.

Bigelow, W. "Inside the Classroom: Social Vision and Critical Pedagogy." In *Becoming Political: Readings and Writings in the Politics of Literacy Education.* Ed. P. Shannon. Portsmouth N.H.: Heinemann, 1992.

Bloom, Lisa A., and Mary Jean Ronan Herzog. "The Democratic Process in Teacher Education: Two Case Studies." In *Democratic Teacher Education: Programs, Processes, Problems, and Prospects.* Ed. John M. Novak. Albany: State University of New York Press, 1994.

Bourdieu, P., and J Passeron. *Reproduction in Education, Society, and Culture.* Beverly Hills: Sage, 1977.

Bowles, S., and H. Gintis. *Schooling in Capitalist America: Educational Reform and Contradictions of Economic Life.* New York: Basic Books, 1976.

Brown, C. *Literacy in 30 Hours: Paulo Freire's Process in North East Brazil.* London: Centre for Open Learning and Teaching, Writers and Readers Publishing Cooperative, 1975.

Buckhalt, J., R. Rutherford, and K. Goldberg. "Verbal and Nonverbal Interactions of Mothers and Their Down's Syndrome and Nonretarded Infants." *American Journal of Mental Deficiency* 82 (1978).

Carter, John Stewart. *Full Fathom Five..* Boston: Houghton Mifflin Co., 1965.

Chall, Jeanne, and Vicki Jacobs. "Writing and Reading in the Elementary Grades: Developmental Trends Among Low SES Children." In *Composing and Comprehending*. Ed. Julie M. Jensen. Urbana, Ill.: ERIC Clearing House on Reading and Communication Skills, 1984.

Coles, Robert. *The Spiritual Life of Children*. Boston: Houghton Mifflin, 1990.

Collins, J. "Hegemonic Practices: Literacy and Standard Language in Public Education." In *Rewriting Literacy: Culture and the Discourse of the Other*. Ed. C. Mitchell and K. Weiler. New York: Bergin & Garvey, 1991.

Colquhoun, P. *A New and Appropriate System of Education for the Labouring People*. London: J. Hatchard, 1806.

Connolly, Megan Elizabeth. *Paper 1, LAI 563 Language, Society, and Language Arts Instruction*. Photocopied. Department of Learning and Instruction, State University of New York at Buffalo, 1998.

Cross, T. "Mothers' Speech Adjustment: The Contribution of Selected Child Listener Variables." In *Talking to Children: Language Input and Acquisition*. Ed. C. A. Snow and C. A. Ferguson. Cambridge: Cambridge University Press, 1977.

Cremin, Lawrence A. *The Transformation of the School*. New York: Random House, Inc, Vintage Books, 1964.

Cubberly, Ellwood P. *Public Education in the United States*. Boston: Houghton-Mifflin Company, 1919.

Donald, J. "How Illiteracy Became a Problem and Literacy Stopped Being One." In *Rewriting Literacy: Culture and the Discourse of the Other*. Ed. C. Mitchell and K. Weiler. New York: Bergin & Harvey, 1991.

Educators for Social Responsibility. Good Works Job Listing. 1998. (http//www.tripod.com)

Fitzgerald, Jim. "Jury Hears Tapes in Texaco Case." Associated Press: April 29, 1998. http://www.blackvoices.com/news/98/04/29/story07.html.

Fraser, Thomas W. *Reading, Writing, and Justice: School Reform as if Democracy Matters*. Albany: State University of New York Press, 1997.

Freeman, Ruth S. *Yesterday's Schools*. Watkin's Glen, N.Y.: Century House, 1962.

Freire, P. *Cultural Action for Freedom*. Cambridge: Harvard Education Review, 1970.

———. *Pedagogy of the Heart*. New York: Continuum, 1997.

———. *Pedagogy of the Oppressed*. New York: Seabury Press, 1970.

———. *Pedagogy of the Oppressed: New, Revised 20th-anniversary Edition*. New York: Continuum, 1993.

———. *Teachers as Cultural Workers: Letters to Those Who Dare to Teach*. Boulder CO: Westview Press, 1998.

Gee, James Paul. "What is Literacy." In *Rewriting Literacy: Culture and the Discourse of the Other*. Ed. C. Mitchell and K. Weiler. New York: Bergin & Garvey, 1991, p. 3.

———. "Orality and Literacy: From *The Savage Mind* to *Ways with Words*." In *Language and Literacy in Social Practice*. Ed. J. Mabin. Clevedon, England: Multilingual Matters Limited, The Open University, 1994.

Gilmore, Perry. "'Gimme Room': School Resistence, Attitude, and Access to Literacy." In *Rewriting Literacy: Culture and the Discourse of the Other*. Ed. Candice Mitchell and Kathleen Weiler. New York: Bergin & Garvey: 1991.

Givon, T. *On Understanding Grammar*. New York: Academic Press, 1979.

Glasser, W. *Control Theory*. New York: Harper Row, 1984.

———. *The Quality School*. New York: Harper Row, 1990.

Graves, D. *Writing: Teachers and Children at Work*. Portsmouth, N.H.: Heinemann, 1983.

Halliday, M. A. K. *Learning How to Mean: Explorations in the Study of Language*. London: Edward Arnold Publishers, 1975.

Hamilton, S. "The Social Side of Schooling." *Elementary School Journal* 83 (1983).

Havelock, E. A. *Preface to Plato*. Cambridge: Harvard University Press, 1963.

Harste, J. C., V. A. Woodward, and C. L. Burke. *Language Stories and Literacy Lessons*. Portsmouth, N.H.: Heinemann, 1984.

Hartfield, Ashley. "The Runaway Elephant." In Patrick J. Finn. *Helping Children Learn to Read*. New York: Longman, 1990.

Heath, Shirley Brice. "Separating 'Things of the Imagination' from Life: Learning to Read and Write." In *Emergent Literacy*. Ed. W. H. Teale and E. Sulzby. Norwood, N.J.: Ablex Publishing Corporation, 1986.

———. *Ways with Words*. Cambridge: Cambridge University Press, 1983.

Herbert, Bob. "In America: Workaday Racism." New York: The New York Times Company, 1996. http//www.dorsai.org/~jdadd/texaco3.html.

Hillkirk, Keith. "Teaching for Democracy: Preparing Teachers to Teach Democracy." In *Democratic Teacher Education: Programs, Processes, Problems, and Prospects*. Ed. John M. Novak. Albany: State University of New York Press, 1994.

Johnson, Clifton. *The Country School in New England*. New York: D. Appleton and Company, 1893.

———. *Old Time Schools and School Books*. New York: The Macmillian Co., 1904.

Judd, D. R., and T. Swanstrom, *City Politics: Private Power and Public Policy*. New York: Harper Collins, 1994.

Kelly, Thomas E. "Democratic Empowerment and Secondary Teacher Education." In *Democratic Teacher Education: Programs, Processes, Problems, and Prospects*. Ed. John M. Novak. Albany: State University of New York Press, 1994.

King, M. "Speech to Writing: Children's Growth in Writing Potential." In *Reading and Writing Connections*. Ed. J. Mason Boston: Allyn and Bacon, 1989.

Kohl, Herbert. "The Politics of Children's Literature: What's Wrong with the Rosa Parks Myth." In *Rethinking Our Classrooms: Teaching for Equity and Justice*. Ed. B. Bigelow, L. Christensen, S. Karp, B. Miner, and B. Peterson. Milwaukee: Rethinking Schools, Ltd., 1994.

Kozol, Jonathan. *Savage Inequalities*. New York: Harper Perennial, 1992.

Labov, W., and C. Robbins. "A note on the Relation of Reading Failure to Peer-Group Status in Urban Ghettos." *The Record—Teacher's College* 70 (1969).

Leacock, E. *Teaching and Learning in City Schools*. New York: Basic Books, 1969.

Levitas, Maurice. *Perspectives in the Sociology of Education*. Boston: Routledge & Kegan Paul, 1974.

McCurdy, M. "Writing on Their Own: Kindergarten and First Grade." In *Classroom Experiences: The Writing Process in Action*. Ed. N. Gordon. Portsmouth, N.H.: Heinemann, 1984.

McDermott, J. Cynthia. "An Institute for Independence through Action, Process, and Theory." In *Democratic Teacher Education: Programs, Processes, Problems, and Prospects*. Ed. John M. Novak. Albany: State University of New York Press, 1994.

McEwan, Barbara. "Deliberately Developing Democratic Teachers in a Year" In *Democratic Teacher Education: Programs, Processes, Problems, and Prospects*. Ed. John M. Novak. Albany: State University of New York Press, 1994.

Michaels, S. "Hearing the Connections in Children's Oral and Written Discourse." In *Rewriting Literacy: Culture and the Discourse of the Other*. Ed. C. Mitchell and K. Weiler. New York: Bergin & Garvey, 1991.

_____. "Narrative Presentations: An Oral Preparation for Literacy with First Graders." In *The Social Construction of Literacy*. Ed. J. Cook-Gumperz. Cambridge: Cambridge University Press, 1986.

Miller, Kerby, and Paul Wagner. *Out of Ireland: The Story of Irish Immigration to America*. Washington, D. C.:Elliott & Clark Publishers, 1994.

Morrison, R. *We Build the Road as We Travel*. Philadelphia: New Society Publishers, 1991.

National Coalition of Education Activists. "Community Organizing: The Missing Piece in School Reform?" *Action for Better Schools: The Newsletter of the National Coalition of Education Activists 5, 3* (Fall/Winter 1997).

Natriello, Gary, Edward L. McDill, and Aaron M. Pallas. *Schooling Disadvantaged Children, Racing Against Catastrophe*. New York: Teachers College Press, 1990.

Ogbu, John U. "Cultural Diversity and School Experience." In *Literacy as Praxis: Culture, Language, and Pedagogy*. Ed. Catherine E. Walsh. Norwood, N.J.: Ablex Publishing Corporation, 1991.

Peck, M. S. *The Different Drum: Community Making and Peace*. New York: Simon and Schuster, 1987.

Persky, J., E. Sklar, and W. Wiewel. *Does America Need Cities: An Urban Investment Strategy for National Prosperity*. Washington, D.C.: Economic Policy Institute and the National Conference of Mayors, 1992.

Peterson, R. E. "Teaching How to Read the World and Change It: Critical Pedagogy in the Intermediate Grades." In *Literacy as Praxis: Culture, Language, and Pedagogy.* Ed. C. E. Walsh. Norwood, N.J.: Ablex Publishing Corporation, 1991.

Pianco, S. H. "A Description of the Composing Process of College Freshmen Writers." *Research in College Teaching 13* (1979).

Reich, Robert B. *The Work of Nations: Preparing Ourselves for 21st Century Capitalism.* New York: Vintage Books, 1991.

Resnick, Daniel P. "Historical Perspectives on Literacy and Schooling." *Daedalus* 119, 2 (1990).

Salmore, B. G., and S. A. Salmore. *New Jersey Politics and Government: Suburban Politics Comes of Age.* Lincoln: University of Nebraska, 1993.

Sampson, Susan Marie. *Paper 1, LAI 563 Language, Society, and Language Arts Instruction.* Photocopied. Department of Learning and Instruction, State University of New York at Buffalo, 1998.

Schatzman, L., and A. Strauss. "Social class and communication." *American Journal of Sociology* 60(1955).

Scollon, R., and S. B. K. Scollon. *Narrative, Literacy, and Face in Interethnic Communication.* Norwood, N.J.: Ablex Publishing Corporation, 1981.

Scott, Foresman Publishing Co. *Golden Streets.* Glenview, Ill., 1980.

Shannon, P. "Reading Instruction and Social Class." In *Becoming Political: Readings and Writings in the Politics of Literacy Education.* Ed. P. Shannon. Portsmouth N.H.: Heinemann, 1992.

Sieber, R. T. "The Politics of Middle-Class Success in an Inner City Public School." *Journal of Education* 164 (1981).

Simon, B. *Studies in the History of Education: The Two Nations and the Educational Structure 1780-1870.* London: Lawrence and Wishart, 1960.

Smith, Hilton. "Foxfire Teachers' Networks (Viewed Through Maxine Greene's *The Dialectic of Freedom*)." In *Democratic Teacher Education: Programs, Processes, Problems, and Prospects.* Ed. John M. Novak. Albany: State University of New York Press, 1994.

Snow, C. E. "The Development of Conversation between Mothers and Babies." *Journal of Child Development* 4(1977).

Sola, M., and A. Bennett. "The Struggle for Voice: Narrative, Literacy, and Consciousness in an East Harlem High School." In *Rewriting Literacy:*

Culture and the Discourse of the Other. Ed. C. Mitchell and K. Weiler. New York: Bergin & Garvey, 1991.

Sowell, Thomas. "Three Black Histories." In *Essays and Data on American Ethnic Groups*. Ed. Thomas Sowell. Washington, D. C., Urban Institute: 1978.

Spufford, M. *Small Books and Pleasant Histories: Popular Fiction and Its Readership in Seventeenth-century England*. Cambridge: Cambridge University Press, 1981.

Swift, David W. *Ideology and Change in the Public Schools: Latent Functions of Progressive Education*. Columbus: Charles E. Merrill Publishing Company, 1971.

Thompson, E. P. *The Making of the English Working Class*. New York: Vintage Books, 1963.

University of Wisconsin, Milwaukee, Center for Urban Community Development. "Designing Pathways to Parental Involvement in School to Work: A Template for Planning and Action," by Participants in a Milwaukee Public Schools' Action Learning Seminar, facilitated by P. Bangura, D. Folkman, and K. Rai.

U. S. Commissioner of Education. *Annual Report of the Commissioner of Education Made to the Secretary of the Interior for the Year 1870*. Washington, D. C.: 1875.

Weis, Lois. *Working Class without Work: High School Students in a Deindustrializing Economy*. New York: Routledge, 1990.

Wells, Gordon. "Apprenticeship in Literacy. " In *Language as Praxis: Culture, Language, and Pedagogy*. Ed. C. E. Walsh. Norwood, N.J.: Ablex Publishing Corporation, 1991.

Wells, Gordon. "Language as Interaction." In *Language through Interaction*. Ed. Gordon Wells. Cambridge: Cambridge University Press, 1981.

Wigginton, E. *The Foxfire book: hog dressing; log cabin building; mountain crafts and foods; planting by the signs; snake lore, hunting tales, faith healing; moonshining; and other affairs of plain living*. Garden City, N.Y.: Doubleday, 1972.

———. *Foxfire 2: ghost stories, spring wild plant foods, spinning and weaving, midwifing, burial customs, corn shuckin's wagon making and more affairs of plain living*. Garden City, N.Y.: Anchor Press, 1973.

——. *Foxfire 3: Animal Care, Banjos and Dulcimers, Wild Plant Foods, Butter Churns, Ginseng, and Still More Affairs of Plain Living.* Garden City, N.Y.: Doubleday, 1975.

——. *Foxfire 4: fiddle making, springhouses, horse trading, sassafras tea, berry buckets, gardening, and further affairs of plain living.* Garden City, N.Y.: Anchor Press/Doubleday, 1977.

——. *Foxfire 5: ironmaking, blacksmithing, flintlock rifles, bear hunting, and other affairs of plain living.* Garden City, N.Y.: Anchor Press/ Doubleday, 1979.

——. *Foxfire 6: shoemaking, gourd banjos, and songbows, one hundred toys and games, wooden locks, a water powered sawmill, and other affairs of just plain living.* Garden City, N.Y.: Anchor Press/Doubleday, 1980.

Willinsky, John. *The New Literacy: Redefining Reading and Writing in the Schools.* New York: Routledge, Chapman and Hall, Inc., 1990.

——, and J. O. Hunniford. "Reading the Romance Younger: The Mirrors and Fears of a Preparatory Literature." *Reading- Canada-Lecture* 4, 1 (1986).

Wood, George. "The Institute for Democracy in Education: Supporting Democratic Teachers." In *Democratic Teacher Education: Programs, Processes, Problems, and Prospects.* Ed. John M. Novak. Albany: State University of New York Press, 1994.

Willis, Paul E. *Learning to Labor: How Working Class Kids Get Working Class Jobs.* Westmead, England: Saxon House, 1977.

Zinn, H. "Why Students Should Study History: An Interview with Howard Zinn." In *Rethinking Our Classrooms: Teaching for Equity and Justice.* Ed. B. Bigelow, L. Christensen, S. Karp, B. Miner, and B. Peterson. Milwaukee: Rethinking Schools, Ltd., 1994.

Index